The Reformatic
Breaking the Bar.

The Reformation of Canada's Schools provides a much-needed look at the problems plaguing the educational system in Canada. Challenging the one-size-fits-all approach to educational policy, Mark Holmes argues that we need a broad range of schools to accommodate the wishes of parents and the goals of a pluralist society. He suggests that if children are to get the education they deserve, instead of centralizing all decision making in the provincial departments of education, we should be moving to a system characterized by central control over money and accountability combined with much more parental choice. He explores the reasons behind the mediocrity of Canadian schools and sets out the reforms necessary to make them successful.

Holmes presents a textured picture of the difficulties facing schools in Canada. He examines the social background of students and the competing goals of parents, teachers, and governments and criticizes progressivism, or child-centred education, speaking out against the closed-mindedness of the educational establishment. He also looks at current research on effective and ineffective schools, as well as on educational achievement in national and international terms. His findings show that the difficulties facing Canadian schools are not caused by a lack of money but by poor allocation of funds and inappropriate priorities.

Increasingly frustrated parents, dedicated teachers, and discouraged citizens will find *The Reformation of Canada's Schools* a welcome source of ideas, information, and thought-provoking possibilities for combating the crisis in Canadian education.

MARK HOLMES is professor emeritus of the Ontario Institute for Studies in Education, University of Toronto, and has been a teacher, elementary and secondary school principal, director of programs, director of education, researcher, academic, and policy analyst. As well, he has worked with many parent groups to promote reform, notably the Organization for Quality Education, of which he was a founding member. His other books include *Educational Policy for the Pluralist Democracy, Making the School an Effective Community,* and *The Educator's Guide to Student Evaluation.*

√

The Reformation of Canada's Schools

Breaking the Barriers to Parental Choice

MARK HOLMES

McGill-Queen's University Press
Montreal & Kingston · London · Ithaca

© McGill-Queen's University Press 1998
ISBN 0-7735-1745-6 (cloth)
ISBN 0-7735-1746-4 (paper)

Legal deposit third quarter 1998
Bibliothèque nationale du Québec

Printed in Canada on acid-free paper

This book has been published with the help of
a grant from the Donner Foundation.

McGill-Queen's University Press acknowledges
the support of the Canada Council for the Arts
for its publishing program.

Canadian Cataloguing in Publication Data

Holmes, Mark, 1935–
The reformation of Canada's schools:
breaking the barriers to parental choice
Includes bibliographical references and index.
ISBN 0-7735-1745-6 (bound) –
ISBN 0-7735-1746-4 (pbk.)
1. Educational change – Canada. I. Title.
LA412.H65 1998   370'.971   c98-900612-3

Typeset in Palatino 10/12
by Caractéra inc.

Contents

Tables

Preface

Canada's school system needs reform. The precise policies required vary from province to province. The urgency of reform is far less in British Columbia and Alberta, the provinces with the best educational record, than in Ontario, with the worst. Both the causes of and the solutions to the educational problems should be examined within the international, federal, and provincial social and economic context.

When one talks of school quality, the issue that first springs to mind is academic achievement. Canada as a whole performs less well than the international leaders, and Ontario's achievement is below the Canadian average. But school quality goes well beyond academics; parents and the public look to the schools for many things. Their level of satisfaction with school performance is possibly the most relevant indicator of quality. There is concern about violence and inadequate discipline, particularly in secondary schools. Underlying the visible disorder and the verbal, as well as physical abuse (mainly of students by students) lies the question of values and, more crucially, virtue. The moral framework of our schools is poorly defined and poorly implemented, reflecting the moral confusion of our adult world. In practical terms, Canadian schools do a notably poor job of preparing young people for work, primarily because most schools do not consider such preparation to be their mandate.

The reader may mistakenly expect that I am writing to urge the schools to adopt my own educational world-view instead of imposing the view of the educational establishment. To avoid any implication that I claim to be an objective, disinterested observer, I should stress that my educational life has increasingly been one of an outsider, as a heretic who rejects the Progressive dogma of Canada's educational establishment. My own philosophy is essentially Traditional, in the

sense that I believe that the education of young people should be
grounded in the fundamental virtues of truth, moral integrity, courage, justice, humility, and consideration of others (representing the
good), together with such associated virtues as industriousness, personal and civic responsibility, and perseverance. Those fundamentals
usually, but not always derive from religious belief. Resting on that
moral and social base, schooling should embrace an openness to life
driven by apprenticeship in the basic skills, by the disciplines of
knowledge, by aesthetic expression, appreciation, and understanding,
by physical fitness, by the preparation of young people for a useful
place in society, and by generally promoting the attitudes and skills
required for both competence and more specialized excellence.

I would be delighted if most parents were to adopt a broadly
interpreted version of my world-view and may at some point write
a book with that end in mind, but this is not that book. It does not
prescribe my own philosophy for all, although my strong opposition
to a monopolistic system that ignores or even ridicules my own and
others' deeply held views will become evident. Even so, it is not my
goal to replace one monopolistic system with another. Such an
imposition would be wrong and impractical: wrong because the
attempted enforcement of alien values would continue the corrosion
of the schools' integrity, as well as being improper in a pluralist
society; impractical because such an attempt would be opposed by
the vast majority of educators, as well as a substantial portion,
perhaps a majority, of the public.

Clearly then, while I believe that the establishment's thirty-year
capture by Progressivism has been harmful, unjustifiable, and
undemocratic, I do not propose the replacement of Progressivism by
Traditionalism, Technocracy, liberal Culture, Individualism, Egalitarianism, or any other ideology or set of compromises. (These terms
are explained in more detail in chapter 3.) The aim of this book is to
justify educational reform through a balance between parental
responsibility and the underlying educational needs of society.

I develop the case for the reformation of our schools by looking at
the financial support for different kinds of schools in the various
provinces, the social context of the school and its students, the practice and consequences of schooling today, relevant research on
instructional and school effectiveness, and the experience and world-
view of teachers. Finally, I recommend a set of reforms designed to
reflect responsible parental choice within the context of a principled,
pluralist democracy. I attempt to take account of the available knowledge about Canada's schools and to make my own assumptions and
values visible. I use anecdotal stories, some personal, not because

they prove any of my arguments, but because they illustrate some of the points that I am trying to make.

I do not expect to convince every reader, but I sincerely hope that readers will reach a better understanding of the intricate issues facing public education in Canada at the end of the twentieth century. I would like those favourable to the status quo to recognize that there are problems which require serious thought and action, and those dissatisfied with things as they are to recognize that there is no quick and easy solution.

Acknowledgments

I appreciate the strong support of Dr Joe Freedman, President of the Society for Advancing Educational Research, without which this book would not have been written and published. It was he who elicited financial support from the Donner Foundation, to which I am also grateful.

My wife, Nora, with the benefit of teaching experience in elementary and secondary schools in three provinces, has been a continuing source of practical and emotional support and education. My four children have also taught me much, through their own educational experiences and those of their spouses, friends, and children.

I owe the greatest professional debt to my first permanent employer in education, Dr William MacKenzie, at that time Superintendent of Schools in Saint John, New Brunswick. He made a lasting impression on my educational beliefs. His was a straightforward educational philosophy. He believed strongly in the value of the traditional disciplines of knowledge and in educational excellence in all fields, physical and technical education, music, art, and drama. He had a caustic disregard for passing fads, believing that professional principals and teachers should be left alone to teach, without interference from administrators or politicians. Unfortunately, with the pride of youth, I did not recognize at the time how unusual among educators he was. If his spirit had prevailed in Canadian schools, this book might have been unnecessary.

I appreciate my fellow members of the Organization for Quality Education, who give voice to so many parents and dissenting teachers. They have provided support and fellowship in what was for me once a lonely and constantly besieged campaign.

The Reformation of Canada's Schools

Introduction

Does Canadian education require fundamental, structural reform? Certainly not, if one believes most employees of the systems of public education. I was one of them for sixteen years. They are, for the most part, sincere and hard-working people who know that they are doing their best for the students. Most recognize that there are problems in education, as in every other sphere of life, but they believe, unlike many parents, that the essential causes lie outside the school.

The situation is not so simple. In 1993 my wife (a public school teacher) and I (a professor working in educational policy) decided to take early retirement. Our motives were complex, as human motives often are, partly financial, partly a longing for the freedom to spend time in the open air, and partly a feeling that we had made our formal contribution, that it was time to make room for younger people. My wife was the subject of envy and congratulation from her colleagues in the school system; retirement (typically not long after reaching age fifty-five) was seen as a delight. Many of her co-workers were counting the months and days. My academic colleagues, in contrast, were amazed at my peculiar decision.

Life in academia is usually less stressful than it is in the school; professors often choose to ease their way into retirement. In contrast, the daily demands on teachers cause more stress as the years go by, not less, mainly because schools have become more stressful places. Teachers are legitimately and understandably defensive of their role in education, which is increasingly difficult; but there is broad recognition, even among them, that schools are not the educational places they should be. Critics say that teachers have an easy life today, without real accountability. Experienced teachers argue that their task gets more difficult every year. Perhaps both opinions are correct. It is possible to endure as a mediocre teacher in most schools, but the challenge of uninterested and undisciplined young people, together with the inconsistent demands of parents and ever-changing administrators, makes life difficult, if not impossible, for the truly professional teacher who wants to make a difference in the lives of young people.

In early 1994 I met by chance in downtown Saint John a teacher whom I had not seen for over twenty years. He had taught in Millidgeville North High School, where I was principal when it opened in 1969. He said that he wanted to thank me for the most professional years of his life, when he had really believed he was a true educator. His comment surprised and saddened me – surprised because the early 1970s were a time of student rebellion and because ours was an uphill fight to compete with the established and well-equipped high schools in the centre of Saint John; saddened that his best years should be among his first. This teacher went on to say that there was a continuing downward drift in standards and expectations, a trend that most senior teachers acknowledge, at least in private.

For a variety of reasons, many of our best teachers are disappointed and frustrated. No doubt, cutbacks across the country add to the tale of woe, as the unions insist. Before the cutbacks began, however, there was already a strong feeling of alienation among many teachers, particularly at the junior high and high school levels, which resulted from a sense of declining standards of work and work habits, a lack of discipline and disorder, and the imposition from above of a series of passing fads.

Teachers sound defensive because they have much to defend; schools are under attack, and they not unreasonably believe that they are the ones singled out for blame. They tire of being told of their five-hour workdays, their long summer holidays, and their professional days "off." Although many experienced teachers recognize the problems in much the same way as does the general public, it is fair to say that teachers as a whole do not see the problems as being as serious as the public at large does, and there is disagreement about the causes. Teachers claim that most of the problems stem from social change and the resulting evolution in norms within the school. Parents more often attribute the problems to changes in the schools: in curricula, instruction, evaluation, and discipline.

Public opinion polls tell a distressing tale. In Ontario, over the five polls taken between 1979 and 1994, a increasing proportion of people came to believe that the quality of education in high schools during the previous ten years had deteriorated. The same question was asked about elementary schools in three biennial polls (Livingstone,

Hart, and Davie 1995). Slightly more people believe that there has been deterioration rather than improvement. As the limited evidence available suggests that the greatest period of deterioration in achievement was from the late 1960s to the mid-1970s (i.e. more than ten years ago), it may be that this question underestimates the actual discontent. My own judgment is that the most rapid deterioration in academic performance took place between 1970 and 1985. The most recent poll discontinues those specific questions (Livingstone, Hart, and Davie 1997). It does repeat a general question concerning the "current situation," with which 50 per cent are satisfied, compared with 36 per cent in 1988, before the current spate of Technocratic reforms began, and 50 per cent in 1979. Most agencies, public or private, would be unhappy with a 50 per cent rating. The flashpoints of public dissatisfaction remain fairly constant: 40 per cent express satisfaction with value for money, 30 per cent support student discipline, and 42 per cent agree that teachers should have the right to strike.

The polls can best be interpreted as a continuing warning; Ontario public schools are not satisfying significant minorities or even a majority on major issues. While it would be unwise to assume that poll results would be the same in the rest of Canada (this book argues that Ontario is the moribund canary in the educational coal mine), there is strong evidence that there has been some polarization of opinion over the last ten or so years, when, for the first time, education has become a major policy issue right across the country. Although the level of dissatisfaction probably varies, there is strong and focused discontent among minorities in the four largest provinces.

The educational glass can be seen as half-full or as half-empty. Educators typically claim that the public elementary and secondary schools are facing unprecedented problems and demands which are not of their making. They are working hard to cope, and although far from perfect, the schools are still of a generally high quality and bear comparison with any others in the world. The Japanese? Their schools are rigid, with learning based on memorization. Their strong international standing can be attributed to the homogeneity of the Japanese people and the strong value placed on educational success. The Germans? They stream their children from the age of ten, and there is little access to postsecondary education – unthinkable in Canada. The English and the Americans? Look at their inner-city schools and compare them with their elite private and suburban schools; we in Canada have preserved an enviable level of equality of opportunity and still manage to perform as well as the two countries most comparable with us.

External critics point to evidence of declining standards in the expansionary decades of the 1970s and 1980s, of Canada's inadequate international standing, and of high illiteracy rates, even among those students who have graduated from high school. For the critics, there is too little "bang for the buck" – and time brings less rather than more. We, like the Americans, are educationally disarmed when it comes to global competitiveness.

My purpose in this book is to dig beneath both sets of well-worn clichés and to examine both the condition and the context of Canadian education. There can be no final answer to the question as to whether Canadian education is good or bad. Compared with what? Using which criteria? According to whose philosophy? Presented with the same set of facts and opinions, people will inevitably make varying judgments because they either select different criteria or weigh the same criteria differently, and because they begin with disparate ideas of what makes good and bad education. What we as a people must decide is whether or not Canadian education would benefit from major reform.

Because I am a well-known critic of Canadian education, it is tempting for friends and foes alike to assume that I follow the popular corporate and media position that the basic skills should be the content of instruction in the elementary grades and that the role of the secondary school is to prepare workers for a globally competitive economy. That is not an accurate summary of my philosophy.

There are two parts to my argument in this book. First, there is no possible consensus on what schools should be doing. As long as most public schools are of the one-size-fits-all kind, there will be widespread dissatisfaction. Maude Barlow and Heather-jane Robertson (1994), like many others, assume that because I am a critic and most criticism in the media comes from a Technocratic standpoint, I must therefore be a Technocrat and want all schools to be turned into Technocratic clones, preferably privatized. The reality is that there are many different criticisms of public education, just as there are diverse defenders. Therefore, while many defenders and critics agree on one thing – that they alone have the correct answer – my position is that there is no single answer and that we should welcome a variety of schools of choice. So unlike Barlow and Robertson, who ask for "one over-arching idea" to govern policy, I do not argue, still less expect, that every sensible person should endorse my preference in a school. This book is concerned with policies for Canadian schools that will satisfy both parents, diverse as they are, and the larger society. Second, I have outlined in the preface my own strongly held philosophy, which inevitably influences parts of the argument in this book. Trying to put that point of view to one side, I attempt to develop solutions that will reasonably satisfy the breadth of public opinion – those who agree with me, of course, but also the many who do not.

There is no contradiction between the two positions. I am an educator, a parent, and a grandparent. Parents should be able to choose the kind of education that I would like, because I am far from being alone in my views. At the same time, I believe that parents should be able to make very different choices from mine, including those advocated by Barlow and Robertson, provided that they do not demand the recruitment of everybody else's children to their cause. My argument is less with Barlow and Robertson, and other zealots for various educational causes, as with their insistence that one educational prescription, theirs, is good for everyone, that they should be able to dictate the education of my grandchildren.

The most important aspect of the education of the child, in my Traditional view, is one of character; becoming a good and virtuous person is more important than either skills or material success (not that I believe one should have to choose). Not all education takes place within the school, and it can play only a supporting role in character building; but I am not one who believes the school should ignore morality and spirituality in a vain attempt to be value-free and simply concentrate on practical skills. I recognize that the virtue I want to be the central focus of a school is very different from the Progressive values desired by some others. I do plead guilty to the belief that schools should demand excellence in academic areas, fitness, and the arts and that the secondary school should prepare young people for either work or postsecondary education (or both). If those views make me a member of a corporate conspiracy in the eyes of left-wing writers, so be it.

Because an important theme in the book is the harm done to our schools by Canada's adoption of the Progressive philosophy, it may be helpful for me to explain at this point just what the term means. In chapter 3 Progressivism will be discussed in the context of five other competing world-views of education.

Progressivism has its philosophical roots in Jean-Jacques Rousseau's book *Émile,* in which an ideal education is prescribed for children, assumed to be born innocent, good, and free. Imposition from adults should be reduced to a minimum; they should instead provide a rich environment from which the child, with a natural desire to learn, will choose appropriate and individual educational paths. The underlying motif is one of "self-love," more familiar today as high self-concept. Early in this century, John Dewey placed Progressivism in a social and "democratic" context; so Rousseau's rich environment (which was of course carefully determined by his rationalism, rather than, for example, France's Roman Catholic tradition) has become one that is politically and socially "relevant." Progressivism today, although it still owes much to those ideological origins (which rejected the good and God in the name of the individual and society), is most immediately recognizable from its methodologies. These have achieved the status, notably in primary education, of a received dogma. Progressive schools and classrooms (the vast majority serving the early grades) are "child-centred" and individualized, giving students a maximum of choice over their learning activities. There is emphasis on the integration of different subjects, because children do not experience compartmentalized ideas in their everyday lives. There is also a focus on collaborative small-group work, with the stronger children helping the weaker ones. Learning takes place in "learning centres."

Progressivism opposes the teaching of traditional virtue. It is also inconsistent with the following: clear, sequential objectives coupled to whole-class instruction; organization in grades to facilitate sequential instruction (Progressives prefer multi-age classrooms); objective report cards showing the achievement of children according to a common standard; the establishment of personal responsibility for the achievement of externally determined objectives; strong control and discipline: and standardized testing (or indeed, any testing based on the assumption that there are some things most children should learn by a certain stage).

Opponents of Progressivism usually emphasize the inadequacy of its methodology. One could infer, then, that the solution is easy: we should simply change the methodologies adopted by our schools or find some compromise. There are many reasons why this solution has not worked and will not work. Progressivism is a strongly held dogma, not just a set of how-to-do-it instructions. The resistance to change stems more from a kind of religious enthusiasm than from any reasoned argument. And there is not just one alternative to Progressivism. Methodology is only one component of good education, and not the most important one, even in terms of academic achievement.

Progressives are not alone in having deeply held beliefs about what education really should mean. Most important, there is fundamental dissent about education, its purposes, and its practice. There can be no consensual solution, no ready compromise. My strong opposition to Progressivism does not lead to a recommendation that it be banned (as Progressives have banned the values and methods associated with different world-views). But parental selection of Progressive schooling should be based on informed choice.

This book's focus is on educational policy, more specifically, policies for educational reform. Unlike most works on the subject, it is not essentially a reflection of the kind of schooling I would like young people to have. Those interested in getting a better picture of my personal perspective might begin with a contribution of mine to *After Liberalism* (1998). My goal here is to reflect the kind of education that parents as a whole and as groups would like for their children. I assume that my size does not fit all parents.

There is probably not a single educator who does not agree that dissent in education is greater today than it has ever been. Evidence of fundamentally differing world-views is found in focused research that I carried out among educated Ontarians, as well as in more general opinion polls. More than twice as many Ontario directors of education, in my survey, favoured the Progressive ideology, as compared with any of five other world-views. Educators in general also ranked Progressive education first, but by a narrower margin. In contrast, a sample selected to compare similarly aged and educated non-educators with directors of education ranked Progressive education fifth out of the six choices. Only the Egalitarian option was placed lower. Samples of nurses and engineers ranked Progressive education second and fifth respectively. The first choices of the comparison group, nurses and engineers, were Cultural and Technocratic tied (in the case of the comparison group), Cultural (nurses), and Technocratic (engineers) (Holmes 1995). One can generalize that educators are more Progressive than most other educated groups. Individuals without university degrees, whom I did not poll, are probably even less Progressive in outlook.

Equally important are differences among educators (between males and females and between elementary and secondary teachers) and among non-educators. My samples were all drawn from selected groups of graduates of the University of Toronto; imagine the differences if a broader representation of society, including such groups as black Canadians, Asian Canadians, unmarried mothers, Baptists, Orthodox Jews, the media, and blue-collar workers had been included, the results might have varied. As always, the differences among human beings are even greater than those among groups. Differences among groups actually underestimate the real variations within our atomized society. Among supporters of my own Traditional world-view, there are significant differences, and not all Traditional parents – Muslim, Jewish, and Christian, for example – would necessarily choose the same school.

There is no longer a consensus about education with a few dissenters at the extremes. There is not even an obvious centre. Some may argue that the dissent is a reflection of public unease about most policy matters, of people's dissatisfaction with politics, and of concern for the economic future, at both the individual and the national levels. I believe that the confused dissent (I say "confused" because some people want contradictory things, such as both common, neighbourhood schools and selective French immersion) goes well beyond the current social malaise and economic uncertainty. It is a necessary condition in an increasingly pluralist, multicultural, and multi-faith country; further, the malaise may itself be an ongoing, rather than a transitory, phenomenon.

People do not disagree about educational issues simply because they are angry, insecure, or unemployed; they do so because there are important matters on which it is reasonable to disagree. Is early French immersion socially divisive? If it is, should we still have it? Should we have racial, gender, and ethnic quotas for admission to university programs? (Many universities do have advertised or unadvertised preferences.) Should we fund Jewish or Protestant or Roman Catholic schools? Is it reasonable, as the Supreme Court claims, to favour Roman Catholicism simply because it was favoured in 1867? Should our area public schools be Progressive and child-centred? Or should they emphasize academic results and high standards of behaviour? Should we keep students together in a single program for most or all of high school, or should we encourage separate university-entrance programs, cooperative education, vocational programs, and school-to-work apprenticeships? Should schools prepare young people for work at all, and if so, how? How much influence should parents have on their children's education?

There is no consensual answer to these and other important questions. Even where there is, or appears to be, a majority answer, to what extent should a majority opinion on education be forced on dissenting parents? Should public Pentecostal schools be banned in Newfoundland if most people do not like them? And what about francophone schools in Alberta?

The pattern of Canada's education system was first established in the late nineteenth century. Two basic assumptions underlay that pattern. Jurisdiction, according to the British North America Act of 1867 (since incorporated, in amended form, in the Constitution Act of 1982) was granted to provinces to run a system of public schools, with the understanding that Roman Catholic and Protestant (in Quebec) minority schools would be provided for their respective denominations where there was historical precedent. Local public school boards (which were de facto Protestant in Ontario) were to serve as buffers between the provincial departments of education and the local population that they served. Those two assumptions, which are still broadly entrenched in the contemporary Canadian educational scene, are questionable in the modern world. In particular, the local school board is most irrelevant in the large urban and suburban centres where most Canadians live and least so in the traditionally rural agricultural areas.

The French and English languages have overtaken Roman Catholicism and Protestantism as bases for affiliation in schooling and social division. School districts have grown so much in size (many representing a population several times greater than that of Prince Edward Island) that they no longer serve a recognizable, let alone consensual, community. Peel and Halton, in Ontario's golden horseshoe, are two large districts without any common historical or contemporary identity.

The first assumption of this book is one of widespread dissent about educational purposes, policies, and practices. The second is the unlikelihood of increased funding. Alberta and Ontario, two of the three most affluent provinces, have already made major cuts. British Columbia did so some years ago, and Quebec is following suit. That the existing structure of educational delivery is based on nineteenth-century conditions which have long passed is the third assumption behind this book. It does not lead necessarily to a conclusion that the basic structure should be radically changed; the problems of change are not automatically lesser than those of obsolescence and incremental development. The three assumptions taken together do, however, suggest that minor adjustments to the status quo are unlikely to be helpful if the inherent educational problems are deemed to be serious.

The assumptions of this book are very different from those that actually guide educational policy and practice in contemporary Canada. The first ingrained assumption, outside New Brunswick, is that local school boards reflect the needs of their local geographical communities, an absurd idea outside a few traditional areas. The second assumption is that the common school serving young people in a particular area will provide the best education for all. This belief is flawed, not only because it is undermined by dissent within geographical communities, but because the next assumption contradicts it. Defenders of the status quo like to argue, at one and the same time, that the public school provides for the democratic mixing of different children and that it is sensitive to the needs of various people. You cannot have both characteristics. Either you have a common, homogenizing school for everyone, or you divide children up in one or more ways. The idea that the public school can and should treat dissimilar children in varying ways is both false and harmful. It sets up false expectations in parents and tacitly encourages discriminatory, inconsistent, and condescending treatments of different children by teachers. If they treat children the same, they can be accused of enforcing one culture on everyone; if they treat them differently, they can be faulted for ethnic, religious, or racial stereotyping.

In reality, the notion of a common public school is a desiccated fig leaf that fails to conceal quite different treatments within and among schools. They are already widely, if haphazardly, differentiated. There are French-immersion schools and programs, schools of the arts, academic high schools serving affluent neighbourhoods, schools of low academic standards serving immigrant neighbourhoods, Roman Catholic schools, and so on.

Those two contradictory assumptions (that schools are both common and differentiated) are made more understandable by the fourth assumption. This strongly held belief must be confronted by any program for genuine reform. It is that educational experts generally know best what is suitable for all children's education. Parents are not usually allowed to decide for themselves the kind of education that their children should have; the policy choices, if any, are substantially determined by officials, whose decisions are normally approved by school boards. There exists a patchwork quilt of educational options across the country, a condition having less to do with the wishes of individual parents than with local politics and establishment control. Where the educational establishment has the greatest power, in Ontario, Nova Scotia, and Saskatchewan, the choices are few. Where government has at times taken on the establishment, in Alberta, British Columbia, and Manitoba, the choices are more numerous. Within the classroom, the educational establishment's chosen practices with respect to individual and group differences prevail.

The first two of the four assumptions (that school districts comprise genuine communities and that a common, area public school serves everybody except Catholics best) may have made sense when they were developed in the late nineteenth and early twentieth centuries. All four beliefs are absurd in contemporary Canada. School boards cannot, with the best will in the world, represent the myriad dissenting communities in their district. The common school, however desirable it may be in countries such as Denmark and Japan, where a common culture is deeply ingrained, is impractical in a country like Canada. Indeed, to introduce a common school would be even more difficult to accomplish than the ambitious reforms I propose. Imagine the public reaction if French-immersion, middle-class neighbourhood schools, schools for the arts, and Roman Catholic schools were all to be abolished and if the recently established schools for francophones outside Quebec were to be replaced by bilingual ones.

It should be obvious that minority choices cannot be determined fairly on a day-to-day basis by representatives of a local majority; there must be some governing principles beyond immediate majoritarian self-interest. Asking school boards to decide which choices should be allowed is rather like asking unions to decide which work would be better contracted out. School administrators and trustees naturally think that they are doing a pretty good job running their schools and are unlikely to be favourably inclined towards a group that wants something very different from the masterpiece created by the board. School districts find it difficult enough to develop schools that suit the majority, let alone address the interests of minorities.

I have stressed the unfair treatment of minorities. The educational establishment shows its real power through its contemptuous attitude towards the majority. In Ontario, parental resistance has been strong ever since Progressive ideas were first introduced in the late 1960s and early 1970s following the Hall-Dennis report. There was a peak of resistance in the mid 1970s, leading to the construction of walls in Progressive open-area elementary schools. But the establishment never let go; it just slowed down. By the 1980s, Progressive imposition of language process (i.e. teaching reading and writing by means of practice rather than by sequential instruction, now transformed into the concept of Whole Language), watered-down mathematics, and intellectually empty, often integrated science, geography, and history programs in the elementary schools was again in full force.

Each generation of parents believes that change can be accomplished by efforts at their local school or school board, or by changes in provincial policy. The evidence is, however, that the deeply committed educational experts who dominate our faculties of education, provincial departments of education, and school district administrations have learned well how to dig in and wait until the wave of protest stops, and then to carry on from where they left off. Indeed, it is natural for large bureaucracies to move slowly, the more so when their own ideology is challenged.

Many people who share my analysis of the current educational scene, and who would like to see many of the same changes in classroom practice, believe that the current system can be altered; all that is needed is for teachers to be introduced to recent research on instruction and for schools to be held accountable for their results. That belief is naive; it is contradicted by experience in many provinces, as well as in other countries. My argument is that the conditions of pluralist democracies today, coupled with the dead hand of the educational establishment in this country, make simultaneous, radical reform on many fronts necessary if parents and the public are to establish a satisfying and successful educational system. Even then, it will not happen quickly.

This is not a contest between rich and poor (as liberals and Progressives would have it) and not simply one between left and right. The children of the underclass are the ones who suffer most from current practices, simply because their parents are usually least equipped to do anything about it. The rich and famous are scarcely involved; their children attend elite private schools. Many of the families supporting religious, independent schools are impoverished by any standard. In contrast, the leaders of the educational establishment – professors in faculties of education, administrators in school systems, officials in teachers' unions, and those in provincial departments of education – are among the highest paid professionals in the country.

Although Progressive ideas are often given an egalitarian gloss, there is nothing in them to appeal to the thoughtful and knowledgeable Marxist left, and indeed, they are strongly opposed by many Marxist academics, such as the much-published American Michael Apple. The Egalitarian (socialist) world-view was ranked very low by educators in my survey, who were far more Progressive. The real struggle is between a self-governing and self-perpetuating professional elite and parents. Even that generalization should not be taken too far. The elite could not have maintained its power without strong allies in the media and the chattering classes.

In this introduction, I have tried to give a flavour of what this book is about. It is an argument for the radical reform of education. It is an argument for tilting authority in education away from educational leaders to parents – collectively, in groups, and individually. Far from being an advocate of strong individualization, I should like to see the schools bond more closely with communities, from which they have largely been separated over the last fifty or so years. Those communities, however, will differ from ones that some may imagine from an idealized view of rural Canada. In urban centres and suburbs and increasingly in the "exurbs," they will be based in ideas and values, not in geographical neighbourhoods. We cannot return to earlier, simpler times even if we wanted to.

My aim is to provide parents with choices, many of which will be opposed to my own, but all of which will be within the reasonable bounds of a pluralist, democratic society. Those choices will be Progressive for some parents. They are less likely to be Egalitarian, partly because that view is so narrowly shared and partly because its adoption, I shall argue, necessitates its imposition on virtually everybody. The Egalitarian educational policy is definitively authoritarian. That fact distinguishes it from other world-views more in theory than in practice. The one-size-fits-all approach to educational policy has been adopted by advocates of all philosophies; it is that ingrained idea which I am challenging. Too many people who agree with many of my educational ideas think that all that needs to be done is for "us" to gain power and to impose "our" good ideas, instead of Progressive "bad" ones.

The proposed reforms are intended to provide a balance between parents and society, both of whom have a legitimate interest in the education of young people. Today, parents, individually and collectively, have minimal power when it comes to the schooling of their children. I am not plotting to abolish the public school; indeed, my hope is that most parents would eagerly choose among local public schools (as happens in the Netherlands). They would have real choice, but there would be publicly defined, agreed on, and defensible limits to those choices.

We should reject the idea that the state must endow all children with significant educational choices in the classroom. In practice, they choose, as they must, from only what the teacher has to offer, which typically does not include direct, sequential instruction in foundational knowledge and skills, all founded in fundamental values. Instead, parents should be encouraged to make genuine decisions about their children's education and to take responsibility for the consequences. Society does have an interest in ensuring that young people have a foundation on which to make informed choices when they reach adolescence, but parents have a legitimate interest in selecting the values and educational practices that build that foundation.

– 1 –

The Funding of Elementary and Secondary Education

Money is not the most important problem facing Canadian schools, even if readers in some provinces, hearing the screams coming from school boards and teachers' unions, may think so. Even where money is a part of the issue, increased overall spending is unlikely to contribute to the solution. Moreover, most provinces are either holding the line or cutting back. What we cannot do any more is to identify problems and throw money at them. That is just as well. Profligate spending has not produced educational excellence, but it has created a well of bad feeling in taxpayers.

Too many administrators have been conditioned to think first in dollars when school board members suggest any change. Instead, they should be thinking in terms of educational priorities. Faced with budgetary cuts, they are always tempted to eliminate the most visible items from the budget, ones which will produce such a public outcry that the government will be hard pressed to continue the proposed reductions. It is as if a young couple, facing money troubles, decide they must put the baby out for adoption and then call the CBC. Canada simply cannot afford that kind of game playing, even if some may think it morally defensible. When Ontario announced funding cuts in the winter of 1996, my local district, Northumberland, reacted by issuing notices of termination to hundreds of teachers. By June the decision had been virtually nullified. The initial action caused a furor; the cancellation of the notices went largely unobserved.

When I was a senior administrator with a suburban district outside Montreal, the board considered a voluntary late French-immersion program beginning in grade seven, with follow-up in the later grades. In the 1970s French was obviously important for anglophone school boards (ours was a Protestant board, but it served most anglophones in the area: non-religious, Protestant, Jewish, and Catholic). As director of instruction I developed a program that did not cost the board a single additional dollar. Class sizes were larger than the average, to allow for drop-outs, and the purchase of program materials was made possible by delaying the acquisition of English-language materials for the same grades. Later, we developed a two-track French program from grade seven to the end of high school (as well as the grade seven immersion), permitting students to be placed at any grade level in either the slow or the fast track irrespective of their formal grade level or their age. The school board was never asked for a single additional penny for any part of this program. We did not have more students or smaller classes or more materials; no more money was needed. (There may have been a slight increase in transportation costs paid directly by the province. The increase would have been minimal because nearly all students in the district were bused to school, and there was already choice of program in any school.)

That is the gist of the argument in this chapter. Better education does not need more money. We should consider our priorities and the fairness and common sense of spending educational dollars the way we do. Cutbacks do not mean that we should stop considering improvements; on the contrary, they are an opportunity to review our priorities carefully and provide all students an effective program in conformity with their parents' wishes at the least cost.

DOES CANADA SPEND TOO MUCH OR TOO LITTLE ON EDUCATION?

Between 1961 and 1991 educational spending in Canada at the elementary and secondary levels steadily increased in real (i.e. constant) dollars. During those three decades, real per-student spending increased at rates of 6.7, 3.5, and 2.3 per cent per annum respectively. For the same period, administrative expenditures are estimated to have increased by 8.4, 10.6, and 2.9 per cent per annum (Newton et al. 1992, 92). In the two years of low inflation from 1990–91 to 1992–93, enrolment in elementary and secondary education increased by 2.5 per cent, and expenditure by 13.4 per cent.

During the period 1960 to 1988, the pupil-teacher ratio (the famous PTR) fell from 25.6 to 17.8 (Newton et al. 1992, 71). PTR is not the same as class size. It is possible for it to go down while class size increases. There are several reasons for this, and the facts are impossible to determine from either Statistics Canada or most provincial statistics. Teachers have bargained for more release time for course preparation and other duties; that provision requires more teachers or larger classes. In addition, most school systems and provinces count as teachers anyone in the system who is qualified to teach, with the exception of administrators.

Some large urban and suburban school boards have armies of qualified teachers who rarely if ever instruct a class. They are usually the best teachers, promoted out of the classroom to be program consultants, for example. No one has ever shown that school districts with consultants do better academically as a result. That is not a question that school boards and administrators who are building bureaucracies want to have answered. My bet would be that over the last twenty years, when school boards have been busy enforcing unhelpful fads, there has actually been a negative effect from taking excellent teachers out of the classroom and paying them to train teachers to adopt child-centred teaching, integrated subjects, and project-based, instead of sequential, programs of study. There is a possible double effect. The outstanding teachers are replaced by, on average, less outstanding ones, and they spend much of their time implementing dubious or downright harmful programs.

My argument is not that we should have smaller classes instead of preparation time and out-of-school experts. Preparation time may be more useful than a slightly smaller class: there is no evidence that decreasing class size by a few students has any positive effect on learning. Teachers do need time to prepare good lessons, and the bureaucratic requirements have continually increased. The money spent on consultants and other experts should be either saved or devoted to other more useful ends. Pulling the best teachers out of the classroom, to become either administrators or expert helpers is like paying the best lawyers and doctors to stop practising law or medicine and join a government bureaucracy to advise other lawyers and doctors how to practise.

Overall, the provinces have devoted an important proportion of their economic growth and debt to elementary and secondary education. The increased funding appears to have been directed to improved teachers' salaries (which grew faster than the overall increase), to a lower PTR, and to greatly expanded services outside the school. The time of increased educational spending may now have passed, mainly because so much of our higher level of spending was paid for by debt. Greater federal and provincial awareness that we cannot go on charging public spending for services to our credit card makes a new spending spree less likely.

It is ironic that a nation should pay out so much for the education of young people – in the form of good salaries for teachers, small classes, and a large supporting bureaucracy – only to turn over to those young people the debt payments and accumulated interest. Is this incurred indebtedness really in their best interests, or is it more in favour of the quasi-monopolies that provide the service? The intentions may have been good, but the consequences are morally unacceptable. If we really want to waste money doing perverse things in education, we should at least waste our own and not our children's and grandchildren's.

Good teachers should receive good salaries, competitive with those of other professionals. But there is something wrong when unionization results in teachers getting increases solely on the basis of their years in the classroom and paper qualifications, and when a mediocre kindergarten teacher receives the same salary as an excellent teacher of university-entrance physics.

Exactly how Canada ranks in international spending on education is very difficult to determine. Many statistics are published, but they are subject to questionable assumptions. If one compares actual spending, one is faced with the problems of variations in rates of exchange. Thus the recent low value of the Canadian dollar (as against the American dollar and most European currencies) has had the effect of decreasing the comparative spending level of Canada on education. That problem can be avoided by looking at educational expenditure as a percentage of GNP or GDP, a comparison that is confused by differences in the level of wealth, or as a percentage of overall governmental spending. (The assumption behind those comparisons – not necessarily valid – is that education should receive the same proportion of a country's wealth irrespective of the amount of that wealth.) As Table 1 shows, Canada spends more on education as a percentage of GNP and of government expenditure than do most of the OECD countries with which we usually compare ourselves. These figures would change if postsecondary education were excluded; but most comparisons have similar results.

Another indicator is a comparison of the economic standing of teachers in different countries. There can be little doubt that Canadian teachers fare better financially than those in England, the United States, or Australia. An unbiased international comparison was made for the period 1980–84 (Economic Council of Canada 1992, 29). That survey, based on purchasing-power parity, shows that Canadian teachers were generally 25 to 40 per cent better off than their counterparts in other countries – Denmark, Sweden, Germany, Britain, the United States, and Japan. A more recent survey (also based on purchasing-power parity) was carried out by the American Federation of Teachers (F. Howard Nelson, *Fiscal Proceedings of the*

Table 1
Expenditure on education by selected Western countries

	as % of govt expense	as % of GNP
Canada 1992	7.6	14.3
USA 1990	5.3	12.3
Japan 1991	4.7	16.6
Austria 1992	5.8	7.7
France 1993	5.7	na
Germany 1991	4.1	11.6
United Kingdom 1991	5.2	na
Sweden 1992	8.3	12.6
Australia 1991	5.5	14.1
Median (excluding Canada)	5.4	13.2

SOURCE: *Statistical Yearbook 1995* (UNESCO and Bernan Press, Lanham, MD, 1995).

National Center for Educational Statistics [1993, Washington, DC]). As well as finding, unsurpisingly, that American teachers are not paid enough, the survey shows that Toronto elementary teachers receive maximum salaries second only to those in Zurich. Saskatchewan and Quebec pay higher maximum salaries than most other places (e.g. the United States, France, England, Germany, the Netherlands, Hong Kong, Sweden, and Australia), being exceeded only by Japan and Switzerland.

Overall, it is fair to say that elementary and secondary education remains very well funded in Canada. However, in the context of our national debt, it would be foolish to anticipate continued growth in educational expenditure. It would be unreasonable to expect the education sector to escape the inevitable cuts resulting from a twenty-year spending spree (from which educators have certainly benefited). The real test is to cut spending without harming children's education. The challenge is to improve that education while spending less. To pass the test and address the challenge, governments need a honed knife rather than a bludgeon.

The evidence is that the bludgeon is the weapon of choice in Alberta and in Ontario. One problem is that cuts are being left to the bureaucracies to make. In the spring of 1996, major school districts in Ontario, like my local board, gave thousands of teachers notice of termination in order to be ready for whatever level of cuts would be imposed. Most of those teachers were not laid off, but harm is obviously done when the youngest and in some cases the best are seen as so readily expendable. The unions' last-in/first-out rule, accepted

by most school districts in their union contacts, is one major problem; another is the inevitable tendency of unfettered bureaucracies
to put bureaucratic maintenance ahead of teachers and students; and
a third lies in the rigidity of collective agreements that prevent any
kind of discrimination in teachers' salaries, except on the basis of
qualifications and experience.

IS MONEY FOR EDUCATION SHARED FAIRLY AMONG THE PROVINCES?

Some readers in the rich provinces may consider this question irrelevant. After all, they will argue, everyone agrees that elementary and
secondary education is a provincial jurisdiction. From that perspective, the question is whether the federal government should have a
continuing role in postsecondary education, not whether it should
develop one at the elementary and secondary levels.

The provinces have, and will continue to have, almost total authority over educational spending, which they may or may not delegate
to school boards or schools; but there remains the question of where
the money comes from. The federal government makes two fairly
general and substantial grants to the provinces: equalization payments to the poorer ones and the Canada Health and Social Transfer
to all provinces. The latter transfer is not designated for elementary
and secondary education; but since the grants are not tied to spending, they can be seen as fairly general transfers provided that federal
policies in certain areas (e.g. in health care and social welfare) are
respected.

Tables 2 and 3 illustrate the interprovincial variations. Ontario
spends about 30 per cent more per student than does Prince Edward
Island, with a similar difference in teachers' maximum salaries. I am
not assuming that spending should be identical from coast to coast.
Wages in the Maritimes, for example, are generally lower than in British Columbia for all employees, not only teachers. In previous times,
the discrepancies may not have been of great interest; schools
throughout Canada have been reasonably well supported. But these
are not previous times. The danger is that services in the poorer provinces may fall below a reasonable minimum standard as provincial
and federal governments alike face their unsustainable levels of debt.
For example, between 1986 and 1993, educational salaries increased
by 38 per cent in affluent Ontario and British Columbia, but by only
18 per cent in Saskatchewan and 25 per cent in New Brunswick.

The federal government should, in consultation with the provinces, ensure that reasonable minimum standards are maintained in

Table 2
Total expenditure per elementary/secondary pupil and teacher and pupil-teacher
ratio (PTR), 1992–93 (by province, with rank order in brackets)

	$ per pupil	$ per teacher	PTR
Canada	6518	115 750	15.8
Newfoundland	5313 (8)	82 984 (10)	14.7 (1)
Prince Edward Island	5228 (10)	93 796 (8)	17.1 (7)
Nova Scotia	5248 (9)	86 044 (9)	17.0 (6)
New Brunswick	5763 (6)	98 089 (7)	17.1 (7)
Quebec	6875 (2)	122 558 (1)	15.7 (4)
Ontario	6918 (1)	119 401 (2)	15.0 (2)
Manitoba	6356 (3)	106 692 (6)	15.1 (3)
Saskatchewan	5433 (7)	107 548 (5)	17.6 (9)
Alberta	5915 (5)	111 750 (4)	17.7 (10)
British Columbia	6343 (4)	116 175 (3)	16.6 (5)

SOURCE: *Education in Canada* (Statistics Canada, 1995).

Table 3
Mean salaries for teachers with five years of postsecondary education, 1991–92
(by province; rank order in brackets)

Province	Minimum	Maximum
Newfoundland	28 394 (10)	40 786 (10)
Prince Edward Island	29 189 (9)	45 235 (9)
Nova Scotia	31 678 (5)	50 448 (4)
New Brunswick	29 424 (8)	45 371 (8)
Quebec	30 593 (6)	46 113 (7)
Ontario	35 158 (2)	61 255 (1)
Manitoba	32 993 (3)	49 953 (5)
Saskatchewan	29 535 (7)	47 975 (6)
Alberta	32 262 (4)	53 169 (3)
British Columbia	36 663 (1)	54 673 (2)

SOURCE: *PAPT Sentinel* (1993).

all basic areas under provincial jurisdiction: health, welfare, education, roads and transport, and police and justice. In place of the current confusing and provocative social transfer and equalization
programs, it would be better if every province were guaranteed a
certain percentage of the national average spending in each area, say,
between 80 and 90 per cent. This would be paid for by means of a
set number of percentage points of personal income tax and of the
Goods and Services Tax. The share for each province, in the case of

elementary and secondary education, would be based on the number of young people between the ages of six (or younger, if there is consensus on early education) and eighteen, whether or not they are in school, in order to provide the utmost flexibility to provinces for educational services. There is nothing in this proposal to prevent differences in levels of income tax and GST among provinces. It will be argued that they would never agree to such a change. That is far from certain: the proposal would give them stronger influence over the amount of money to be devoted to basic services and over the taxes used to support them. As provinces would be differentially advantaged by the high or low level of support guaranteed, a federal decision would be required on that one central issue; but federal tax points would be the means of providing the money.

There should be a deduction from each province's basic services grant, representing its potential revenue from a tax on real estate, a traditional source of support for educational spending. The deduction might be, for example, 0.6 per cent of 85 per cent of the true (or actual) market value of each province's residential and business and professional property (based on a three-year rolling assessment, with the percentage rate varying according to national fluctuations in property value). The numbers used here are for purposes of illustration only and would be subject to intense negotiations. The level and basis of real estate taxes actually assessed in each province or school district for educational and other purposes would be left to the discretion of the provinces. If a province wished to abolish them altogether and substitute higher provincial income or sales taxes, that would be its decision. The deduction at the national level for all provinces simply serves to reflect the differences in potentially taxable business and residential wealth. It also reflects the fact that property is taxed in all provinces.

The great advantage of the proposed system is that, symbolically, transfers would be made from richer individuals to poorer ones, not from province to province. A taxpayer would pay the same taxes for basic services (including education) irrespective of the province of residence. Provinces would retain the right to tax as much or as little as they liked for additional educational (and other) services. There would be no more playing with the formulas to help provinces that are "squeaky wheels" or supporters of the government in power, and the intensity of bad feeling between have and have-not provinces would be eased. It would no longer be Ontario supporting the Maritimes, or Alberta supporting Quebec, but rich people everywhere supporting the poor throughout the country. Torontonians like to oppose the equalization of taxes within Ontario, or even within the greater Toronto area, using the argument that there are more poor children in the city than in the Atlantic provinces. Poor people would not pay much tax under this plan (as is the case at the moment); and the better off would pay the same rate for basic services wherever they lived.

If, as seems to be the case, current formulas are arranged to the advantage of Quebec, as compared with the more needy Atlantic provinces, Quebec could be expected to object to the policy proposed here. However, when discussions develop with that province, as they surely will, concerning increased autonomy, there will inevitably be some trade off between its current high level of subsidization and increased independence. The fact that Quebec, a have-not province, is able to spend almost as much as Ontario on education is in part a reflection of its favourable grant status. Quebec is also one of the most highly taxed provinces, with heavy spending on administration and subsidies.

It will be objected that this proposal will increase the effective level of interprovincial transfer (although that will depend on the percentage of average national expenditure on basic services covered by the plan). Currently, however, there are gross disparities in the percentage of provincial personal income devoted to education (including the postsecondary level), which varies from under 9 per cent to over 11. The additional cost to the more affluent citizens in some of the richer provinces would be reduced once the excess spending in their own provinces was curbed. There need be no sudden upset to individuals if the new grant structure were introduced gradually over five years.

Once a base level of funding per student, or foundation plan, is established across Canada, it becomes easier for minorities that are discriminated against by the large educational bureaucracies to be granted their share. The principle that it is the schools attended by students that deserve educational support, rather than the school district bureaucracies, would be established. In the current battles over educational jurisdiction, parents and students are forgotten as school boards fight with provinces, and provinces with other provinces and the federal government. From the federal level to the school, from the school district to the courts, the current working assumption is that educational funding is a matter for competing bureaucracies; parents and students are of no account. This is an outdated and unsupportable assumption. It also encourages wasteful spending on the part of affluent school districts, particularly those with a high commercial property base with ownership spread outside the local tax jurisdiction (e.g. Toronto and Ottawa).

IS IT FAIR TO HAVE BIG DIFFERENCES IN
EDUCATIONAL SPENDING WITHIN PROVINCES?

Canada, like the United States, has traditionally organized schools under school districts. In the United States the school district used to have, and still does have in some places, a certain degree of logic. Believers in popular democracy founded school districts to ensure that local communities ran their own schools the way they wanted them. The schools were integral parts of the community and avoided the class distinctions that Americans believed European, particularly the English and German, systems supported. Traditionally, the state was a weak part of the educational hierarchy, and the federal government weaker still.

Over the years that pattern has changed in the United States. Large urban and, in some cases, suburban school systems no longer serve distinct communities. Some small suburban school boards strung around the large metropolitan centres continue to serve distinct (often bedroom) communities, but they no longer function to democ ratize and homogenize; most of these small school districts are distinctive on the basis of relative wealth, some also being so by ethnicity or race. The authority of the local district has rested largely on its power to tax. The stronger the state department becomes and the more egalitarian the state in providing equal resources among schools, the weaker the district becomes.

In Canada the local school district has never had the distinguishing virtues (and corresponding limitations) of its American equivalent. Since Confederation, education has been more centralized at the level of the province. The district, usually far from being autonomous, has served more as a buffer between the government and the local people in the district, rather than as an autonomous authority. Further, Canada was not founded on a separation of church and state. Since before Confederation and reinforced by the articles of union, Ontario and Quebec have had entirely separate systems for public and separate schools (in Ontario) and Roman Catholic and Protestant schools (in Quebec). The confessional system is changing in Quebec to one based on language, but it seems likely that Roman Catholic schools will remain in some form. Although the other founding signatories to Confederation, Nova Scotia and New Brunswick, did not and do not have systems differentiated by religion (New Brunswick has recently developed two systems distinguished by language), they both retained a few de facto English-language Roman Catholic schools. Public schools in Canada were, until comparatively recently, by law as well as by practice, Christian (effectively Protestant in English

Canada), with morning Bible readings, occasional formal services, and religious teaching.

Overall, Alberta, Saskatchewan, Ontario, Quebec, Newfoundland, and the Northwest Territories have, for many years, run overlapping school districts differentiated either between Catholic and Protestant or, more recently, between Catholic and secular. I shall return to the problem of religious schools, and Newfoundland's unique situation, later. My concern here is with the nature of the school district. Obviously, there is a limit to the extent that a school board can reflect a genuine geographical community if it serves only a part of the population and is based on religious affiliation. This is a complete contradiction of the American ideal, where there have been no explicitly denomination-based public schools.

Over the years, Canadian school boards have become even more divorced from genuine community than they were at the outset. There have been many reasons, the most important being the changing character of the population and the growing size of the school district. The population has become more diverse: by religion, ideology, race, ethnicity, social class, and culture. Cities, suburbs, and even rural areas are increasingly divided by type of housing and therefore by type of resident; I refer here to differences within municipal boundaries much more than between municipalities. Most provinces have tried to make public education more efficient by increasing the size of school districts, although there is no evidence that the enormous bureaucracies are more efficient than medium-sized school districts. If efficiency means lower cost per pupil, then the small rural districts in Ontario are more efficient than the large urban and suburban ones. In British Columbia, Peter Coleman found a negative relationship between school board size and both per-pupil costs and academic achievement (even after allowing for differences in social background).

So what do school districts and their history have to do with the fairness of differences in funding within provinces? The answer is, Everything. I have suggested that the relative autonomy of the American school district has traditionally depended on its ability to raise most of its revenue from local taxpayers. Ontario is the only province in Canada that still permited, at the time of writing, a high degree of local fund-raising for education. In all other provinces, either school funding is essentially centralized or else the local financial autonomy is in practice rather slight.

Interestingly, the one other holdout against centralization was, until recently, Alberta, another affluent province. When Premier Ralph Klein came to make across-the-board cuts in all areas of government including education, the first thing he did was to centralize

Table 4
Selected school board expenditures, Ontario, 1990 (in dollars per pupil)

Board	Elementary	Secondary
AFFLUENT URBAN BOARDS		
Metropolitan Toronto	4703	7870
Ottawa	5630	7609
Mean	5667	7740
LESS AFFLUENT BOARDS		
Lanark	4291	5510
Elgin	3760	5164
Sault Ste Marie	4703	5651
Windsor	4687	6625
Mean	4360	5738
ROMAN CATHOLIC BOARDS		
Lakehead	3900	5300
Frontenac/Lennox/Addington	4485	5006
Hastings/Prince Edward	3500	4400
Mean	3962	4902
SUBURBAN BOARDS		
Carleton (Nepean)	4584	6037
Peel (Mississauga/Brampton)	4661	6469
York Region (Markham)	4562	6089
Halton (Burlington/Oakville)	4426	6185
Mean	4458	6195
PERCENTAGE TORONTO/OTTAWA GREATER THAN		
Less affluent boards (selected)	30	35
Roman Catholic boards (selected)	43	58
Suburban boards (selected)	28	25

SOURCE: *School Board 3 Year Statistics* (Ministry of Education, Toronto, 1990).

funding and to cut the powers of local school districts. Poor provinces simply cannot afford much local autonomy, and even affluent ones, such as British Columbia and Alberta, when they come to make cuts, find that local autonomy has to be sacrificed.

We thus come to Ontario, the province still wrestling with the interrelated problems of cutting costs and the traditional financial autonomy of affluent local school boards. Table 4 provides a snapshot of the variation in expenditure of some Ontario boards in 1990. The Progressive Conservative government under Michael Harris initially imposed cuts in its grants to school boards from which the

Toronto and Ottawa boards were exempt because they were ineligible to receive government grants in the first place. The high taxes on business and commercial property and low taxes on the extremely valuable residential property in the city of Toronto means that its affluent residents can enjoy the best of both worlds: relatively low property taxes and per-pupil expenditures more than 50 per cent higher than in some rural districts. The Toronto-based media have strongly opposed any real equalization, favouring taxes based on services, a policy that recalls the infamous poll (head) tax that Margaret Thatcher tried to introduce in Britain – to universal condemnation from the Canadian media. No one seriously argues that only the parents of children in school should pay educational taxes, which would be the logic of taxes based on service.

The Ontario government is planning to centralize all educational expenditure. The educational property tax, residential and commercial, is likely to be equalized at a considerably reduced level as municipalities assume financial responsibility for some other services. It remains to be seen if the new enlarged (metropolitan) city of Toronto will be able to resist equalized tax rates in the old city of Toronto, and if it will be able to continue to subsidize its rich homeowners by means of taxes on national and international corporations that are unavailable to the rest of the province.

City dwellers in Ontario argue that urban education is inevitably more costly than rural, but that is not the case generally in Canada, except where historical discrepancies have been maintained (e.g. in British Columbia). Problems of poverty and of immigrants are seen as causes. In Quebec and New Brunswick, where provincial funding has been predominant for several decades, urban and rural expenditures are essentially equal. The greater cost of transportation in rural areas balances the increased need for special programs in the cities.

I am not arguing that a provincial monopoly is more efficient than a local one, but I am underlining both the inefficiency and the unfairness of centrally sanctioned local monopolies. A high degree of centralized funding is essential, but it does not imply the centralization of all policies. New Zealand, for example, has centralized funding, but there are no school boards, and each school's parent council effectively controls local school policy. The Netherlands has centralized funding for secular and denominational school systems, as Quebec has had for Catholic and Protestant systems and New Brunswick for English- and French-language ones. Alberta saw the need to centralize funding if cuts in expenditure were to be fairly applied.

Ontario will end up with (at least) central funding and budgeting for public and Roman Catholic schools.

The main argument for local funding is that it permits a community to set its own priorities, but school districts today hardly ever represent distinct communities. Beyond that, the argument is only legitimate if members of the school district bear the additional costs. The use of a business and commercial property tax to the advantage of the affluent over the poor is totally unjustifiable, and even abhorrent in a pluralistic democracy.

One important issue at the heart of this discussion is the fairness of a tax on residential property. Some people argue that property taxes are unfair anyway, and others that true market value taxes are the problem. The idea that any government would abolish property taxes in the current financial context is a fantasy. The use of some form of true market value as the base for residential property taxation is virtually uncontested outside Ontario. The justification is very simple: expensive homes are an indication of ability to pay, and the property tax is harder for the rich to evade than income or sales taxes. Certainly, under true market value taxation, elderly residents are sometimes compelled to sell their relatively expensive homes if they have little income, but that is normal for many people as they grow old. Higher income taxes would also force people – for the most part, poorer people than those who own $300 000 homes – to sell their homes, perhaps with negative equity.

The only strong voices opposing true market value come from residents of major cities, particularly Toronto, whose taxes would increase under a more just system. It is worth noting that the inflated gains in Toronto homes have been tax-free. If the owners have been long-term residents, they make enormous tax-free gains on the sale of their homes. If they have purchased them recently and have not experienced capital gains, they must have been sufficiently affluent to raise the required funds or loans.

In short, the original idea of the local school district no longer has currency in contemporary Canada. The real question is whether school boards are needed at all, or whether their few remaining tasks (planning new schools, providing a range of program options, arranging transport) would be better carried out by a single public agency reporting to the province. If school districts have little or no financial autonomy and do not represent a distinct community, what should be their responsibilities, if any? As currently constituted and funded, school boards, particularly in Ontario, are an expensive barrier to constructive change. New Brunswick has taken the lead in

abolishing them, but the changes may well lead to more centralization of educational policy rather than less.

WHAT IS THE FEDERAL GOVERNMENT'S ROLE IN ELEMENTARY AND SECONDARY EDUCATION?

The role of the federal government in the funding of education is and
will remain a minor one, except in areas under direct federal jurisdiction. Even in the Yukon and Northwest Territories, the educational influence of British Columbia and Alberta respectively is at
least as great of that of the federal government. Those who argue
that funding of Roman Catholic schools is simply a historical relic of
the British North America Act should note that Roman Catholic
schools are federally supported in the Northwest Territories.

I shall not describe the detailed ways in which the federal government is and has been involved in educational funding, but will
mention areas of relevance to major policy issues for the future.
While subordinate to the provinces in education, the federal government is not irrelevant to its funding and direction. It provides
funding for second-language programs, thereby contributing to the
rapid growth of French immersion, an alternative program that
does not appeal equally to a random cross-section of the population. (Middle-class people often prefer French immersion, particularly if they do not like their local school.) The emphasis on choice
of education by first official language and on the mandatory teaching of the second language is federal in origin; the policy has not
always received strong support from all provinces. It is not obvious
why the federal government should continue to interfere in this
particular area, promoting as much social tension as it resolves.
Either there should be a federal act, comparable to the legislation
on health policy, assuring non-discrimination on the basis of official
language, religion, race, and ethnicity, or the federal government
should get out of the field completely. Piecemeal involvement
distorts spending.

By far the largest federal source of funding for elementary and
secondary education consists of the transfers (equalization grants) to
provinces, already discussed. My argument is that these grants
should be more directly related to the basic funding needs of the
provinces and determined by distinct tax points, in order that taxpayers may see exactly how much they are paying for the basic
provincial programs, and how much extra they are putting out
within their own province. Transfers should be seen as being from
rich to poor taxpayers, not from rich to poor provinces.

THE FUNDING OF INDEPENDENT
AND RELIGIOUS SCHOOLS

There are some generalizations that can be made across Canada about the support of public schools. Provinces provide a major share. There is a tendency to increased centralization (despite the rhetoric about school-based management). Ontario was the only exception, but even there, centralization of control is certainly not weakening; provincial regulations cover the most minute details of school operation, and current policy legislation has led to increased centralization of funding.

In the case of private or independent education, on the other hand, there is no safe generalization to be made for Canada as a whole. The terms "private" and "independent" are used interchangeably, but they cover a wide range of accommodations and denials. Strong supporters of a centralized monopoly controlled by the educational establishment use the word "private" pejoratively to suggest profit and unequal accessibility. The majority of independent schools are far from being financially profitable, however; most are hard put to survive. Independent schools are private in the sense that they are not public, but they may be more accessible than are some so-called public Roman Catholic schools (which refuse admission to non-Catholics). I have already described the enormous disparities in accessibility within Ontario's public school system. People often think of private schools as elite institutions for the wealthy, disregarding the more numerous religious schools that serve parents of average means. The independent school is an important area for educational policy because there is no common understanding of what it is, and no logical policy in most provinces to determine the dividing line between fully supported, partially supported, and unsupported schools.

British Columbia, Manitoba, Alberta, and Quebec all provide partial funding to support independent schools that meet certain conditions. These provinces differ in their treatment of Roman Catholic schools, with British Columbia and Manitoba treating such schools on the same basis as Seventh-Day Adventist or Dutch Reformed institutions, while Alberta and Quebec have fully funded Roman Catholic systems as well as partially supported religious and secular schools.

British Columbia has the most sophisticated set of funding criteria and, together with Manitoba, cannot be accused of discriminating by religion. It has five categories of independent school. The first category receives approximately 50 per cent of the public school level of funding. To qualify, such schools must report to the department; not

Table 5
Changes in public and private school enrolment from 1988–89 to 1993–94, and private enrolment in 1993–94 as a proportion of total enrolment (in percentages)

	Public (change 1988–89 to 1993–94)	Private (change 1988–89 to 1993–94)	Private as % of total (1993–94)
Canada	+5.9	+15.0	4.96
Newfoundland	−11.1		
Prince Edward Island	−2.2		
Nova Scotia	−1.7		
New Brunswick	+1.6		
Quebec	+0.4	+4.4	9.01
Ontario	+9.4	+18.6	3.52
Manitoba	−1.5	+18.2	5.34
Saskatchewan	−2.1	+5.1	1.50
Alberta	+11.1	+32.8	3.55
British Columbia	+11.4	+32.0	7.92

SOURCE: *Education in Canada* (Statistics Canada, 1995).

NOTE: Private enrolments in Atlantic Canada are too small for changes or percentages to be meaningful.

teach racial superiority, religious intolerance, or violent social change; employ only certified teachers; follow the provincial curriculum; and not spend more per student than the local school district. The second category receives about 35 per cent of public school funding, but does not have to restrict costs to the level of public schools. The third receives only 10 per cent of public school funding and does not have to employ certified teachers or follow provincial program requirements. The final two categories receive no funding.

In British Columbia, only 14 per cent of independent enrolment is in schools belonging to the Independent Schools Association, a group committed to high academic standards and high values (often referred to as the elite schools); most of the remaining enrolment is in schools with a religious focus. There has been a gradual increase in the private school population, recent statistics showing over 7 per cent of the total enrolment in such schools. The NDP government under Premier Michael Harcourt moved to reduce funding for those religiously based schools most independent of government policy, the ones often described as fundamentalist. Alberta supports independent schools in a somewhat similar manner. Manitoba is the most generous supporter of private schools and attaches the fewest strings, with target funding at 80 per cent of the public level.

Quebec has an elaborate protocol for the funding of private schools not entirely unlike that of British Columbia, but in practice it does not appear to be easy for institutions to know exactly how the criteria will be applied. Nevertheless, in 1993–94 the province had the highest enrolment in private schools of any (9.01 per cent of total enrolment). Many of the private schools are Roman Catholic, which is not the case in the provinces with publicly funded Catholic systems, probably because the public Catholic schools in Quebec, particularly the large secondary *polyvalents*, have been secularized.

Quebec is in the process of changing to two public systems, one French, the other English. One nominally Protestant board (Laurenval) has an enrolment that is only 28 per cent Protestant, with greater proportions of Jewish and Roman Catholic students. It seems likely that Catholic schools are more Catholic where they are a minority denomination (e.g. in Ontario and Newfoundland) than in Quebec. The future of religion in the publicly supported schools of that province must remain in some doubt once their constitutional protection is removed.

Saskatchewan and Ontario are the most discriminatory provinces in their treatment of independent schools. Both fully fund public Roman Catholic separate schools, but provide no support for the independent schools attended by members of other denominations or religions. (Saskatchewan provides support for independent schools for children with special needs and for a few academic high schools historically receiving partial support.)

Ontario, the largest province with the most varied population, is the most overtly discriminatory in its treatment of religion, just as it is the most unfair in its financial support of public schools. The problem has been exacerbated by the deliberate political (as distinct from judicial) decision in the mid-1980s to extend funding of Roman Catholic education from grade ten to the end of high school. Similarly, a nominally judicial decision, welcomed by government and establishment alike, to forbid the teaching of Christian religion, previously mandatory in elementary schools but frequently not carried out in practice, created an anomalous situation where the traditional Protestant majority is denied any schools representing its beliefs, while the traditional minority has a fully funded system. To be fair to government, the mainstream Protestant denominations, notably the Anglican and United churches, with their secularized and politicized liberal leadership and declining congregations, have either supported (as in the case of Newfoundland) or condoned the secularization of the schools and have not supported the Roman Catholic Church's attempt to retain a genuine Christian influence. It is ironic that in the second half of the twentieth century, when the Christian tradition is waning, some of the strongest criticism of publicly supported Christian schools has come from the leaders of the mainstream Protestant denominations.

The NDP government in Ontario eagerly reinforced the judicial decision to ban religious teaching by refusing to permit public boards even to provide optional programs during the lunch break. Thus the various minorities desiring a religious education, including the substantial evangelical Christian denominations, Orthodox and Conservative Jews, and the increasing Muslim population, are left with a publicly financed education that is strongly secular in character. Even a preference by non-Catholics for a publicly funded Catholic education is not always recognized, some districts requiring baptismal certificates for admission. It is possible that right of access is more abused by publicly supported, than by independent, schools, since the latter are often desperate for increased enrolment to keep them afloat.

In my discussion of discriminatory funding, I am clearly not implying that all members of religious groups would prefer religious to secular schools. Just as some Roman Catholic children attend public schools rather than fully funded Catholic ones, one may assume that higher proportions of non-Catholics with nominal religious affiliation, whose traditional commitment has been to public schools, including members of the mainstream Protestant denominations, Reform Jews, and westernized Muslims, would choose a secular public school. The gradual secularization of traditionally Christian public schools in most provinces, accompanied by comparatively little public protest and by media celebration, is evidence of the acceptance by many Christians of a secular system.

New Brunswick, Nova Scotia, and Prince Edward Island are similar to one another in that none has a strong independent school tradition. The Maritime provinces are less overtly discriminatory than Ontario and Saskatchewan. None was bound by the BNA Act of 1867 to provide either religious or French-language school boards. In practice, the English-language public schools have generally been Christian and Protestant, but, as in the rest of the country, they are rapidly becoming secularized. Traditionally, Moncton, Saint John, Charlottetown, and Halifax, all with significant English-speaking Catholic populations, have had publicly supported Catholic schools, administered by their public school boards. They are currently under siege in Saint John, where they were most strongly entrenched.

All three Maritime provinces provide French immersion to anglophone students and French-language schools for francophones within the public system. New Brunswick, Canada's only legally bilingual province, has two essentially autonomous school systems, one French and the other English. This situation contrasts with Quebec and Ontario, each with large anglophone or francophone student populations, which have fairly centralized patterns of program delivery, based on the majority language, delivered in two languages.

Newfoundland may at first sight appear to be similar to the Maritime provinces in that it lacks an independent school tradition. It is, however, unique in that it funds all the major religious groups equally: there is no legal secular school system. That situation is changing in practice and constitutionally. The Integrated (mainstream Protestant) schools are typically not strongly religious, and there is a high level of support, particularly from their teachers and religious leaders, for a move to a secular public school system. The gradual trend has been towards greater association between the Catholic and Integrated schools, evidenced by an increasing number of joint service buildings. The Pentecostal schools have so far fiercely maintained their independence. Newfoundland is the only province where parents do not have access to avowedly secular schools. There is little overt demand, probably because the Integrated schools are often de facto secular.

In 1995 and 1997 plebiscites were held on the question of the legal authority of the churches over education. The government argued that government control would make for greater financial efficiency and that religious teaching would still be retained. A large majority favoured the move in 1997, and the federal government supports the constitutional change requested by the Newfoundland government. The move was strongly opposed by the Roman Catholic and Pentecostal churches, but not by the mainstream Protestant ones. It is remarkable that, in the late 1990s, when so much is spoken about individual rights, a plebiscite should be the justification for the removal of rights from two religious minorities.

Why should there be objection to the constitutional change, it may be asked, if religious education is to remain an option? Compulsory religious education in England has had little influence on the beliefs of that country's people. I was at one time the principal of the first combined Roman Catholic and public elementary school in Saint John, New Brunswick. The absence of a religious community in the school undermined the Catholicity of the optional religious program. Religion survives best in a school that is a part of a genuine religious community.

I recently attended the first (Roman Catholic) Communion of one of my granddaughters. For the special service the large, modern, suburban church was filled by parents, siblings, relatives, and friends of the forty or so first communicants. The school attended by these children was very much a part of the service, with heavy involvement by the principal, vice-principal, and teachers (very different from the experience of my Anglican grandchildren). Although some of those Catholic children will undoubtedly be secularized by the powerful mass culture of the general society – not all will remain practising Catholics – the strong sense of community and belonging invested in occasions such as this impresses Catholicity much more strongly on children than anything provided by the mainstream Protestant churches. The school prepared these children for Communion. In contrast, the public school attended by mainstream Protestant children is at most neutral to religion; many strongly religious parents see it as actively hostile, with teachers ignoring religion as a factor in morals and values, and some sarcastic or derisive.

The provision of religious education in public or independent schools is a crucial part of the debate about educational policy in Canada. Some readers will consider this discussion of religion as irrelevant in a chapter on funding. But in my judgment, the grossly discriminatory funding of religious schooling in Canada is the single most important issue in this area. It is precisely because the issue affects minorities (a majority of parents are highly unlikely to choose religious schools, even if discrimination were abolished across the country tomorrow) that it is so important.

Most independent schools in Canada have a religious or denominational focus. The same is true elsewhere. In the United States and Australia, both English-speaking democracies with Roman Catholic minorities who do not have their own public schools, Roman Catholic schools account for a substantial part of the independent sector. Much of the opposition among the elites in Canada to independent schools is attributable to anti-religious sentiment. There was widespread negative reaction to the increased public funding of Roman Catholic schools in Ontario, partly based on residual Orange Protestantism, but much more, at least in the media, on opposition to religious schooling in principle. In the Netherlands, where secular and denominational schools have been equally funded for over half a century, the various schools exist peacefully side by side, and parents have free choice.

The discrimination in Canada becomes most obvious when one compares the situation of committed Roman Catholic and Protestant parents in different parts of the country. In Toronto, Catholic parents have a choice between fully funded Catholic and public schools. In Winnipeg the choice is between a public school and a substantially funded Catholic independent one. In Fredericton there is no choice, simply a secular public school. Dutch Reformed Protestants in the Toronto area may have the choice of a Catholic school, depending on where they live, but they will probably have to pay full fees or put up with a strongly secular public school. In Calgary they will have a partially funded Calvinist option, but in Fredericton there is not even a Catholic one. No province funds schools in accordance with parents' spiritual or secular values without discrimination; only British Columbia and Manitoba treat all denominations and religions equally. So discussion of independent schools has little national meaning; their definition depends on the province in which one resides.

The question of independent and religious schools underlies much of the policy discussion that follows later in this book. If my assumption that there is considerable and increasing dissent about education in Canada is correct, then the line between the public and the independent school is an important one; but it cannot be discussed without reference to the kinds of choices available within the public system.

At the national level, the decision has been made that education in the minority official language shall be provided, although the terms of that provision are debated in British Columbia, Alberta, Manitoba, Ontario, and Quebec. Simply, provincial jurisdiction in educational policy is not and never has been sacrosanct. Provinces (most obviously British Columbia and Ontario) have, ostensibly for judicial reasons, gradually changed the public school from being vaguely Protestant or Judaeo-Christian to determinedly secular, with the approval (or at the behest) of the courts.

The Supreme Court has been politicized by the Constitution Act and the entrenchment of the Canadian Charter of Rights and Freedoms. The Charter effectively grants an improbably impartial Supreme Court legislative authority; appointments to the court are left in the politically partisan hands of the prime minister. In that context, it is not surprising that the Supreme Court has done much to promote the interests of, for example, francophones, homosexuals, common-law spouses, and native peoples, but nothing for religious minorities where they are not protected by the original BNA Act of 1867. This is not to suggest that the Supreme Court's judgments have been judicially incorrect, but that their interpretations have been permeated by the dominant liberal and politically correct ideologies of the elites, including Canada's major law schools. No recent federal government has seen much advantage in protecting religious rights. Prime ministers from Quebec have shown determination to defend the educational rights of francophones outside the province (notably in Ontario and Alberta), but no interest in protecting educational religious rights, either inside or outside Quebec.

Provinces and local school boards have offered a variety of alternative schools and programs. In Ontario at least 40 per cent of students in fully funded schools do not attend anything approaching a common school (defined as a school attended by a reasonable cross-section of young people living in the immediate area and following a relatively undifferentiated program). Most, but by no means all, of this 40 per cent are in the Roman Catholic system or in French-immersion schools or programs. So one can no longer distinguish, in terms of selectivity, between a supposedly common public school and a distinctive independent one.

Independent schools can best be defined in Canada, not as schools for dissenting minorities (some of which have their own public schools), but as those which the provinces decline to fund. Ontario is the province with the largest number of unfunded independent schools: the elite schools along the Belleville–St Catharines axis are far outnumbered by such poor (in terms of finance, not quality) schools as the Netherlands Reformed in the Norwich area. In Canada as a whole, per-student spending is about the same in private schools as it is in public institutions.

Excluding the Atlantic region and Saskatchewan, the schools in provinces with a significant independent enrolment receive between 40 and 45 per cent of their funding from fees; in Ontario the proportion is 68 per cent (Newton et al. 1992). Day-school fees in Toronto's elite independent schools are well over $10 000, with total per-pupil spending about 40 per cent higher than in the expensive public system. Although in Ontario, independent school expenditure on the average slightly exceeds that of the public schools, there are many independent schools whose per-student spending falls well below the public levels. The difference is most evident in teachers' salaries and facilities and in the lack of a bureaucratic structure and support service outside the school.

Several conclusions can be made at this point. Minority schools are funded on a greatly variable basis in Canada. It is not simply a matter of different levels of public funding, but of different definitions of what constitutes independent education. That education costs about the same as public instruction, but this fact hides enormous variations, with elite schools costing much more and many religious schools getting by on much less. A large part of the saving stems from lower teachers' salaries. Enrolment appears to be sensitive to the level of provincial financial support. The patterns of funding for schools, particularly religious ones, across Canada are grossly discriminatory. Some provinces, notably British Columbia and Manitoba, have made genuine attempts to deal with the problem gradually, comprehensively, and fairly. Ontario, with its unjust system of financial support for public schools, is exceptionally discriminatory in its treatment of religion.

Although the statistics are not broken down, it is reasonable to assume that publicly funded Catholic schools spend a little less than the public school norm – certainly, this remains the case in Ontario, although the gap is narrowing. Other minority schools (notably French-immersion) probably spend more than regular public schools (for smaller classes and transportation). Non-publicly funded religious schools generally spend less than public ones.

It may seem contradictory for me to assume that cuts will have to be made in educational funding and then to suggest that independent schools should be funded fairly. There are two answers. First, there are other areas where increased spending could be justified, and not only on the basis of fairness and the elimination of unsupportable discrimination. School districts often cut first anything that does not involve personnel. Such an approach may seem humane, but I argue that education should be for students, not for the people providing the service. Many schools are sadly lacking in up-to-date textbooks, and many school libraries are a disgrace. Music and art programs are sometimes so badly cut that genuine expression and skill development are rare. Later, I shall show how badly school-to-work programs have fared in recent years. Student evaluation is totally inadequate in many provinces, including big-spending Ontario.

Across-the-board cuts by a monopoly (as in Alberta) are generally ineffective in terms of program maintenance, let alone improvement, even though they do save the money intended. Unfortunately, there is no reason to assume that future cuts by large provincial bureaucracies will be made in those areas that parents and the public would most approve. With increased decentralization of programs, more school choice, and more parental authority, parents would be able to influence the cuts and, more important, would be able to choose the schools that have not sacrificed the program of most importance to them. Unfair discrimination is one reason for reallocating school funding, but it is far from the only one. I have earlier pointed out the need for changes in the funding of education among provinces and within the province of Ontario.

Second, in the long run, providing partial funding to minority schools may save money. It is impossible to forecast exactly what proportion of parents would choose schools with a religious orientation if they were partially funded at different rates. In British Columbia, independent enrolment has been steadily increasing and now exceeds 7 per cent, as is shown in Table 5. In Australia, where support has been provided for many more years (and where there are no public Catholic schools), independent enrolment is over 30 per cent. Manitoba, Alberta, and British Columbia provide partial funding to independent schools based on open criteria; in each case, the rate of enrolment continues to grow steadily.

If Ontario funded independent schools at half the public rate, by the time that 10 per cent of students were enrolled in independent schools, the saving to the province would be about $300 million per year; that figure assumes that all current enrolment would be funded. If only those schools spending amounts equal to or less than comparable public schools were to receive funding, the eventual saving would be increased and the initial cost reduced.

WHERE DOES THE MONEY GO?

Unfortunately, it is very difficult to determine exactly how money is spent on elementary and secondary education. The best resources for factual information on Canadian education are the complementary publications of the Economic Council of Canada, *A Lot to Learn* (Economic Council of Canada 1992) and *Education and Training in Canada* (Newton et al. 1992), to which I am greatly indebted. The authors of the latter study conclude, with commendable restraint, "we have frequently been struck by the paucity and poverty of data." These two documents are recommended to those who want more information about many of the factual aspects of this section.

I was responsible for developing a questionnaire circulated to the provinces by an independent, non-partisan agency concerning funding and administrative policies. The lack of consistency and, in many cases, of important data makes informed provincial comparison and national discussion difficult. There is no agreed definition of what constitutes "administrative," for example, so that interprovincial comparisons are of limited value.

I have referred to the convenient confusion of out-of-school personnel with teachers in the classroom. Manitoba defines teachers as "all certified teachers on the school division payroll who render direct and personal services which are in the nature of teaching or *the improvement of the teacher learning situation*" (my emphasis). While "supervisors" are appropriately classified as administrators, the combining of non-teaching consulting personnel with classroom teachers makes the intelligent analysis of expenditures and potential economies impossible. There is no single area of school board expenditure where the number of personnel per thousand students is more varied than that of consultants (part-time and full-time.) Put a different way, consultants (the term is used generically to include all curriculum and special-service personnel who are qualified teachers but not classroom teachers) constitute the single greatest area of discretionary spending.

When teachers are asked to suggest where spending cuts can be made, as Peel teachers in Ontario were in 1991–92, I have been informally told that consultants are high on the list of suggestions. Peel teachers never heard the results of their questionnaire; one has to wonder if the answers were unflattering to the central bureaucracy. While it may be that teachers are more willing to throw consultants out of the lifeboat than jump themselves, many teachers do see them as an unnecessary luxury, even though they have respect and affection for the individuals with whom they work. Whereas a school district must have a superintendent (director), clerical personnel, and custodians, there is no necessity for consultants. Further, it is not at all clear that additional spending on out-of-school personnel is related in any positive way to changes in students.

In Newfoundland, the poorest province, the heaviest spender on education in comparison to personal income, and the second lowest on education overall, the numbers of "others" (defined as guidance counsellors and specialist teachers) in the Integrated and Roman Catholic systems increased from 632.5 in 1988–89 to 648 in 1989–90 (a 3.5 per cent increase in one year) and to 653.65 in 1990–91. There were nearly two and a half times as many "others" in 1991 as there were school board administrators. ("Others" do not include special-education teachers.) So official "administrative costs" tell only a small part of the story about out-of-school spending.

There is no surprise, then, that teachers wonder how the official PTR can go down so remarkably while class sizes decrease more slowly or not at all. Those who hold non-teaching responsibilities – guidance counsellors, curriculum developers, consultants – should not be counted as teachers for that portion of their time not devoted to teaching. The administrative convenience of including department heads and lead teachers (who spend all their time in the school, but only part of it teaching) in the teacher count is understandable. But it is not justifiable to include those who do not teach at all on a regular basis and those who never take responsibility for an entire class (e.g. music and special-education teachers acting on a pull-out basis instead of teaching entire classes).

When school districts are faced with limiting or cutting their budgets, they usually see union agreements as sacrosanct. The result is that a major determinant of expenditure in schools – the collective agreement, governing teachers' terms of employment, and the other rules, laws, and regulations so prevalent in the educational quasi-monopoly – becomes a matter of public discussion only when a province decides to override such provisions by arbitrary legislation or when a naive school board tries to make cuts on educational, instead of contractual, grounds. Left-wing governments (in Quebec and Ontario) have seen, on occasion, the necessity for legislative recourse as readily as right-wing ones.

Publicly funded schools are staffed by unionized teachers. In most provinces, they must join the union in order to be employed in the public sector. It is not a question of teachers in a particular district choosing whether or not they wish to unionize and then selecting their union; they have no choice by law. Similarly, although the majority of people, when asked, state that teachers should not have the right to strike, teachers in Canada generally do have that right. The strike is the approved method of resolving disputes between teachers and their employers. So we have a government-legislated public quasi-monopoly providing an essential (in my opinion, largely because it is monopolistic) service, with workers given the right to strike as members of a monopolistic union. The employer pays the costs resulting from negotiations and strikes by taxing the public. The salaries of all concerned on both sides come, directly or indirectly, from the taxpayer, as does payment for the grievance tribunals, very active where agreements run to tens or even hundreds of pages. The combination of the right to strike and a legislated monopoly is not made in the best interests of students.

Important questions concern the value of a public quasi-monopoly and the consequent structure of the teachers' salary scales. A salary of $60 000 for an educated, experienced, and competent teacher of high school mathematics is not over-generous. There is no rush to enrol in difficult mathematics and science programs in universities, and good engineers with similar experience and competence within their profession earn similar or higher salaries (and they themselves are poorly paid compared with comparable managers, lawyers, and physicians).

But the $60 000 salary is not at all based on the subject and grade level being taught or on the level of competence. A major consequence of the unionization of elementary and secondary education is a salary scale equal across grades, subjects, and competence. In Canada a mediocre kindergarten teacher is usually paid the same as a superb teacher of high school math or science. The rationale provided for these apparent anomalies is that the teacher's competence cannot be measured and that kindergarten teaching is just as valuable as mathematics teaching. The salary policies, outside the perspective of collective bargaining, are absurd. Whereas it would be possible to double the supply of kindergarten teachers in a matter of months with no ill effects by reducing the qualification from five years of postsecondary education to one, it would take many years to increase the supply of well-qualified physics teachers, who require a minimum of excellent results in high school followed by four years of demanding postsecondary work. There is an enormous supply of people with general degrees in the arts and social sciences; there is a much smaller pool of people with advanced qualifications in math and science, and greater competition for their services.

Credentials, which in many cases have nothing to do with teaching effectiveness, play an important part in determining salary levels. For example, there is no reason to believe that obtaining a master of education degree makes a teacher more competent in the classroom, although, as an ex-teacher of MEd students, I do believe that the degree may sometimes have professional and educational value. The value is greatest in cases where the students' motives are more educational than financial. But generally, an MEd, however irrelevant to the teacher's work, increases salary and provides employment for more professors in the university, also paid by the taxpayer. Degrees in education have ballooned in Canada over the last twenty-five years. On balance, the proliferation has done more harm than good.

All provinces require teachers to have qualifications, but there is no clear evidence of the benefits of a teacher preparation program, which some universities are now extending to two years from one (at the taxpayer's expense). Nova Scotia, facing an exceptional level of debt even by Canadian standards, has accepted recommendations that, while reducing the number of teachers in training and the number of faculties of education, will double the length of teachers' preparation programs! One may anticipate that most of the intending teachers refused admission will enrol in programs elsewhere or in general arts programs in Nova Scotia, thereby actually increasing the overall cost of postsecondary education. The recommendation came, as one would expect, from members of the educational establishment. As well, there will be the inevitable costs of reorganization. It is strange that experts would argue that because one year has little perceptible value, the experience should be doubled.

The state of New Jersey permits school districts to hire teachers with university degrees but without teacher training, provided that they take courses as they teach. A financial advantage of having training take place at the same time as intern teaching is that it is feasible (and reasonable) to transfer much of the cost to the teachers-in-training. If these teachers were to pay much of the real cost from their internship salaries, they would likely look for efficient and helpful programs. They would also expect value for their money, rather than see it as an irritating, bureaucratic, irrelevant hurdle which the province insists that they jump to get their credentials. Instead of looking for the easiest or most entertaining course, interns would seek courses that were of most practical help.

It is rare for a university to fail teachers-in-training. As a member of admissions committees at the Ontario Institute for Studies in Education for many years, I hardly ever saw a grade less than A minus on a transcript; we routinely ignored education grades (they did not discriminate), preferring the undergraduate transcripts. At OISE, a graduate school, grades included failure and a six-point range from B minus to A plus. I had the undeserved reputation of being a tough marker (I occasionally gave B minus and B grades and once or twice a fail). In fact, I tried to give grades close to the average in the department; in the university as in the school, a single teacher cannot stand out against the system. In the school, the principal soon deals with the teacher who marks too low; in the university, students themselves simply avoid courses if they think they will receive a low grade for the amount of work they put in. My argument is that the system must be reformed from outside; it will not and cannot reform itself without powerful incentives.

Ontario even insists on its senior administrators having their own provincially defined and delivered qualifications. The training programs are publicly subsidized and function principally to exclude any administrator from outside the province (or anyone from inside who fails to conceal unconventional opinions). This fact may help to explain Ontario's narrow provincialism in education and exceptional inadequacy overall. No other province has such a completely closed shop. There could be no clearer example of how an increase in irrelevant credentials serves only to ensure a lower level of service.

One other important area of waste is transportation. Many provinces delegate this service to local districts, which either operate their own or contract out routes or groups of routes. There is frequent overlap between separate and public boards. The Ottawa area is an extreme example of administrative overlap, where there are French and English buses and separate and public ones, not to mention the special-education and French-immersion vehicles, all paid for by the public. Because districts are funded largely on the basis of head-count, there is sometimes competition between boards (separate and public) to provide better transportation. Whereas competition among schools has many potential advantages, rivalry between public bureaucracies to provide ever more elaborate "free" services is not in the public interest.

Most provinces insist that transportation be free. As the variety of schools and programs increases, French immersion being an enormous instance, districts may or may not initially provide transportation. What they cannot do, by regulation, is charge, even a partial sum, for the service. The parents of French-immersion children – and those of many other children receiving special programs – are typically vocal and ambitious. They are often themselves well educated and able to form a lobby group to obtain free transportation. Funding for French-immersion transportation is an example of additional money being directed to those parents who need it least.

For a variety of reasons, there is minimal integration of school and municipal or private bus services. In all but the biggest cities, students going to school use the public bus service to a very limited extent. The basic assumptions underlying the provision of school bus service in much of Canada are that children live in rural areas, have housewives as mothers, and attend the local public school closest to them. No more than a fraction of the school population today probably meets those three criteria. It is also assumed that, except in the biggest cities, municipal services cannot be adapted for students and that taxpayers prefer to support dual, triple, or even quadruple services, all provided by generally non-competitive public monopolies.

Junior kindergarten (for four-year-olds) is common in affluent Ontario, and the children's schedule is often different from that of, say, grades one to six. More bus trips are needed, since streets are dangerous for four-year-olds. We begin the educational transfer from the poor to the rich at age four. Low-paid workers have schedules that often interfere with supervising kindergarten attendance, and they cannot afford nannies. (When the wealthy class goes on to university, including the French-immersion graduates, most of whom continue to postsecondary education, less well paid workers, whose children are not so likely to attend university, pay taxes to subsidize the higher education of middle-class children, just as they have subsidized kindergarten years before.)

Junior and senior kindergarten, like postsecondary education, is outside the scope of this book, and the complex policy issues involving early childhood education will not be fully explored here. Nevertheless, expenditure on kindergarten is a major item in the education budget and a wasteful one. A strong argument can be made for some form of early childhood education, particularly for disadvantaged children whose parents do not usually give them the vitally important stimulation provided by more-affluent parents. No rational argument can be provided for the inefficient and ineffective pre-school programs generally found in Canada, which are an extravagant obsolescence, providing neither the focused education required to help children master the basic skills and a second language nor the day care needed by two-income or single-parent families.

In short, the spending of money on elementary and secondary education is marked by deception (by obscuring the amount of money spent outside the school), inertia, inefficiency, and perverse waste. Internal reform is next to impossible because nearly everyone concerned is a beneficiary of the system. Only radical change to the structure of the educational monopolies can bring about both improvement and reduced costs. The danger is that governments by simply cutting available funds, but leaving the inefficient and ineffective monopolies in place, will inflict damage on the classroom.

Tables 2 and 3 (p. 22) can be used to give a rough picture of the relative overall efficiency of the provinces' educational spending, which will be put into more complete perspective later when it will be seen that Alberta, British Columbia, and Quebec obtain the best academic results and Ontario the worst. That province is the biggest spender overall, partly as a result of paying too many teachers (it has a low pupil-teacher ratio) the highest salaries. Its spending per teacher is high, probably as a result of its large out-of-school bureaucracy as well as its well-paid teachers. The three westernmost provinces, although their spending patterns vary, are particularly efficient, with relatively high pupil teacher ratios. Newfoundland, with the lowest ratio, is also, contrarily, one of the lowest spenders per pupil and the lowest per teacher. Its inefficiency is largely a product of geography and climate, aggravated by its unimaginative method of funding education; it continues to fund systems (i.e. bureaucracies) rather than students. The province is exceptional in its high proportion of very small and isolated villages. In most of the rest of northern Canada, the small populations tend to be concentrated in mining or logging centres, reducing the inefficiency of educational spending. Quebec stands out as having high spending on services other than classroom teachers.

Reasonable targets for the more-affluent provinces would be the following: $6000 per pupil; $115 000 per teacher (this figure includes total spending and all overheads); a pupil-teacher ratio not below nineteen, excluding teaching aides; and a teacher salary range from $20 000 (for interns) to $70 000 (for exemplary senior teachers in high school academic programs). It should be possible to reduce expenditure in Ontario by 10 to 15 per cent while improving quality. The potential in other provinces is much less, and savings in the poorest provinces could well be more than offset by needed increases in areas of neglect (e.g. school-to-work programs, texts and library books, early childhood education for the disadvantaged, better paid excellent teachers, and programs in the arts).

ISSUES IN THE FUNDING OF EDUCATION

At a time when overall expenditure on education should be (and probably will be) reduced or held constant, it is appropriate to consider spending across the country, spending within provinces, and the general issues of efficiency and effectiveness. Although the discrepancies among provinces appear large, substantively they are less important than the problems within provinces and the more general problem of inefficiency. Much of the disparity may be attributed to justifiable differences in salary levels. Even so, the destructive system of federal grants in place today should be replaced by a more straightforward foundation plan that permanently guarantees a reasonable level of services in all areas throughout the country.

Ontario, by far the most populous province, is the only remaining one with egregious unfairness in funding based on geography. The fact that the discrimination is partially concealed by excessive overall spending in the province in no way justifies its continuation. Although some form of centralized funding is being implemented in Ontario, it is far from certain, at the time of writing, that the current inequity in residential and commercial property tax will be eliminated, leaving either lower than desirable spending or unjustifiably high taxes for those who can least afford them.

Even more important than the system of financing public schools is determination of the line between public and independent schools. One of the factors that enables Ontario's educational juggernaut to continue its wasteful ways is the inability of independent schools to compete effectively. Cause and effect is notoriously difficult to establish in education, but the two factors that most distinguish the relatively effective schools in British Columbia, Alberta, and Quebec from the ineffective ones in Ontario are the former provinces' strongly competitive independent schools and effective systems of student evaluation; put more simply, the successful provinces have standards, while Ontario has none.

Not so obvious as the factors that distinguish provinces are the problems of inefficiency that pervade most or all of them. The notion that school systems, rather than students or schools, should be funded still persists outside New Brunswick. This assumption leads directly to unbalanced priorities. Some Toronto trustees who pay themselves salaries in excess of $50 000 are an obscene example. (If trustees are needed, they should be paid a nominal honorarium.)

Teachers are (appropriately) the most important item of expenditure. Compulsory union membership and bizarre systems of collective bargaining (between associated members of the monopoly all paid by the taxpayer) exclude the possibility of competition, efficiency, payment by results, emphasis on quality in teaching, payment in relation to relevant qualifications, and the speedy termination of the incompetent. It is not that the best, most qualified teachers are paid too much (as many members of the public conclude), but that there is no justifiable differentiation among individual teachers' salary levels, an outcome that only serves to promote even stronger unionization and even greater misuse of public funding. Teacher education, itself in the hands of a self-serving cartel without criteria of quality, is another expensive program with little in the way of positive results. It is currently doubling, or trying to double, the length of its unproductive program to compensate for decreased demand for teachers.

School districts and elected school boards should not necessarily be abolished, but their authority and incentive to build empires must be curbed. This reform is best achieved, as is usually the case, through external competition rather than through regulation. Was Air Canada a fat and lazy monopoly before deregulation? Senior officials of the corporation would today agree that it was. Still more regulation and centralization did not solve the problem, but rather, deregulation and competition.

Regulations can always be bent or avoided. When parents vote with their children's feet, however, there can be no avoidance of the painful reality. School districts should be open to competition from both inside and, more vitally, outside the system. Two school districts, Edmonton and North York (now part of Toronto), have led the way in providing significant internal choice and transparency, attempting to serve rather than rule the public; but it would be unwise to believe that others will rush to follow. After all, Edmonton's leadership goes back over twenty years, and other cities, including Saint John and Calgary, have backtracked. Independent schools should be seen as part of the solution. There is strong evidence of dissatisfaction with the offerings of most public boards, and provinces with even moderate levels of financial support for independent schools show increases in their enrolment.

I do not make the argument for the wholesale privatization of schooling. Education, like health care for serious problems, should be funded from the public purse. There are three reasons for this. First, just as individuals cannot predict or avoid most extreme ill-nesses, children cannot be held responsible for their own education. Neither can impoverished parents. Although parents can and should be held largely accountable for determining the pattern of their chil-dren's education, it is vital that the state ensure that disadvantaged children not be additionally handicapped at school and that no chil-dren receive systematic miseducation as a result of the ignorance or malevolence of their parents.

The second reason is that schooling is a necessary and vitally important benefit to society as well as to children and their parents. Thirdly, in a pluralist, democratic state devoted to such competing values as freedom, security and self-sufficiency, responsible and democratic government, order, excellence, and civic virtue, it is a matter of fundamental principle that all young people have a fair opportunity to flourish in an open and law-abiding society. The idea of equal opportunity (which should not be confused with equal results or identical instruction in common schools) is a difficult one to which I shall return. At this point, suffice it to say that it is a value held by nearly all Canadians, even if their interpretation of it is understandably vague. I am obviously not defining equal opportu-nity as requiring the same schooling for everyone, just as a health system does not need identical medical treatment for each individ-ual. It does mean that the youngest child from the largest and poor-est family should be able to attain an advanced education, something that is possible in Canada today. Equal opportunity is an idea that must not be lost in the legitimate search for reduced costs and increased choice.

A pressing problem facing most provinces' educational systems today is how to cut. That is not the major concern of this book. At the same time, educational reform does not take place in a vacuum. The problem addressed in this book is how to reform and improve schools in a context of cost-cutting. There are several approaches. The simplest in the nine provinces with centralized funding is across-the-board cuts in all areas. However unfair and unreasonable such a policy may appear to be, it is the easiest to implement, as the Alberta experience illustrates very well. If special areas are exempted, everyone will argue that his or her area is unique; special-interest groups emerge, and the government is put in a terrible light by the media, who drag out every case of "special" hardship that does not get favoured treatment. The more exemptions that are made, the harder the general cuts must be. The public sees the rough justice in everyone being cut by an across-the-board percentage.

More delicate approaches can be made by selecting certain areas for special cuts. In education these tend to be areas where political support is less vocal and where fewer human beings are involved. Typical school district cuts are to secretarial support in the schools, building maintenance, and teaching materials (especially textbooks and library books, neither of which are fashionable with Progressive educators). In my view, those are generally just about the last places where cuts should be made. Failing to maintain sound and clean buildings leads to serious problems. A good school secretary (a job more managerial than clerical) is often a vital, underpaid employee. As for teaching materials, one of Canada's serious problems is a lack of adequate texts in key subject areas. Many school libraries and resource centres have too few unattractive and aging books and too many expensive and not very educational gadgets.

Teachers are laid off when cuts are serious. Yet in most cases, this means that the youngest, most vigorous (and sometimes the most able) people are dismissed on a last-in/first-out basis. Alternatively, teachers may be asked or legislated to take pay cuts in lieu of extensive lay-offs of their members. The problem with this policy is that it makes the job of senior high school physics teacher even less competitive with the market, without doing anything to decrease the number of less able and less well educated people seeking to become overpaid pre-school and primary teachers.

The argument in this book is that radical reform, rather than tinkering, is necessary for the improvement of education. Such reform will make intelligent cost-cutting easier and the negative consequences far less severe. By this point it will be obvious to the reader that reducing the negative effects of cost-cutting will not necessarily be a commendation to members of the educational establishment, whose first interest is to fend off cuts altogether and whose second is to keep them out of their immediate domain. Doing more with less has not been a favourite dictum in public bureaucracies.

Provincial funding of schools should provide a high degree of equity among schools and, at the same time, a high level of flexibility for them to spend money in the best interests of their students. The scope of collective agreements should be reduced to safeguard the best interests of students. School district and provincial regulations should be heavily pruned. Instead of maintaining the system, incentives should encourage educators to provide the best possible education for children, one that meets the approval of their parents. Large, inefficient, bureaucratic monopolies do not create such incentives.

– 2 –

The Social Context of the School

Critics of education often blame the schools for all sorts of things over which schools themselves have no control, according to defenders of the status quo. Such defensiveness is often justifiable because schools are just one factor, and not the most important one, in determining what young people are when they leave. For that reason, schools are better off concentrating on the things that they can demonstrably do, rather than on trying to do all kinds of things that they either cannot do at all or can only influence very slightly. School people weaken their position when they make public claims to be educating the whole child and solving all manner of social problems. This opinion may appear inconsistent with my own Traditional philosophy of education, which puts character before material accomplishment. While the school of my choice would be grounded in values, its program – the content of regular instruction – would be heavily academic and, in the later years, vocational. Although we often think of education as what goes on in school, strictly speaking, a person's entire education is only in part a result of formal schooling. The school can overcome moral corruption outside it even less than it can counter anti-intellectualism.

Defenders of the school system may justifiably assert that educational reform must take into account the kind of society in which we live, provided that such an argument does not imply, as it often does, that we should incorporate the negative aspects of society into the compulsory schooling of everyone. Some reformers do appear to think that schools can be made to do anything they want, irrespective of what society in general and parents in particular are doing. In this chapter I take a brief look at the context in which young people are growing up. The picture I draw is intended to ask the reader to consider the question: If this is the context, how can we reform schools to address the problems of the educational system and meet the reasonable wishes of parents and the larger society? I take it as a given that the school (with its 1000 hours a year) cannot provide an effective program that runs entirely counter to the wishes and values of their parents and their peers, operating 4000 hours a year.

SCHOOL, WORK, AND THE SOCIAL ORDER

Employment is a major concern of adolescents and their parents. During the prosperous 1980s, I had the opportunity to interview a selection of children from the fifth to the eleventh grade in a suburban school district in greater Toronto. I asked them why they were in school. The answer of the majority was astonishingly uniform at all grade levels and in both academic and non-academic classes in secondary schools. It boiled down to, "I need an education to get a good job." Some students began by saying that education was important or valuable, but when they were asked why, there was only one answer – to get a good job. A minority response in several non-academic secondary classes was more dismal: "We have to be here; there is no other choice." Even when I tried to draw more academically correct answers (such as the value of education in itself, the love of learning, the love of literature and the arts, understanding the world around one, or civic responsibility), I was brought back to work, money, and the material things one can buy with money. If that was the case in the 1980s, how much more is it likely to be true today, when jobs are less available and when competition for the best ones is even stronger.

I am not implying that preparation for work is or ought to be the paramount concern of the school, but work is the single most important issue for the vast majority of young people in the context of their schooling. That concern should not be ignored. Even parents, whose educational goals for their adolescent children are much more varied and who see their children's lives over a longer time-frame, assume that schooling should be followed by good employment. I cannot count the number of parents, some of them reformers, who have told me in apparent surprise about children – their own or of those friends and relatives – who have not been able to find work, despite their good educational qualifications.

My guess is that academics in the social sciences are among the least realistic about this issue. They sometimes encourage their children to do whatever interests them, which often changes from year to year, and they are then surprised and upset when the children end up neither prepared for nor committed to hard work in a job they do not much want, a condition for which government action or inaction is often blamed. Their advice to teachers and policy makers is unhelpful. It is rare to hear an academic in education discuss preparation for work for those not continuing to postsecondary education, or even to accept its inevitability. It is easier to blame government for not providing more good jobs. The fact that there are not enough jobs, particularly ones they want, is obviously a major problem facing young people. Even if schools did an excellent job preparing them for work, something that Canadian schools do not do, the current high probability of unemployment among young people is about the worst preparation for a responsible adult life that one can imagine.

Making international comparisons in unemployment is notoriously difficult even for experts in the field, which I am not. Nevertheless, a few obvious facts stand out. I compared overall unemployment rates in six countries – Canada, the United States, France, Germany, the United Kingdom, Austria, and Japan. I then looked at the discrepancy between the unemployment rates for people in their early twenties and in mid-life (generally between the ages of thirty-five and forty-four). Those two factors, the overall level of unemployment and the relative size of the youth unemployment rate, combine to give me an estimate of the job-related prospects facing young people.

Canada ranked first in having the worst prospects. Now, obviously, international statistics vary over time – Germany's situation looks worse since the old East Germany has been included in its national statistics. In the 1990s the American (particularly) and Canadian economies have held up better than the European and Japanese. Still, it is very obvious that Canada has a major, if not unique, youth unemployment crisis. Generally, in good times and bad, our youth unemployment rate runs close to twice as high as that among the middle-aged. The United States is like Canada in having a relatively higher youth, than middle-aged unemployment rate, but its absolute unemployment rate is considerably lower than ours, and the gap appears to be widening. With both economies flourishing in 1997, the contrast in unemployment rates is stark. The countries with the lowest *relative* unemployment rates for young people are the Germanic ones: Germany, Austria, and Switzerland. While it is impossible to prove cause and effect in such a complex and changing field, the fact is that those countries do a comprehensive job of preparing young people for work. Canada not only does an extremely ineffective job; it is not even making a reasonable effort, as I show in chapter 4.

Whether or not we should free our economy more to increase job creation following the American pattern is beyond the scope of this book, but a smug sense of superiority over our neighbours makes it difficult for Canadians even to consider the negative effects of our more controlled economy. Recent surveys of the most successful economies show that those which are most open are the most successful – Singapore, Switzerland, the United States with Canada ahead of most of the rest of the industrial world.

Thus this country has an unfortunate combination in the important area of job accessibility. We have high overall unemployment rates, compared with the United States (but not Europe). When these rates are high, they are disastrous for young people, who get much less than their share of jobs. Canada's efforts to smooth the passage from school to work (compared with Germany's, for example) are almost invisible. Our young people have the worst of both worlds, benefiting from neither the controlled employment of Switzerland nor the open, competitive economy of the United States. Our elites, in contrast, have the best of both worlds, neither the insecurity of the American way nor the lack of opportunity and mobility, the inertia, of European planning.

If there is to be a choice, more employment is preferable for those in their twenties and less for those in their late fifties and early sixties. Yet mandatory retirement has been phased out in some places, and there is even talk of raising the pensionable age! It would pay universities, for instance, with their generally good pension plans, to retire highly paid senior professors, who are often less productive, and hire younger ones. They could set an example and provide more of the jobs most desired by young people. Why do they not do so? Universities, like the schools, are run too much in the interests of those providing the service. Ontario universities long bemoaned the poor state of their libraries and scientific equipment. But when the NDP government under Bob Rae granted massive increases, most of the money went into benefits for faculty and staff – I was one of the beneficiaries. The OISE library remained inadequately stocked with current educational literature.

We should be doing much more to give young people the opportunity to move smoothly from school to work. While it would be simplistic to suggest that merely producing more employable people would increase the size of the job market commensurately, the fact is that some vacancies remain unfilled because many young people have become essentially unemployable. This conclusion is obvious from the number of relatively unskilled immigrants and visiting workers who have jobs and, less apparent, from the number of jobs that are exported overseas when uncompetitive industries (including some agricultural activities) move, not only to low-wage countries such as China but to the United States. The serious problem of the unemployable means that even if the changing age structure reduces the number of young people eligible for the workforce, and therefore the youth unemployment rate, many young people will remain unemployed as a result of their lack of aptitude and preparedness for work.

These lacks – of attitudes, values, and skills – have multiple causes: too few jobs, the breakdown of the family resulting in uncontrolled behaviour at home, an adolescent culture that encourages immediate gratification of wants (in the form of sex, drugs, entertainment, alcohol, and pleasure rather than work), and the breakdown of the traditional values of work, personal responsibility, and commitment. The school is too often part of the problem, rather than of the solution, for those young people most at risk.

An important theme of this book is that, although parents are usually an important element in the problem, often its crux, they are not helped by our social system in general and by the school system in particular. If government is soft on crime (and the Young Offenders Act and the Charter of Rights and Freedoms are both generally perceived, sometimes correctly, as supporting wrongdoers rather than public order), then weak or busy parents and educators find it easier to ignore minor misdoings. If government makes divorce easier and encourages common-law relationships through the tax system, then family breakdown accelerates. If the media focus on casual sex, crime, and materialism, then sex outside marriage, crime, and materialistic world-views flourish. It is unlikely that many parents deliberately encourage their adolescent children to participate in casual sex, crime, or drugs, but many do so tacitly and indirectly by providing the opportunity and looking the other way. The provision of schools of choice that actively promote different and more desirable values (more desirable than the "more for me right now" philosophy) would give parents the opportunity to select a better environment for their children. Today, they are apt to give way by default: they feel they cannot fight the tide.

A middle-class parent, a teacher, was overheard to say that her rebellious fourteen-year-old daughter was now attending school regularly and that she even occasionally smiled. The parent went on to report that she had given up on her daughter's dress and appearance as being beyond her immediate control; the school, of course, like most others, has no rules about dress and appearance. Association with other parents and a school that made the same choices would help to provide an environment where sex, violence, and material-ism are not seen as inevitable aspects of life, real or vicarious, at school and at home. A dress code would become feasible, as it is in so many of England's new grant-maintained schools.

There is one further, frequently overlooked factor that inhibits young people from becoming usefully employed. With the best of intentions, educators and government agencies bombard adolescents with a message that staying in school is important if they are to get the best jobs. They are told that postsecondary education, sometimes university, is essential for a good future and that all the new jobs require specialized skills.

The advice is well intentioned. As individual parents, my wife and I encouraged our own children to prepare for adult life as workers, and all four completed university with at least one degree. None has yet experienced lengthy unemployment, and all are working in jobs that are both highly specific in their demands for skills and well rewarded financially. So when I criticize the universal advice of edu-cators and others, I can be accused of hypocrisy. It will be said that I want the best for my own children, but not for others; that I am like the left-wing leaders, academics, and politicians who prescribe Egalitarian common schools for everyone else, but quickly turn to elite private or public education opportunities for their own children.

The truth is more complex. First, my wife's and my first concern for our children was not that they attend university and get highly paid jobs, but that they become truthful, decent, responsible, dili-gent, and independent adults with a respect for family values. It is not appropriate to judge their personal values publicly, and I am hardly impartial; but it is a fact that all are married with children. They were bright youngsters who found school work relatively easy; it is hardly surprising that, coming from an educated family, they all went to university.

More important, I am not suggesting that other parents, unlike my wife and me, should not encourage their children to get a good edu-cation. On the contrary, I believe that it is a prime responsibility of parents to give their children strong guidance in terms of fundamen-tal values and choices – moral, social, material, and spiritual – at the same time recognizing that they will make their own decisions as independent adults. While it is not sensible to encourage ambitions well beyond one's children's evident limits, it is worse to condone or protect a young person's choice of a life of sloth and irresponsibility.

Thirdly, my criticism of left-wing leaders is not that they fail to sacrifice their children on the altar of their own ideology. Sacrificing one's children is not something I admire. No, my criticism of the left-wing ideologues is different. Like the animals in George Orwell's *Animal Farm*, these people promote a seductive ideology that, inevitably, they will not and should not apply to themselves. Egalitarianism is wrong because of the social engineering and authoritarianism that it necessarily entails, not because its advocates are all hypocrites or evil people. Indeed, the decay of Western democratic society has resulted more from sincere, well-intentioned ideology than from evil and hypocrisy. It is inevitably one thing to exhort or compel other parents to take actions not in their children's best interests in the name of the alleged good of society; it is another to take harmful actions against one's own.

This subtle point leads to the other policy promoted by many leaders of educational opinion in current times. It is not enough for such people that every child be encouraged to continue to postsecondary education; as well, they argue that successful graduates from various groups in society should mirror the size of the group in the general population.

There are, then, two distinct, but widely accepted and generally promulgated policies with respect to participation in the more advanced areas of schooling. First, every young person should be strongly encouraged to continue to postsecondary education; and second, there is something wrong if certain groups are not represented proportionately in postsecondary programs. Indeed, the absence of proportionality is seen as straightforward evidence of unfair discrimination; it offends the Egalitarian ideal. I believe that both policies are wrongheaded and contribute to the negative qualities of our educational system.

The argument for everyone completing high school and continuing to postsecondary schooling goes like this: first, nearly all the growth in the job market is in the highly skilled areas; second, unemployment is much higher among high school drop-outs than among those who have finished high school, and higher among high school graduates than among those with some postsecondary education, a diploma, or a degree; and third, the less-educated who do find employment usually end up in low-paying, dead-end jobs. These three assertions all have a factual core. The problem is that they are selective parts of the economic and employment picture and convey a distorted and unhelpful message to young people. Taken together as the key to the future, they are seriously misleading and harmful.

Consider the first statement: it is itself far from the whole truth. Over the last ten years, there has been enormous growth in the service sector, exceeding that in the areas requiring high technical skills. Proportionately, the highly skilled areas (particularly the technical ones) may still be increasing at the fastest rate, and in time of recession they have even seen the greatest absolute growth. Many of the generally more numerous new service jobs have required little or no technical training, and they have been in the low-wage sector. It is also untrue to imply that all highly skilled jobs are increasing; there has been little demand in Canada over the last five or so years for doctors, lawyers, and teachers, and even within the math, science, and engineering areas there are sectors that have not expanded. The rapidly growing area is relatively narrow, requiring some combination of computer, engineering, and mathematical skills. Clearly, there is a limit to the proportion of young people who can qualify for such positions. Math and science are not exceptionally popular in high schools, and the inadequate teaching in math in the elementary grades is not helping that situation. While it does make sense to encourage more bright young people to take advanced math and science in high school and computer science, engineering, and mathematics in college and university, the effect on the problem of youth unemployment will be marginal; these are not the young people who are unemployed and unemployable at the moment. "Get yourself qualified" is too often interpreted by the young as meaning "Fulfil yourself in sociology," rather than the more accurate "Become qualified in computer programming."

The second statement is particularly misleading when applied to a social, rather than an individual, issue. The individual does generally increase his or her chances of getting a job with more schooling, though it depends on what kind of schooling. But if the high school drop-out rate decreased by 40 per cent and the proportion of young people qualifying for postsecondary education increased by 25 per cent, the effect on unemployment and the unemployable would be negligible.

That more-qualified people generally get paid more than less-qualified ones in an industrialized, capitalist, free society is true by definition and will always be so as long as those social conditions hold. Large numbers of employed people are what economists call "underemployed." This does not mean that they are not working hard; it means that they hold jobs which do not require their levels of qualification; they are, in a technical sense, overqualified. Within reason, an employer will usually hire a more educated person before a less educated one because, on average, the more educated person will probably have qualities that are difficult or illegal to measure directly. He or she is more likely to be intelligent, diligent, and responsible ("compliant" would be an equally accurate, if less flattering term). My first principal, when I began my teaching career, had never earned his BA. He was an excellent, if eccentric administrator with a first-rate mind. But he was poor in math, which he never taught, and he refused to spend the necessary time and effort to get the pass in that subject required for his degree – he was prepared to accept the loss in salary. In short, he was not compliant. Today, he would not get a job as a teacher, let alone be promoted to principal. Increasing the educational levels of the population does not magically change the size of the employment market.

There are, it must be allowed, two areas where the type of schooling probably will have an effect on the numbers (as distinct from the individuals) employed: development of stronger and larger programs at the cutting edge of invention in the highly relevant areas of computers, science, and technology, and development of programs to help the least-educated (the potentially unemployable) move from school to responsible work.

The implications of the second statement (that highly educated people will, by definition, get jobs) are belied by government policy at another level. Enrolment in postsecondary education is not enhanced by financial cutbacks; clearly, governments, provincial and federal, do not really believe that we need overall increases in the size of university programs. We do not require massively greater numbers of mediocre sociologists, psychologists, social workers, elementary teachers, or generalists in the humanities and social sciences; we already have too many. All financial cuts to universities are not wrong, but it is foolish to tell young people as a whole to go to university at the same time as cuts are imposed.

The third statement is also essentially factual: the jobs available for those with little schooling are, as I have pointed out, generally low paying. They are also dead-end, in the sense that working as a service employee in a hotel or fast-food restaurant does not lead by a normal and orderly process to promotion to management. Even so, this is perhaps the most harmful of the three statements when it is generalized, rather than used in the context of sensitive counselling to an individual.

If we except the most highly qualified jobs in the expanding technical sectors, for which only a fraction of the population has a chance of qualifying in terms of intelligence and education, the service sector, predominantly low skilled, is the one most able to hold its own in the new economy. To deride one of the most important and persistent sources of employment is at best a luxury of academic and social snobbery, at worst an unintentional torpedoing of one of the most important areas of potential growth. Canada's tourist industry does not have a good reputation for service, and if its employees are dubbed failures, that reputation will continue to be justified. In Switzerland and even in parts of the United States, employees in tourism are not failures, and this fact shows in their demeanour and deportment.

The "dead-end" epithet is easily dealt with. Many of the most sought-after jobs are dead-end in that they typically do not lead to steady promotion to more-fulfilling and better-paying jobs. For the most part, teaching, nursing, family medicine, and law are dead ends as much as being a hotel worker. But those jobs are well paid, frequently fulfilling, and much in desired by young people.

What is fulfilling about a job is a highly subjective issue. I know teaching best. For some teachers (in school, college, or university) pedagogy is far from fulfilling; such is the case even for some effective teachers. Academics may try hard to avoid teaching assignments (some being good at research and others at neither), often with success. We are all different and have varying wants and needs. It is as much the holder of the job as its substance that defines fulfilment.

Admittedly, there is a substantive difference between teaching and cleaning a hamburger outlet. But all necessary jobs can provide at least some fulfilment from a sense of an appreciated job well done. Some fast-food workers get more satisfaction from their jobs than do certain teachers. The advice that we give to an entire generation of young people serves to feed a culture of unfulfilment, a culture of failure. If everyone is supposed to go to university, 80 per cent of young people are immediately failures (more, if we also demand graduation). If all young people are supposed to go on to a job defined as fulfilling, the percentage of failures will gradually increase as all are taught to raise their ambitions and criteria of success.

What is the alternative? Just as we should stop assuming that one kind of school fits everybody, so we should cease believing that everyone should have the same or comparable material and psychic ambitions. A good place to begin is by telling young people that what is important is doing a legitimate, worthwhile job well, not how much one is paid for it and whether it will lead to managing other people. There is no such thing as a job with guaranteed fulfilment, but there are fulfilled and unfulfilled people in all walks of life. Even fulfilment itself is inappropriate as a major goal, for it assumes a self-centred world-view, one that is by no means universally shared. A sense of satisfaction – self-respect, a recognition of one's strengths and weaknesses – is a better goal than expecting to be truly fulfilled. The discussion about fulfilment in "good jobs" often implies that government should provide fulfilment; it becomes a right (along with money, health, and everything else one may want). Surely, the bad job is one that involves demeaning others and criminal or immoral behaviour, irrespective of how much it pays.

Sometimes forgotten is the importance of the balance between work, family life, and leisure. People find different levels of satisfaction in those various spheres, not directly tied to wealth and materialism. If some parents wish to stress fulfilment in work and material goods above all else, that is their prerogative. But it should not be imposed on all children in a state-run educational system.

The second bad policy concerns the goal of equal educational outcomes between groups of people. This goal is as misguided as the first, and it leads to many of the same social problems. Equality is arbitrarily demanded with regard to some groups but not for others. Those for which equal educational outcomes are typically demanded today are racial groups, particularly as between blacks and whites, some ethnic groups, the sexes, and social classes.

There is unquestionably a big difference between the outcomes of different religious groups, with Jews and Presbyterians attaining higher results than Baptists and the fundamentalist and evangelical denominations. It is not at all clear why these differences are fair, but those between the other groups are unfair. Even between racial groups, there is intense concern about blacks (sometimes including black Asians), but little interest in the relative success or failure of Asians compared with those of European origin. In North America Asians from the Pacific rim outperform all others in computer science and math, but they underperform in the humanities. With regard to ethnic groups, there is social ambivalence, concern being expressed about some and not about others. In the United States much emphasis is placed on Hispanics, complicated by the very different outcomes among various groups of Hispanics (between Cuban Americans and the less successful Mexican Americans, for example).

A crucial point too often lost lost in the push for egalitarianism is that increasing the share of some groups means decreasing that of others. Some universities in Canada used to have quotas on Jewish students, to prevent them from getting more than their share of places. I suspect there are covert attempts to place unofficial quotas on Asians in some faculties, such as medicine, today. It is not clear why members of successful groups should be penalized to help people from less successful communities unless there is evidence of discrimination against them as individuals on the basis of their group membership.

There are three conceptual causes of unequal outcomes between groups. They may be the result of genetic factors inherited from parents; culture, in which is included treatment before and immediately after birth, as well as the more obvious factors of family and the associated social upbringing and, in the broad sense of the word, education; or prejudice, which may differentiate the treatment received by groups within the school.

The three factors are easily defined, but in practice they are less readily separable. The effects of differing treatment on the development of intelligence, for example, are not fully understood. On the one hand, there is no evidence that for a country to begin formal schooling at age four is better than for it wait until age seven. On the other hand, intellectual stimulation from birth to the age of ten appears to have particularly important effects. (One explanation for the apparent contradiction is that most pre-school education is not intellectually stimulating.) The family itself may be a repository of prejudice that truck driving, for example, is an unsuitable goal for a girl. If that is classified as prejudice rather than as culture, then one has to be careful not to blame the school. This is not a trivial point: primary teachers often claim that they are fighting prejudice (based on sex, ethnicity, or race) arising from the family. If that is the case, the school should not subsequently be blamed if girls choose not to take up truck driving. The issue raises the broader one of whose culture the child should be taught. Some parents, for example, do not want their boys to be expected to play at dressing and undressing dolls in kindergarten.

The first and most controversial explanation of educational differences between groups is one of genetic inheritance, particularly with respect to intelligence but also more generally with regard to behavioural characteristics. The simple fact is that nobody really knows to what extent intelligence and characteristics of personality (which may be helpful for success in our society) are inherited. Part of the reason for our ignorance is the complexity of the topic. Within a narrow, homogeneous population, a family, or an isolated community, differences in intelligence may well be accounted for largely by genetic inheritance. Among larger, more heterogeneous groups that differ greatly by culture, the proportion of intelligence attributable to inheritance is probably considerably smaller. Another part of our ignorance stems from an understandable reluctance on the part of researchers to address such explosive issues. I shall argue later that the answers are not particularly relevant to schooling in the future. Their apparent importance hinges on the fallacious assumption that the state should dictate one basic form of education, differentiated only according to the educational "needs" (as determined by experts) of various groups of children.

Whatever the cause and the consequences, we simply do not know precisely how important the first possible cause of difference in group academic performance is. There are, of course, people on both sides of the debate who claim they do know, but their answers are factually opposed. Educational policy should be based on neither an assumption that there are important inherited differences between groups nor a belief that there are none. It is important that I emphasize that that restraint is not a handicap once we accept the enormous differences among individuals, their complex causes, and the importance of an educational balance between the expectations of society and those of parents. In that context, one agreed fact is significant. Whatever differences, minimal or substantial, there may be between groups in intelligence (however defined) and personality, they are consistently exceeded by variations among individuals. There is no pedagogical or ethical justification for the state to set up mandatory segregation of students on the basis of sex, ethnicity, social class, or race. That fact has nothing to do with the question of what parents may wish to choose for their children as individuals; the two issues are ethically and factually unrelated, even though ideologists frequently try to confuse them. My statement may seem so obvious and weak as to have no practical implications for policy. That is not the case. Many schools do have regulated zones that effectively recapitulate social class and occasionally ethnic boundaries. I have referred to some funded Roman Catholic schools that demand proof of Catholic baptism. The issue of segregation on the basis of official language is not perfectly comparable (it can be argued on pedagogical grounds, for example, that anglophones should not be admitted to francophone schools), but there is a serious question as to whether accessibility, if not totally open, should be based on the child's linguistic competence instead of the parents' cultural or linguistic background.

The second explanation for differences between groups in terms of educational success is culture, broadly defined to include all the factors, physical and social, familial and societal, that impinge on the child before and after birth, excluding only genetic inheritance and the effects (physical, academic, psychological, and social) of formal schooling the other two possible explanations for the differences.

There is abundant research showing differences in family upbringing by social class, ethnicity, and race. It is always difficult to separate nature from nurture (impossible, if one wishes to achieve consensus among proponents of both), but there is no dispute that nurture has an important independent effect, particularly when one is considering heterogeneous populations where the cultural backgrounds are enormously varied. The important point here is that, from a policy perspective, it does not make much difference exactly how great each component – nature or nurture – is because neither is readily changeable. Genetic characteristics of groups may evolve over time through interracial and interethnic marriage and by regression to the mean, and cultural variations may also change gradually over time through immigration and the influences of the larger society, including the mass media. In the short run, neither is noticeably sensitive to formal instruction.

In the past, many educators assumed that genetic factors could not be changed by education while cultural ones could. Not only is it becoming clear that it is extremely difficult to separate the two, but it is also becoming irrelevant. Some genetic characteristics (related to the abnormal functioning of the brain) can be helped by good instruction, and many cultural factors are deeply ingrained in even the youngest children. Moreover, the appropriateness of educators taking it upon themselves to change cultural dispositions that they do not approve of is also increasingly under attack. This is most obvious in the case of Canada's native peoples, but it is also a matter of concern in urban multicultural classrooms. For example, should the state enforce the coeducation of Muslim boys and girls? If the answer is yes, should it enforce sex education for them? Should it require coeducational swimming lessons? Should it enforce dress codes for swimming and for physical education?

As members of the educated elite increasingly intermarry and as the number of less-educated single parents grows, the intellectual differences (resulting from nurture, nature, or both) between children of high and low social classes also increase. In short, the technical reasons for intergroup differences are increasingly irrelevant; the educational reality is that children differ enormously depending on the kind of home background from which they come. In an increasingly differentiated society, it may well be all the more important for the school to identify and stimulate children with real academic potential (however defined) from deprived backgrounds. There is also a strong argument for pre-school instruction, provided that it is intellectually stimulating and demanding, rather than child-centred play. For this reason, children in the impoverished inner city should not be confined to their local school (which is usually intellectually impoverished).

A third possible explanation, and one that is qualitatively different, for varying outcomes between groups is systemic prejudice within the school. Some groups may be, by this argument, routinely denied equal opportunities by the state's educational agencies. The extreme politically correct often jump at this explanation as the only possible cause for differences in outcomes among or between groups. Are females "under-represented" in engineering schools? Then the explanation must be prejudice in the elementary and secondary schools and the engineering schools themselves. Are blacks "under-represented" in postsecondary institutions, particularly in the most skilled faculties – engineering, computer science, medicine, and dentistry? The explanation once again must be prejudice.

Looking at Canada in the second half of this century, I conclude that all three explanations probably have some validity. Any genetic advantage or disadvantage, however trivial, is enhanced by the enormous cultural differences, which are themselves increasing. The access of professionals to travel, the arts, and computers and their involvement in the ever-increasing activities (swimming, skating, summer camps) of their children are many times greater than those of the underclass. One of the reasons that many educators feel uncomfortable about segregated classes or schools for the intellectually gifted (often defined as having IQs over 140) is that the children are so predominantly of middle- and upper-class origin, frequently having two professional parents. Differences in nutrition should also not be overlooked. Social activists claim that the poor cannot afford nutritious food. Another factor is that children from less-educated families are likely to have diets dominated by potato chips, fast food, doughnuts, sweetened cereals, and sugary carbonated drinks, irrespective of the question of what poor families can and cannot afford. There is an evident physical difference in appearance between the children of the most advantaged and the most disadvantaged. Early instruction in the home is also increasingly seen as an important differentiating factor among groups.

While class differentiation is steadily increasing, ethnic and racial separation is more fluid, except in those cases where race and ethnicity are combined with social class. In Toronto there are neighbourhoods where Orthodox and Conservative Jews, unusually successful educationally and financially, still live together, close to a synagogue and an appropriate, often independent, school. At the other end of the social spectrum, blacks of Jamaican origin are disproportionately represented in underclass neighbourhoods. But those are not, as yet, the norm; in many cases, races and ethnic groups gradually integrate, their differences becoming defined more by social class than by race or ethnicity. Intermarriage is increasingly common. Such integration does not contradict the fact that schools in the Toronto and Vancouver areas have become increasingly different from one another; immigration of non-traditional groups, notably East Asians, outpaces the slower process of integration.

In terms of religion, those truly committed (to Christianity, Judaism, Islam, or a sect) are becoming more psychologically, though not physically, separate as the mainstream religions are increasingly absorbed into the secular world. While religion becomes a subsidiary factor in the lives of most people and in educational policy, it necessarily differentiates more the Orthodox Jews, the fundamentalist Moslems, and Pentecostalists and Jehovah's Witnesses, whose commitment alienates the family from current social trends and their children from other young people. One trend continues, in contrast to the fluidity of ethnic and religious differentiation: the role of social class is steadily increasing. That fact demands recognition. Even where there is a genuine local school, it is unlikely to be a truly common one that represents a microcosm of the people.

Two conclusions emerge from this discussion. First, it is both impossible and unnecessary to distinguish between the effects of inheritance and culture because they so often seem to work together. Intelligent people become successful and use their material advantage to gain benefits for their children not available a hundred years ago. I have argued that the relative weight of each effect is not very important in terms of educational practice because both are persistent and not easily influenced, except by extreme social engineering and perhaps not even then. The excessive assimilation attempted in the Soviet Union for seventy years and in Yugoslavia for forty hardly had the effect of reducing ethnic differences. Secondly, although the definition and nature of significant groups within society change gradually over time, their existence does not. Today, we live in a materialistic, hedonist, and individualist society; we should hardly be surprised that social class (based essentially on financial success) is gradually becoming the most important defining factor.

What about prejudice? While I have no doubt that ethnic and racial prejudice in the schools seriously affected some young people's life chances in the past, I know of little evidence of its strength today. Suppose we consider the most successful groups – Jews and Presbyterians – as examples. It is difficult to argue that their success is attributable to favourable prejudice on the part of schools, compared with negative attitudes towards evangelical Protestants. Far more likely, the differences between materially successful and unsuccessful religious groups are the result of parallel differences in culture and values.

As for women, the evidence that prejudice in the schools negatively affects them today is slight indeed. Women now constitute more than half the undergraduate population in Canada. To be sure, men and women are not equally distributed in the various departments within universities, but it is difficult to see why one should assume prejudice as a cause. More likely, differences are due to a variety of background and circumstantial factors. By circumstantial I refer, as one important example, to women calculating the ease of combining a particular job with having children. As a matter of interest, two of my daughters are professional engineers; both experienced, they say, as much positive as negative prejudice in university. The third is a financial analyst. They received strong support from their parents to make choices within our family values, but they did not meet sex-based opposition from school or university. All three attempt, against difficult odds, to juggle work, household, and family.

Would it be desirable, even if it were possible, to eliminate the cultural differences among young people to create equal educational outcomes between groups? It would be reprehensible for the public school to arrogate to itself such a function. It is difficult to imagine any Western democracy passing the necessary legislation. The idea that there is a complete set of cultural priorities, a single secular world-view, which the state should approve for all people is unacceptable in a democratic, pluralist society. The state already goes too far in its attacks, deliberate or not, on the survival of minority religious groups by means of a compulsory secular educational system. This is not to deny that there may be groups and individuals who suffer from widespread prejudice and other forms of disadvantage. Clearly, the state has a duty to eliminate negative discrimination against groups and individuals by the public school system, where it exists. But action in those areas requires evidence of wrongdoing, not statistics open to various reasonable explanations. While I have no doubt that prejudice does exist, since human beings rarely approach a model of perfection in any area of life, I am unconvinced that prejudice in the school (as distinct from the group's own culture and values and others' unavoidable reactions to them) is even a significant minor cause of varying group outcomes. At the very least, a careful study should be carried out of the home backgrounds of different groups and of their academic aptitude on entry to the school system before schools are convicted of prejudice based on the fact of group differences in outcome.

Later, I shall lay out a few common principles that I believe underlie the very nature of a pluralist democracy; they should indeed be taught in the schools. They do not constitute a world-view or philosophy; the very nature of democracy in the modern world assures continuing dissent on all but the most basic political values necessary for the continuation of our society.

So our school system, instead of dealing with the obvious problems of ineffective and inefficient movement from school to work and inadequate academic standards, has to deal with accusations of failing to do enough to distribute the rewards of education equally among different groups. It is even sometimes accused of promoting social inequality, as though the underclass was simply a creation of educational, rather than economic, circumstance. Young people are given well-intended advice that is misleading and potentially harmful: "Stay in school"; "Go to university"; "Avoid dead-end jobs"; "Find work that is fulfilling and meaningful." If everyone took the advice seriously, one would expect the proportions of dissatisfied young adults who classed themselves as failures or victims to skyrocket, and that does seem to be happening. Rather than supporting a genuinely well educated population, the political context promotes a generation of malcontents always looking for that well-paid, fulfilling job that is supposed to be theirs if only they had the right credentials and if mysterious others, notably government agencies such as schools, did the right things and refrained from prejudice. Unfortunately, credentials – notably high school graduation certificates and general degrees in the arts and social sciences from major universities – have little to do with being educated and equally little with leading a happy and useful life. Instead of instilling a sense of personal responsibility, the state and the school system, with the eager help of the media, seem determined to show that every accident, misfortune, failure, or dissatisfaction is the fault of somebody else, the government, or some other organization.

What can be done? The restrictive nature of our labour market, compared with that in the United States, does lead to higher levels of unemployment. Low-level jobs are exported. Industry gravitates to American states with right-to-work laws. If no special effort is made to help the young, they are likely to be those most at risk, for the obvious reasons that they begin without jobs or without experience. Right-to-work laws, the elimination of the closed shop, and the stabilization of minimum-wage laws, with lower rates for those under twenty-five, would all make Canada more competitive in the international sphere. But they would do little to promote the secure, permanent, and "fulfilling" jobs that young people seek; the new employment would be primarily in the service and labour-intensive areas where much of the work is likely to be low paid, seasonal, temporary, and part-time. Further, the removal of some of the safety net for workers (by right-to-work legislation) could augment, rather than moderate, the problem of an underclass of unemployed and unemployable. With work of some kind generally available, those who never work, increasingly unemployable, would become more easily identified and probably even more separated by residence. The problem of unemployability is masked in a country with high youth unemployment, but more obvious in the United States.

It is a debatable question whether a free and open labour market can be combined with a safety net in the form of supplementary income for the working poor. On the evidence, it seems likely that any form of subsidy for not working discourages continued employment. The social and economic choices open to government are not easy ones. Providing more opportunity hurts those who do not or cannot take advantage of it. Providing more security reduces the incentive to be independent and accept personal responsibility. It is clear that criticizing governments for not creating more jobs is empty rhetoric unless one is willing to accept the consequences of genuine, job-creating strategies, which do have negative side effects. If there were an easy answer, would some country somewhere not have found it? But we should not simply accept the status quo.

Government policies that encourage employed people to keep working beyond age sixty and even sixty-five could be changed to promote earlier retirement, at least until the unemployment among young people is resolved. Mandatory retirement should be reinstated; there should be no additional pension benefit for those who work beyond sixty-five, and registered retirement savings plans should be terminated at that age instead of sixty-nine.

The direct cost to government of earlier retirement is not great and might well be offset by the lower level of unemployment among young people. The major cost is borne by those who retire early and eventually by their children, who will inherit less. Young people as a whole would be better served by job opportunities now than an inheritance later, but the people who found employment today would not be the same ones who would lose an inheritance tomorrow.

If the social context is largely the product of national and international forces beyond the reach of the educational sector, that does not mean that educational policy is irrelevant. It is not sufficiently understood that the average educator feels little or no sense of responsibility for developing employable young people. (This topic is addressed directly in chapter 4). There are important things that the educational system could do, either independently or in cooperation with employers.

Maude Barlow and Heather-jane Robertson (1994) defend the status quo of today's public schools. (Robertson is a senior administrator for the Canadian Teachers' Federation, the central agency for teachers' unions in this country.) Their opinion on the question of employable youth is not extreme, but is typical of contemporary educators in the public sector: "Elementary and secondary schools were never intended to be employment training centres. The education [that students] are receiving is supposed to be in the tradition of a liberal education, which means schools are to help [them] acquire the skills and knowledge to live 'in liberty' alongside [their] fellow citizens. [Their] education should be about how to make life, not how to make a living."

Earlier in this chapter, I observed that young people generally see schooling in direct, instrumental terms – getting a job. Educators, in contrast, see the employment problem as someone else's, even though they know that two-thirds of young people do not continue to postsecondary education. The public is more ambivalent. Most parents, if asked, would not describe getting a job as a major goal of education, but at the same time they assume that somehow their children deserve a good job when they have completed their schooling.

There is a problem here. It is natural for teachers to take a longer-term and broader view than young people do, but the difference between them is a chasm. Parents fall somewhere between the two extremes, wanting the best for their own children and expecting that all young people be ready for work, including (for other people's children) the manual trades. Part of the problem is one of social change. My generation did not worry about jobs; they fell like manna from the heavens, and the only problem was choosing.

SURVIVAL IN A HEALTHY SOCIETY

In an affluent country such as Canada, one may take it for granted that life is generally secure and safe for young people growing up. At the same time, the media are full of tales of disease, poverty, and deprivation, usually resulting, it would appear, from governmental inaction and rarely from individual choice or folly.

From an overall statistical perspective, Canada is neither a better nor a worse place to live than other developed, industrialized countries. Despite the tales of horror about the American health system and that country's violence, the life expectancy of American twenty-year-olds is the same as in Canada: fifty-three to fifty-four additional years for men and about six more for women. For the other major Western democracies, the statistics do not vary by more than a year or two. Only Japan has life expectancies three years longer for both sexes (*Demographic Yearbook* [United Nations, 1995].

If we narrow our look to murder and suicide, the violent deaths that parents particularly fear for their children, the situation is somewhat more variable, but Canada remains unexceptional. The suicide rate among young male adults is relatively high, substantially higher than that in Japan and the United States. In contrast, the rate among young women is lower than in other countries and only half the Japanese rate. Canada's murder rate among young men (3.1 per 100 000) is well below the phenomenally high American figure (17.7), but still more than twice as high as rates in other developed countries. Murder of young women is much less common (5.8 per 100 000 in the United States, 2.0 in Canada), but our relative standing is similar (*World Health Statistics Annual* [World Health Organization 1986]). These statistics are just the tip of the iceberg, but they do give a sense of why parents often feel that their children are growing up in a dangerous world. Suicide and murder are both more common than they once were, suicide among youth having increased steadily over recent years.

It would be wrong to suggest that the unemployment situation is the cause of violence. Research on suicide suggests that it is a complex social phenomenon most closely related to changes in the organization of society. Thus Newfoundland, with the highest unemployment rates, has the lowest suicide rate in Canada, and the more affluent western provinces and Quebec have considerably higher rates. Nevertheless, violence, hopelessness, and unemployment are important parts of some young people's lives and may themselves have complex, interrelated social causes.

In 1995 more than 40 per cent of all people charged with robbery in Metropolitan Toronto were between twelve and seventeen, compared with 21 per cent in 1985 (*Globe and Mail*, 16 June 1996). When statistics such as these are published, experts immediately claim that the figures do not mean what they say. In the same article in the *Globe and Mail* and also in a front-page item the following day in the *Toronto Star*, the argument was made that children are charged today when they would hot have been in the past. No evidence is supplied for a claim that goes against most people's experience, that crime has to be significant or frequently repeated to attract the attention of the police in the first place. Another speculatively irrational argument used is that schools' new zero-violence policies increase the numbers of criminal charges. In fact, few school systems have those policies, and those that do experience less, rather than more, violence. School treatment of misbehaviour rarely involves the police, let alone resulting in charges. Liberal experts maintain the fiction that increasing individual freedom and the relaxation of standards of personal dress, behaviour, and sexual relations, coupled with the weakening of the restraints of religion and traditional values, do not lead to lower standards of behaviour and increased crime. Although violent crime rates may have peaked, current levels are extremely high by historical standards.

Violence outside the school pervades the school itself. The Young Offenders Act and the Charter of Rights and Freedoms have together made young people increasingly aware of their "rights," real or imagined. If ten-year-olds are defined as being incapable of criminal behaviour, then their rate of misbehaviour, including theft and violence, increases. Even life within the home is invaded by law and the courts, with their rigid rules of evidence and their assumption of a contest between accused and accuser. Recently, an American tourist in Ontario was held in jail over night and formally accused of violent abuse because he spanked the bare bottom of his young child after she slammed the car door on her sister's finger. The man was eventually acquitted, but it is remarkable that such discipline (even if one thinks it poor judgment on the father's part) should become the business of the legal system. Similarly, there is increased agitation for state intervention against the corporal punishment of immigrant children by their parents. Needless to say, educators are extremely fearful of having any forcible physical contact with students, no matter what the situation. Teachers are sometimes enjoined by policy not to treat a student injured in the playground until they have donned protective rubber gloves (to avoid contact with AIDS and a future law case against the school board). Male teachers touch male or female students at their risk.

This is not just a question of changing standards of punishment, although standards are changing. Corporal punishment was accepted practice in public schools when I began teaching in Saint John in 1958. Originally opposed to the practice, I was soon forced to adopt it because adolescents were conditioned to expect such treatment. The practice was gradually prohibited. I am not advocating a return to the "good old days" of the strap; discipline in schools should reflect the public will. Corporal punishment is ineffective – indeed, unthinkable – in a society where the majority of people, or even a large minority, oppose it. The change in type of punishment is not in itself the problem; it is a symptom of declining belief in order and punishment. Many parents, and schools, maintain excellent order using other forms of discipline.

The more serious problem is a change in the interpretation of mis-behaviour and punishment, the redefinition of what is disorderly and the replacement of the concept of wilful wrongdoing by error, misunderstanding, and faulty upbringing. The knowledge of most ordinary people that the young know when they are doing bad things is considered crude and unsophisticated by our establishment elites. The idea that punishment is an important symbol of recognition of harm done to the community is either not thought of or considered archaic.

Some years ago, Urie Bronfenbrenner (1970) noted the difference in the treatment of misbehaviour of adolescents in the Soviet Union and the United States. If adolescents were unruly in a public place, a park for example, in Russia, any adult, including an old person, would see it as his or her duty to remonstrate, and the unruly behaviour would cease. When I was a boy in England in the 1940s, passing adults would occasionally reprimand children who were rude or rough. Fifty years earlier, my grandfather, fancying himself a squire, had had a village boy strapped by the local schoolmaster for failing to tip his cap to show respect when they passed in the street. In the United States, Bronfenbrenner noted, adults were now too frightened to address a misbehaving youth. How much truer is that observation almost thirty years later! The replacement of established social norms by individual rights is partly responsible for this change. (No, I am not nostalgic for my grandfather's regime; I am simply pointing out how far the pendulum has swung.) The authority of the school principal and the teacher, even more than that of the parent, relies increasingly on contracts, regulations, and rules. Traditional authority is fast disappearing.

Of all social changes, the progression from right to rights may be the most difficult to reverse or even to halt. In Canada the cult of individual rights, and associated appeals to the Charter, continues unabated. A family cannot possibly exist harmoniously if the only ties are rules and contracts. If every parental request is to be challenged on the basis of the rule book, family life has ended. The same is true of the school. There must be some acceptance of norms of behaviour if a meaningful education is to take place in a harmonious social environment; there has to be acceptance of right and wrong in the classroom.

Interestingly, even classrooms whose teachers deny that they have rules are in fact governed by implicit regulations understood by the students (Robert Boostrom in *Curriculum Inquiry* 21 [1991]). The problem arises when parents and teachers as individuals have their own idiosyncratic and poorly communicated rules. If society as a whole becomes disordered as a result of the abolition of punishment and changing definitions of appropriate behaviour, how much more does the compulsory, closed, and narrow society of classroom and school. The replacement of the concept of right and wrong by appropriate (formerly good) and inappropriate (formerly bad) behaviour, and with it the elimination of virtue and guilt, is corrosive.

The public school developed in the context of different times, when authority was recognized. Adults received respect because they were adults; principals and teachers, like parents, had a special kind of traditional authority within their limited sphere of action. If schools are to survive as useful social organizations, there must be some commitment from parents to their authority. That commitment depends on there being clear, shared values. I cannot see the current bureaucracies undoing what they have laboriously built over decades; indeed, I am not sure they could. As an administrator, I shared in the construction of bureaucracy, in which every new event demands new tinkering and new definitions. We need to start over, to permit teachers and parents to come together to build the kinds of schools they both want. This cannot be done by massive new rules for school operation from the centre. Doing so would simply mean more bureaucracy. The idea of an effective, common, state school in a heterogeneous and multicultural Western democracy is full of internal contradictions.

This section on physical survival began with statistics on life expectancy and violent death. How close the link is between crime and social life quickly becomes obvious. Suicide and murder arise from the social climate. Unquestionably, there are always psychological triggers: a normal adolescent does not rush out and commit a violent act after witnessing one on television. But just as pollutants in the atmosphere cause cancer in susceptible individuals, so the moral pollution, the disintegration, of the psychological and social environment triggers violence, theft, and social disorder. The increasing everyday rudeness, in the form of insolence and disobedience, that permeates the family and the school is to be seen as resulting, like murder and suicide, from the norms of daily social life. Road rage is an obvious symptom that most of us see regularly.

A strong traditional society, as Newfoundland is compared with, say, Quebec or British Columbia, is more able to withstand physical hardship, deprivation, and unemployment. But Newfoundland cannot remain unaffected. In 1993 I returned to New Brunswick to live after an absence of twenty years. I was surprised to see how similar social norms were to those in southern Ontario; I had unthinkingly been comparing Ontario with New Brunswick in an earlier age. New-foundland, more distant, is evolving, as the recent constitutional change with respect to educational authority illustrates.

Not only can a society weakened by the erosion of positive values (such as personal responsibility and integrity) not survive the genu-ine hardships characteristic of life, but it sees every slight, disap-pointment, failure, and tragedy as an attack on some fundamental right, as the fault of somebody or some organization. Suicide and self-loathing are reduced in a social framework that provides clear norms of behaviour, clear and legitimate goals, and the caring and education that lead to self-respect and independence. Violence and rebellion are diminished in a firm, fair, and loving context, where the social norms are recognized and internalized, not just as rules and regulations but as part of the normal, necessary, and desirable pat-tern of social life.

The chances of desirable changes in direction being taken in the larger society in the foreseeable future are remote; our times are char-acterized by excessive individual freedom and rights and by a lack of responsibility and sense of duty. Parents will only gain the oppor-tunity to choose a distinctive educational environment for their chil-dren if the problems and choices are openly discussed, and if the power of the state and its elites is reduced. Society cannot be turned around in a single generation, even if there is the political will – and there is no such will.

My argument here is that the social problems which spill over into the school are the inevitable outcome of the political, ideological, and moral (in my view, amoral) choices that we have made, not just in Canada, but in the Western world generally. Educational defenders of the status quo are correct in asserting that the schools cannot reverse the trends of the larger society; too often they shed crocodile tears over trends which they themselves promote. Liberal (Progres-sive and Individualist in educational terms) ideas among Canada's elites have contributed to the changes in our social fabric.

Parents should not have to lose their children to social forces for which there is no evidence of majority support. Even if there were a state majority in favour of liberal Progressivism and lax standards of work and behaviour, the state should not take to itself and its agen-cies the authority to impose a regime of irresponsibility and exces-sive individualism in all schools. Parents should have a major influence on the schooling of their children.

It may seem incredible – contradictory, even – that the establish-ment would impose irresponsibility and low standards with an iron hand. Why would it ban schools based on hard work, clear standards, or good behaviour? Perhaps it is motivated by the same impulse that leads adolescents to destroy the perfect garden next door or scratch a brand new Mercedes, and commentators to ridicule those who try to lead a decent life with spouse and family.

THE LIFE OF THE ADOLESCENT

In 1992 Bibby and Posterski published their second survey of adolescent beliefs and attitudes. Several years earlier, in 1989, Alan King had completed a national survey of young people's attitudes to issues of sex and health. Nationally, according to Bibby and Posterski, 36 per cent of young people saw school violence as very serious and 45 per cent knew of a victim. More than 60 per cent of the sample expected to graduate from university, yet, realistically only 20 per cent would even enrol, if the sample was representative. Similarly, 85 per cent expected to get the job they wanted. These figures illustrate the gap between aspirations and the reality discussed earlier.

The two major sources of enjoyment for young people are friends and music. VCRs, pets, and television are also important. At the bottom of the list are school, jobs, youth groups, and organized religion. The last is in general decline among youth. A question about what was highly valued showed a preference for modern, over traditional, values. When young people were asked about freedom, honesty, and generosity, the national responses indicated that these values were "very important" for 86, 70, and 40 per cent respectively. Those who claimed to attend a religious service every week were more likely to consider fundamental values very important than were those who never attended – 76 per cent compared with 61 in terms of honesty and 75 per cent compared with 48 with respect to forgiveness.

Perhaps most significant are the changes in values between 1984 and 1992: honesty declined from 85 per cent (very important) to 70, politeness from 64 to 53 per cent, cleanliness from 79 to 72 per cent, and, of importance in the school and work context, working hard from 69 to 49 per cent. Values among adults also fell between 1985 and 1990. But in all cases except for cleanliness, they were higher than values among youth.

King's study also shows a relationship between weekly church attendance and other behaviour. Among grade eleven students who said that they had sexual intercourse often, 13 per cent attended church often, while 28 per cent of those who had had no sexual intercourse attended church often. By college and university, where the choice of churchgoing is made more independently and the opportunity for sex is greater, the gap widened to 13 and 35 per cent, or 22 percentage points.

King interprets the negative relationship between churchgoing and sexual activity from a secular perspective. His view is of interest because it illustrates clearly the gap between traditionally religious parents (I refer here to the stronger branches of Christianity, Judaism, and Islam) and the secular world-view predominant in public education. Widely prevalent among Progressive educators, as I have noted, is the primacy of self-concept as a value. Sexual experience, King explains, is positive for young people because such experience is related to higher scores on self-esteem. His interpretation is diametrically opposed to that of the Traditional parent, who objects to the ethos of the secular high school precisely because it is one where sexual prowess is identified with personal success, and where the most important value is self-concept.

The evolving values, behaviour, and attitudes of young people are accompanied by changes in their family structure. William Gairdner (1992) develops a coherent argument, one with which liberal Canadians fiercely disagree: the traditional family – with parents committed to marriage "until death do us part" and children who form a focus of family life – is the necessary foundation for a peaceful, successful, and virtuous society. He argues further that there is clear empirical evidence of the inferiority of single-parent families (particularly those caused by deliberate choice or by marriage breakdown, as distinct from death of a spouse) and that government policy systematically undermines the traditional family.

Many of the facts are not in dispute. Single-parent families are increasing, the greatest numbers consisting of young unmarried women with one or more children and of separated spouses. Divorce is also rising, from 0.46 per 1000 population in 1965 to 2.7 in 1993 (*The Canadian Global Almanac 1996*). The divorce rate is lowest in the Atlantic provinces, where the youth suicide rate is also the lowest and unemployment the highest. More children are being born to unmarried mothers. In 1975, 10.1 per cent of all births were to unmarried mothers; by 1989 the proportion was 23.1 per cent. In the same period, births to unmarried mothers under age twenty expressed as a percentage of all births to women in that age group increased from 39.9 to 80.5 per cent. An interesting indicator of changing attitudes is the fact that statistics concerning such moral matters as births to unmarried mothers, marriage, and divorce are increasingly difficult to come by. It is not that Statistics Canada is unwilling to collect data on which moral judgments can be made;

rather, it only seems to be interested in being able to make Egalitarian moral judgments. Ironically, statistics are readily available on single parents, perhaps because they are viewed as unfairly disadvantaged. It is hard to imagine why anyone would think that the single-parent family could or should be as financially secure as one with two parents.

The last two decades have also been a time of growth in sex-education programs in schools. The relationship between such programs and sexual activity is a matter for heated debate. An important review of sex-education programs in American schools has recently concluded that they do not have the positive empirical effects that their supporters claim (notably, a reduction in the number of unwanted pregnancies). The morality of these programs' emphasis on individual decision making and the consent of both parties (as distinct from postponing sex until marriage or adulthood) is also questioned by Barbara Whitehead in an article in the *Atlantic Monthly* (October 1994).

In another well-supported article (*Atlantic Monthly*, April 1993), Whitehead concludes that in the United States (the one major democracy that generally fares less well than Canada on most of the youth indicators presented in this book), children in single-parent or step-parent families are more likely than others to be poor, to drop out of school, and to have trouble with the law. Whitehead also argues that the happiness of the parents who participate in serial marriages is paid for by the unhappiness and sacrifice of their children. She goes on to emphasize the importance of the father in children's broader education. But, she observes, any discussion of the consequences of changes in family structure provokes angry protest.

In 1996 the Canadian government passed legislation to remove sexual orientation (only vaguely defined) as grounds for discrimination. Conservative opponents see this legislation as another frontal assault on the traditional family, leading ineluctably if indirectly to the courts, themselves only too keen to pass liberal legislation of their own, who will determine that marriage cannot be confined to heterosexual couples and that sexual orientation is irrelevant in determining the custody of children. Similarly, it will predictably become legitimate for teachers of young and adolescent children to display their homosexual lifestyle.

In the late 1980s the Ontario Ministry of Education distributed a comic book called *Condom Sense* to all high school students. Its message was that sexual relations should take place only between consenting couples and that condoms should always be used for "safe" sex. There is evidence that these devices are ineffective means of preventing pregnancy and sexually transmitted disease, notably AIDS. Beyond that issue, adolescents were left to imagine whether consenting couples included an older brother and his twelve-year-old sister or same-sex partners. With homosexual relationships defined as normal, sex with children publicly advocated, and incest increasingly presented as normal in the arts, sex with animals is the last remaining taboo, but for how long? And why, if the animal consents and is loved?

The most important response to Gairdner and Whitehead, other than the hate-filled, emotional diatribes they evoke, is the argument that the key factor causing problems for young people is poverty rather than the single-parent family. In the case of family structure and poverty, most of the research depends on measuring associations between one factor and another, rather than on investigations that might establish cause and effect. There can be little doubt that it is more difficult to bring up good children in a poor environment than in a rich one, in part because there are more problem children as peers in the poor environment. The same is true of schools – parents understandably want friends for their children, particularly their problem children, who will be good role models. This attitude is not selfish and irrational, as it seems to many educators. The social environment may not be the most important influence on the individual, but it is a factor.

The increases over the last three decades in children born to unmarried mothers, the divorce rate, the youth suicide rate, crimes of violence and theft (by both adults and youth), and the incidence of sexually transmitted diseases have been accompanied by a rise in per capita income in constant dollars, increased per-student school expenditures in constant dollars, and a reduction in the high school drop-out rate. Furthermore, the poorest provinces in Canada (with the highest unemployment rates) are no more affected by the negative indicators than are the more affluent ones. Adherence to formal religion is negatively related to some of those unpleasant changes. Thus, while *relative* poverty is without doubt an important trigger in some cases, how it, let alone *absolute* poverty (rare in Canada), can be the only or even the most important factor is difficult to see. To the extent that relative poverty is a cause of social disorder, its effect may well stem in part from a culture of entitlement and discontent, in comparison with one of personal responsibility and integrity. I am not making any argument about the appropriateness or fairness of Canada's tax policies with respect to rich and poor. I am pointing out, however, that relative poverty has always been with us and is unlikely to disappear. By contrast, absolute poverty has diminished steadily over the last hundred years. There are other social factors, such as a decline in traditional values, that do parallel the social problems which have increased over the last few decades.

Families come under stress from declining faith in such traditional virtues as integrity, truth, courage, and industriousness, and increasing emphasis on self-fulfilment, self-concept, and material success; declining affiliation with any community institution either run by adults or based on fundamental values; increased likelihood of there being only one biological parent in the home; a higher probability of both parents, where there are two, working outside the home; decreased probability that parents will work in secure jobs with regular hours; and greater probability of unemployment; thus it is scarcely surprising that young people retreat to entertainment and their peers. In 1990 adolescents watched about eighteen hours of television (including videotapes) in an average week (Bibby and Posterski 1992). If they had perfect attendance at school, they would have had about twenty-five hours of classes, an increasing portion of which would have consisted of discussions with peers. Provinces do not publish attendance data, but I estimate from experience, informal discussion with senior administrators, and other sources that Canadian secondary schools have attendance rates between 85 and 96 per cent, with a probable average in the low 90s.

There is little consensus about the influence of television and popular music on young people, but it seems unlikely that such widespread experiences would be without impact. The direct influence of television on most young people is probably not great: it is simply junk food and tranquillizer for an already poorly stimulated mind and body. The imminent danger is its powerful effect on a small minority who are already disconnected from family and friends. Here, it seems to be not the violence of far-fetched fantasies that is most dangerous, but rather the realistic depiction of sadistic or sexual assault in everyday circumstances "by people like me in situations like mine." One would expect, from this argument, that Koreans would be less negatively affected by watching American television programs than are Americans themselves. Similarly, the fact that Newfoundland thirteen-year-olds, living in a relatively stable society, watch more television than those from other provinces (23 per cent watch five or more hours a day, according to Lapointe, Mead, and Askew 1992) is unlikely to impel a disproportionate number of them into an immediate life of violence, since the scenes they view on American programs are not like their own experiences. Television is largely a background noise, not very beneficial but not very harmful either – except in the case of the increasing numbers of people who are at special risk, for whom it acts as a trigger. A more pervasive effect is an indirect one. Those watching television are not doing homework or household chores, performing community service, reading a challenging book, or getting physical exercise.

CONCLUSION

In this chapter I have drawn a picture of life outside the school which is very different from the one that many readers will themselves have experienced or seen. I have emphasized the changes that young people are experiencing: a more hostile external world and a more stressed family. At the same time, it is important to note that the majority of young people do not encounter most, if any, of these problems. Few commit suicide, become the objects of violence, suffer the stress of a failed family, or face continuing unemployment when they leave school. I tire of educated people asserting that their educated children cannot get work because there are no jobs out there, when the vast majority of young people not in school are employed, even those who have not graduated from high school. Most, although not affected directly, still experience the decaying social climate, even those, particularly in the elites, who do not define the changes as decay. What most people see as decay – increases in divorce, family breakdown, single-parent families, heterosexual and homosexual activity among adolescent and younger children, the use of illegal drugs, and extreme expression of these changes in books and the arts – they see as freedom for the individual and the destruction of inhibiting tradition. They do not accept that theft, violent crime, and family desertion are part of the same trend. Increasingly, the media's opposition to the abrogation of the few remaining standards and values is tenuous and limited to particular contexts – theft by lawyers and business people, violence by the police or soldiers, and family breakdown if it is caused by male chauvinism or violence against women.

The pressures to individualize students within the classroom and the growing differentiation of children (increasing numbers of whom have behavioural problems) makes the idea of classroom norms and standards more difficult to realize in the typical public school today. While there have always been families whose habits have been destructive to school success, their numbers have increased. What is new is the number of families whose values are deliberately at odds with those principles that support constructive behaviour in school. There has always been resistance to school standards (as there is to any standard) from rebels. The change is the increasing proportion of adults, some of whom are educated and affluent, who openly challenge any standard or rule that impinges on their child's freedom or rights.

One of the most important implications of the changes in life outside the school is the increased diversity of children's lives. Some come from extremely traditional, religious homes where television is strictly rationed, if it is allowed at all, and where any involvement with the opposite sex is monitored right into the high school years. Others, with televisions, access to the Internet, radios, and disc players in their own rooms, come from modern families where parents provide advice on the use of condoms to their twelve-year-olds. Some come from immigrant families with no knowledge of English and strong, patriarchal traditions; others have a lesbian parent living with a partner.

Some children receive constructive educational assistance from two loving parents who have helped them learn to read and to use numbers before they begin kindergarten; others have been neglected and shunted from foster home to foster home, where they have encountered many forms of abuse. Some come from homes with two professional parents and a level of affluence that would scarcely have been dreamed of forty years ago; others have unstable families degraded by poverty, crime, drugs, and sexual abuse. Not only are the traditional norms much less common, but those increasingly rare teachers who try to cling to them in the classroom are more and more fearful of the abuse accorded to William Gairdner and Barbara Whitehead. Teachers tell me, as a commonplace, received belief, that they should not, do not, and are not allowed to "impose" their values on children in their classes. In this context, they refer without exception to traditional values, not to politically correct ones. There are many values that teachers want, are allowed to, and are instructed to teach, such as a green environment, non-judgmental approaches to sexual practice, and the harmful effects of academic competition.

Parents can do six things to promote success in school. They can provide help, encouragement, and support; stimulate ideas and involve the family in out-of-school activities; use language carefully for genuine, caring communication; have high expectations of their children in all areas of life and encourage high, but realistic expectations for the future; with their children, practise good work habits; and provide their children with help in the basic skills (Mark and Leanora Holmes, *Parents Guide to CAT/2 Results* [Canadian Test Centre, 1997]). Quite apart from deliberately determined variation in family lifestyles and values, there are obvious limits to the ability of parents to act on that prescription. If most could and did help their children in these ways, this book would be redundant.

Whose culture should the school promulgate? Inevitably, it seeks to compromise, and this usually entails adopting the lowest common denominator, those few values – constituting what I call low doctrine – to which there will be least exception and which are most necessary for the school's survival to the end of the day. These values are typically non-violence, consideration of others, and tolerance. Not always realized in practice, those values are far from sufficient for many parents.

In chapters 3 and 4, I show that the school's instructional practices are quite different from what the public would like. There I disagree strongly with defenders of the educational establishment. In this chapter the establishment and I probably agree substantially on the facts; the values and social climate of the school are not very different from those of the larger society. It is on the interpretation of those facts that we disagree. My argument is that the values of the larger society, with a multitude of sources not all within our own country, should not be imposed on children by the power of the state against the will of their parents. Generally accepted values in the larger society, particularly among the influential media, cultural, and academic elites, in no way represent all parents.

Consider the teacher mentioned earlier who does not like the appearance of her teenaged daughter. She might be happy if the school, supported by the community, insisted on an appropriate appearance for students at school. Whether in the majority or the minority, parents in a pluralist society who want a social environment that does not simply reflect the values of the media and other unsavoury elements in the larger society should not have them forced upon them. So-called broad-minded teachers look back in horror to an age when religious training was mandatory, but have no inhibitions about the state-ordained inculcation of contemporary majoritarian values (or even those held by an expert minority).

At the same time, it must be recognized that educators do not, for the most part, consciously invest the schools with debased values, and when they do (by watering down the dress code, for example), it is sometimes at the behest of influential parents. Reforms that depend on parents' agreement and action are limited by those parents' own values and world-views. The idea that a mass school system could be set up which was essentially alien to the larger society, such as one that closely reflected my personal values or those of other advocates of reform on the Egalitarian left or even the currently powerful Technocratic right, is preposterous. That is why utopian solutions to the school problem are of little more than intellectual value. Even Stalin had limited success using the schools to mould all children to his wishes. Unduly influential as our monopolies may be, their power is far from Stalinist.

There are, then, several implications from this chapter. Schools cannot possibly mend the various social wrongs observed by different groups. Some of the limitations of the school result from the deficiencies of society and of parents. If parents are permitted more choice, at least those who object strongly to the school's informal curriculum – to its values and ideology, whether or not their source is majoritarian – will be able to find a more favourable social climate for their children. Since the school is to some extent a mirror of society, it is vain to imagine that all schools will quickly be able to produce graduates greatly different from their parents. The breakdown of civilization can occur rapidly, as those who deny such breakdown in our own society will at least admit for the past. Constructing a strong society takes much longer, particularly in a democracy and most of all in a pluralist democracy. In attempting to treat the whole child in the name of tolerance, educators fail to recognize the extent to which they themselves end up representing the problems of the whole child, of single-parent families, of variable diluted and flexible values, and of the lack of community. Schools can only be rebuilt one at a time, through the concerted will of those involved. There will be no effective five-year plans to improve all schools in a comprehensive way. Within such a time-frame, parents would not even agree on what constituted improvement.

– 3 –

What Do Canadian Schools Do?

This chapter is concerned with what goes on in schools and the changes that are brought about by them in students. A short overview cannot possibly provide a detailed picture; rather, the major contested policy issues are emphasized. The commentary should be seen in context. It is clear that for the most part money is not the crucial problem. Most Canadian public schools are on the whole well funded, even though the distribution of money is wasteful and unfair. It is equally clear that the Canadian social context is not one that is likely to contribute to an effective and committed education in the disciplines of knowledge and the fundamental values. Traditional beliefs and values are diluted or abandoned; the idea of a common school serving a high level of consensually agreed goals is obsolescent, if it ever existed, while the school is still expected to fulfil some traditional roles and expectations, as well as a host of contradictory and obscure new ones.

The best place to begin the complex task of interpreting today's schools is to consider educational purposes. An important part of the problem facing schools today is simply that people want different and sometimes contradictory things, with the result that teachers face vague ambiguity and high-minded platitudes from the bureaucracies they serve. When parents complain that their children cannot spell, teachers are shocked or condescending, dismissive or defensive. After all, nothing could be further than spelling from the minds of high-level officials.

A single school, even a large comprehensive high school, is not and cannot be a supermarket, providing totally different products for a variety of tastes. The traditional department store is finding it difficult to cater to the wide range in preferences; sectoral marketing seems to be more successful, and department stores try to mimic these niche outlets. One school cannot provide strong discipline and regular homework for some, permissive opportunities for self-actualization and high self-concept for others; both whole-class direct instruction and child-centred learning; both a religious and a secular environment; effective instruction for all and also individualization; both the reinforcement of fundamental values and the acceptance of nearly all cultural differences. The large cafeteria-style high school, with its multitudinous options and levels, cannot genuinely cater to people who want a small, community environment based on strongly shared values. In my terms, the school cannot have both low and high doctrine. Inevitably, it gravitates towards the permissive, the individualized, and the secular and a disinclination for any strongly held values other than its own survival.

WHAT SHOULD SCHOOLS TRY TO DO?

If we could agree on what schools ought to be doing, then we could perhaps concur on how to run a monopolistic system. But if we cannot even agree on fundamental purposes, then the chances of the public school continuing its traditional role are slim.

British Columbia's policy document *Enabling Learners: Year 2000: A Framework for Learning* is close to the middle of the road for educators. It is a good representation of the educational establishment's world-view. Three goals are listed, the first being intellectual development, in which the schools are to be "supported" by the family and community. The second and third goals – human and social development and career development – are "shared" among schools, family, and community. The details of the three goals are discouraging. The intellectual ones, while giving a nod to "basic learning skills and bodies of knowledge," emphasize such rather vague things as "the ability to analyse critically, reason and think independently," the development of "a lifelong appreciation of learning," and a "capacity" for creative thought and expression. These nebulous statements may seem harmless enough, but they downgrade the essence of learning: history, geography, literature, and science. The reality is that critical thinking is of no value at all when coupled with ignorance. I have sat in high school social-studies classes listening to earnest and opinionated discussions of current events in various parts of the world, where easy solutions were reached based on ignorance of important facts. There are no short cuts to "high level" thinking skills; they depend on an educated and knowledgeable intelligence, as well as the ability to apply reason, logic, and, in many instances, empathy. If one visits the average, somewhat apathetic high school classroom, it is difficult to imagine any positive effect lasting five years, let alone a lifetime. How anyone would know if students have a "capacity" for "creative" thought and expression is unclear, and it is even more unclear why capacity should be preferred to result.

Such vague goals lead to vague teaching, with good intentions but equally uncertain methods of evaluation. It is miseducative to encourage young people to discuss important issues critically without their first having a solid background knowledge of the subject. And it is harmful to emphasize students' opinions about historical and contemporary events and their conclusions about character in literature outside a context of disciplined thought and knowledge.

The human and social goals to which families are to be converted are just as contentious. In the same way that critical reasoning is emphasized more than academic knowledge and understanding, so "self-worth and personal initiative" displace the traditional virtues of truth, justice, courage, consideration for others, humility, personal responsibility, and industriousness. When self and personal initiative are encouraged without virtue, it is hardly surprising that incivility, misbehaviour, and crime increase. The closest that the British Columbia document comes to virtue is the development of "social responsibility and a tolerance and respect for the ideas and beliefs of others." This statement is distressingly similar to the lowest common denominator I anticipated in the last chapter. *Enabling Learners: Year 2000* was not accepted quietly in British Columbia, an issue to which I return in the final chapter. At this point, it should be seen as a blueprint that represented the educational establishment and was largely accepted by both Social Credit (presumably without government members having read it) and NDP governments for a time.

Ontario's goals, dating back to the early 1980s, are more extreme, in that they make no reference to bodies of knowledge at all and are even more open to aberrant values. It is not clear why a school system would consider it important to feel good about being a liar and a cheat, and to initiate unkind or criminal activity, but that is the logical consequence of putting self-concept and initiative before any fundamental virtue.

Public opinion in both these provinces has caused the "experts" to modify their documents. British Columbia's is on ice, and Ontario's NDP government set up the Caplan-Bégin commission to examine the entire system (Caplan was a committed socialist, hardly in tune with the public will in the 1990s). Even so, schools do not stop at the stroke of a pen; those written documents substantially represent the current talk and action of educators. The Caplan-Bégin report did recognize some public concerns, but it failed to accept the crucial importance of educational choice. I have been told informally that there was considerable internal disagreement within the commission on that issue, Caplan being adamantly opposed to any expansion of school choice. The commission report does note the total lack of consensus on moral issues, but proceeds to provide a recipe for all as if that fact were of no consequence. It makes no attempt to state a set of educational purposes to replace Ontario's official goals, on which it does not comment. The Conservative government under Mike Harris has also not dealt with the existing goals. They remain as orphans fondly remembered by members of the educational establishment who wrote them (they were never discussed by legislators; merely tabled in the legislature by a Progressive Conservative government).

In the introduction, I referred to research on the opinions of Ontario's directors of education, those of similarly educated people not employed in education, and other educators, nurses, and engineers. The individuals were asked to rank six statements of educational goals (Holmes 1991, 1995). I subsequently labelled the statements Progressive, Technocratic, Cultural, Traditional, Individualist, and Egalitarian, terms that I have already used for differing world-views on education.

The Progressive world-view (or educational philosophy), defined more fully in the introduction, gives priority to allowing children to grow healthily, to express themselves, to be tolerant of others, and to feel at one with themselves. The school does not impose a desired set of outcomes but provides opportunities. This is the world-view favoured by the educational establishment. The directors ranked the Progressive statement first, whereas the equivalent sample of non-educators placed it fifth. Elementary educators are as committed to the Progressive idea as the directors, but secondary educators much less so.

The Technocratic world-view wants children to be prepared for future lives as citizens and workers, and to develop the basic skills, habits, and attitudes required for future success and good citizenship. This is the perspective most opposed by the educational establishment and is the focus of Barlow and Robertson's attack (1994). Engineers are strongly Technocratic, as I assume a majority of the general public are (at least in these complex economic times). Nurses fall somewhere between. The Progressive idea is reflected in Ontario's educational goals and British Columbia's *Enabling Learners: Year 2000*, and less strongly in the Caplan-Bégin report, which is a blend of the Egalitarian, the Progressive, and the Technocratic. It rejects the Traditional and ignores the Cultural world-view, probably because the latter is incorrectly assumed to be well represented in the secondary school.

It is understandable (as well as naive) that Barlow and Robertson should classify everyone who opposes their position (including me) in the Technocratic category. Most of the public debate takes place between adherents of the Progressive outlook (mainly educators and members of the academic, cultural, and media elites) and those of the Technocratic philosophy (mainly business people and most of the middle-of-the-road public). The media quickly place interested parties in one or other of two categories (e.g. progressive, child-centred, and establishment or back-to-basics and reform); not only is discussion reduced to two simplistic choices, but educational purpose is displaced by instructional methodology.

The oversimplification of the debate into a methodological one between two parties about how to teach is unhelpful; discussion is focused on symptoms instead of the disease. Peacemakers then call for a balance between the two methodologies, which is sometimes (but by no means always) possible, while there are fundamental, unbridgeable differences between the world-views. The Progressive, for example, sees the child as essentially good and a natural learner. Children need help and choices within a rich and caring environment in order that they may first develop good feelings about themselves which will in time lead to self-fulfilment. In contrast, the Technocrat sees the child as a young citizen who must be trained and educated to play a useful part in adult life. The basic skills and the education required for useful work are of pre-eminent worth. The first sees the child as decision maker; the second believes that adults must make early choices on behalf of the child – responsibility goes with authority. While those two conflicting ideologies are not readily reconciled, they do share a disregard (occasionally manifested as contempt) for the larger society and for traditional culture and values. That common disregard is based on entirely distinct reasons.

The Cultural view, that we should cultivate the intellect, together with the aesthetic and social senses, is often lumped in with the Technocratic view by Progressive opponents, despite the fundamental differences in their philosophical underpinnings. The Cultural philosophy, promoted by nineteenth-century liberals but often called conservative today, envisages young people being immersed in a rich, inherited culture, including the great books. This idea does not mix well with education based on the individual's own choices or on a vision of the future defined in terms of computers and more material goods.

The Traditional view (summarized in the preface) that education should be founded in virtue, if acknowledged at all by the Progressive establishment, is parcelled off as more negative evidence that reformers want to go back to some imaginary golden age. (It is interesting that reformers can be painted as being at the same time both nostalgic for an imaginary past and conspiring with big business to build a mechanistic future.) I have many times been told that I want schools to return to what I had as a child, by people who have no idea what that experience was. In fact, during and following World War II, I received mixed, but generally poor-quality schooling, inferior to what my children received twenty-five or so years later. It certainly did not reflect the beliefs that I now hold, and the instructional methodology was generally inadequate.

The Traditionalist advocates development of good character and personal responsibility, with an emphasis on family and community. Instruction in the skills, the disciplines of knowledge, and other school subjects – the major content of schooling but not its primary educational aim – should take place within an explicitly moral framework. Ultimately, Traditionalists want the school to cultivate an openness to life based on knowledge, understanding, reason, and faith in the good (or, in many cases, God).

The Egalitarian view is often seen by Technocrats as part of the Progressive idea. In fact, the Progressive outlook is fundamentally non-egalitarian, as Marxists are quick to point out. The Egalitarian world-view, espoused by socialists, wants education to produce a better society, with less social and economic division. It desires equality and the reduction or elimination of differences based on sex, social background, and race. Obviously, children from different environments and backgrounds in Progressive schools make choices of greatly varying educational quality. Progressive instruction promotes greater individualism than either the Technocratic, which has many common objectives for all, or the Egalitarian, which actively seeks the elimination of individual differences.

Finally, the Individualist world-view emphasizes the fullest possible development of the individual's capacities, to promote excellence in all fields by means of reasonable competition. While the Progressive philosophy encourages individual choice, it also stresses group activity and high self-concept (based on frequent praise). The Individualist wants a more bracing, competitive school climate, with constant challenge to do one's best or face failure. The Individualist demand for educational excellence is treated with distaste by Progressives, who believe children should work "at their own rate." Ironically, both Progressivism and Individualism focus on the individual child, but see his or her schooling and ultimate characteristics in very different terms.

By definition, no two of these six perspectives can be perfectly combined, but the Progressive and the Traditional are fundamentally opposed in their primary moral assumptions, as are the Individualist and the Egalitarian. As a Traditionalist, I am not surprisingly most opposed to the prevailing Progressive world-view. Although I have greater sympathy with the Individualist position, I oppose its excesses, represented by the crass materialist values embraced by schools and even more by contemporary Western culture.

Overall, my samples of educated people showed three world-views being particularly strong in some sectors. The Progressive choice reveals the strongest division of opinion; it is ranked very high by directors of education and elementary teachers and very low (fifth out of six) by some lay groups. In contrast, the Cultural viewpoint has the most general support and the least opposition; ironically, the idea that schooling should stress academics first is least popular among directors of education and less so than among other educators and lay groups. Cultural ideas are accepted to some degree by almost everyone, but they are given lower priority by followers of the Egalitarian, Technocratic, and Progressive world-views. The Technocratic perspective is, as one might expect, the mirror image of the Progressive: much more popular among lay groups than among educators. The three philosophies – Cultural, Technocratic, and Progressive – all have strong, influential supporters.

The Traditional and the Individualist world-views are clearly minority perspectives among the educated. The Traditional is the first choice for about 15 per cent and accounts for about 35 per cent for first and second choices combined. If, as I suspect, this perspective is more widely held among the less educated (the strongly religious denominations and sects are scarcely represented among my educated samples), between one-sixth and one-third of the population might favour schools with an overriding moral or religious purpose. The Individualist world-view is fairly stable among groups, but at a level of popularity below that of the Traditional. Aspects of this outlook could be effectively absorbed into a school based primarily on the Cultural or Technocratic world-views. The Egalitarian philosophy is not significantly represented in the samples. As the samples (of educated people) were generally not supportive of left-wing politics, the Egalitarian view would definitely be more popular among a sample more representative of the entire population. My guess is that well under 20 per cent of people would favour it as the foundation for school policy, for reasons that will become apparent later.

Individualism and Egalitarianism, polar opposites, probably have the least support from the population. Individualism, with its emphasis on rugged competition and excellence, is unfashionable in today's schools, where competitive tests are frowned upon by educators and sometimes banned. Egalitarianism is more popular, notably among academics, but it is distorted to a bleeding-heart paternalism of "the whole child" in the schools, an approach understandably opposed by the Marxist left, who are the first to realize that pity and condescension lead to ineffective teaching. "Doing good" is increasingly recognized by representatives of the disadvantaged as trapping educational disadvantage in low expectations. Egalitarian educational ideas are popular in the media and with left-leaning politicians. I argue later that their translation into education within a Western democracy is conceptually unreasonable.

My limited samples are only illustrative. One may assume that if I had been able to sample groups representing those without university degrees, for example, or unmarried mothers, the unemployed, industrial workers, housewives, and workers in service industries, the variation in world-view would be even greater. Generally, the less educated would be more Technocratic, more Egalitarian, more Traditional, and less Progressive and Cultural than the educated. That assumption is generally supported by public opinion polls, with their inevitably more general questions.

There is nothing magically new revealed in the popularity of the six views, and we do not need six types of school to meet the six philosophies. The data do show that, first, there is an important gap between educational leaders and lay people on many key aspects of educational policy; and second, there is major variation in the priorities assigned to educational goals by the educated public. Although the differences between educational leaders and lay people stand out in my analysis (it was that issue that I was emphasizing), there is no reason to believe that similar discrepancies do not exist among different groups of lay people, as indeed they do between engineers and nurses in my samples. My point is not that there are four, five, or six world-views rather than two, but that the complexity of educational goals is so great that it cannot be usefully reduced to a choice of two options, still less two instructional methodologies.

Overall, four philosophical views in my survey (Progressive, Technocratic, Cultural, and Traditional) received substantial support, and a fifth, the Egalitarian, is strongly held by a small, vocal minority. The Technocratic and the Cultural can be substantially combined; the typical Canadian high school of the 1950s represented such a combination, with greater emphasis on the Cultural. It would be conceptually possible to include the Traditional philosophy as well, but it must be remembered that the addition of that world-view would repel as well as attract; in urban areas it could well repel more than it attracted. The Technocratic, the Progressive, and the Individualist outlooks all capture aspects – not necessarily compatible ones – of the modern and postmodern world, notably its individualism. They can all easily stand independent of traditional religious belief and Marxism; they are essentially modern, centred on self rather than society.

The closest thing to a model for the majority (or plurality) remains a combination of the Technocratic and the Cultural, with some Individualist aspects: programs of excellence and a competitive climate. This model is unattractive to followers of the Progressive and Traditional ideas, not to mention the smaller band of vociferous Egalitarians. In practice, some school systems have moved to a Progressive and Individualist elementary school and a Technocratic and Cultural secondary school.

Those surveyed and the graduate students with whom I have discussed the world-views have been unwilling to accept just one position for themselves: typically people combine three or four. Respondents to the questionnaires were asked to rank in order as many philosophies as they felt some sympathy for; most included about four. Sometimes the priority among the three or four chosen is important; sometimes it is not.

My own educational philosophy combines the Traditional with the Cultural and the Technocratic. The Traditional provides a framework for education, the Cultural defines its most important content, and the Technocratic assures practical training for future citizenship. I recognize secondary emphases of excellence and equity respectively from the Individualist and Egalitarian positions.

Until the early twentieth century, the Progressive world-view served the useful function of enabling parents and educators to accept children as young people needing both nurture and freedom, rather than as miniature adults simply requiring strong control, but in recent decades its social and educational influence has become pernicious. Any world-view that is interpreted with fanatical zeal is dangerous, including Traditionalism (in Afghanistan, Algeria, and Rwanda, as extreme examples). But Western society and schools are under greatest attack today from Progressivism (in the form of worship of self, acceptance of mediocrity, and freedom become licence), Individualism (in the form of materialism and greed), and Egalitarianism (in the form of authoritarian state agencies). The harm from excessive Technocracy stems from its coupling with and promotion of excessive individualism and materialism.

PROGRAMS IN THE PROVINCES

It should be clear that, if the goals of Canadians are varied, then the desired content and objectives of the curriculum are equally so. For example, if there is to be AIDS education of any kind, should it be based on the need to have (so-called) safe sex, should it assume the postponement of sexual activity, or should it just stick to the "facts"? Should a class in English literature be dominated by the Eurocentric works of "dead white men," should it "liberate" young people by "deconstructing" old texts and introducing them to the "endemic racism" and "sexism" exposed in new ones, or should it take a broad sample of differing views? That last option is not the easy compromise it may at first appear. One still must develop criteria for inclusion and exclusion. There will continue to be demands, from various groups, for removing from the classroom *The Merchant of Venice* (as anti-Semitic), *The Catcher in the Rye* (as anti-Christian), and *Huckleberry Finn* (as racist).

Should young children learn long division and penmanship or calculators and word processing? Is reading still of primary importance, or is it now surpassed by "people skills" such as constructive collaboration? The debate is not just about instructional methodology, sex education, the content of books in the literature program, or evolution; it is about the substance and purpose of education, beginning in early childhood. Is it acceptable if boys in kindergarten choose to play with trucks (not dolls), and girls with dolls (not trucks)?

Only limited data are available to show the changes in the curriculum in recent years. Tables 6 and 7 illustrate changes in subject enrolments in two provinces. One must be careful in interpreting such statistics since the way in which subjects and courses are organized varies across the country. The following generalizations must therefore be treated with caution. Enrolment in French as a second language and advanced physics has increased. In Newfoundland, by 1991–92, the enrolment of girls in physics was 43 percent of their enrolment in grade twelve English (a high proportion for such a specialized subject). The focus of teaching in geography and history is extremely varied. World Problems is now the most popular senior history course in Newfoundland. Geography has traditionally been a Cinderella subject in Canada, and the low enrolment in grade twelve is remarkable (although there may be compensation in higher enrolments in grade ten or eleven). Only a minority of students enrol in physical education in grade twelve, and those who do are probably of above average fitness to begin with. While it makes sense for students with the greatest interest and aptitude in science to enrol in

Table 6
Student enrolment in selected courses in Saskatchewan in grade twelve, 1980–90
(expressed as a percentage of enrolment in grade twelve English)

Course	79–80	84–85	89–90
French	14	15	22
Physics	37	4	49
Music	2	1	1
Geography	4	2	2
History	72	65	65
Electricity	1	1	1
Food Preparation	13	11	11
Auto Mechanics	3	2	1
Phys. Ed.	27	28	28

SOURCE: Departmental statistics.

Table 7
Student enrolment in selected courses in Newfoundland in grade twelve, 1984–92
(expressed as a percentage of enrolment in English)

Course	83–84[a]	89–90	91–92
French	26	30	36
Physics	30	40	48
Music[b]	1	2	2
Geography	66	74	79
History[c]	54	53	50
Food Service[d]	3	6	4
Electronics	4	2	3
Phys. Ed.	39	47	49

SOURCE: Departmental statistics.

[a] First year for grade twelve in Newfoundland.

[b] Instrumental music. There are other music options; students may choose one or more.

[c] Includes a course in world problems, in which enrolments have increased.

[d] Offered at grade eleven.

advanced physics, it is strange that the least fit should not take physical education; it is like allowing those who misbehave to be exempt from education in civic values.

There is only one relevant comparative study of international curricula. While the international programs that test achievement increasingly analyse the "intended curriculum," the "delivered curriculum," and the "achieved curriculum," their emphasis is on their test items and their applicability, as distinct from curriculum content in the various countries.

A joint study of math and science by the Alberta Chamber of Resources and the Alberta Department of Education in 1992 found that concepts are generally introduced earlier in the comparison countries (Hungary, Japan, and Germany) than in that province. Equally important, there was much less repetition of concepts, notably in Japan, the country most like Alberta in its timing of the introduction of topics. Effective instructional systems use carefully developed, sequential programs rather than the spiral approach popular in North America. Sequential programs teach a concept once thoroughly, before going on to the next – like putting building blocks on a foundation. Spiral programs touch on ideas every year, each time going a little deeper. It seems strange that the growing awareness that sequential programs are more effective has had no impact on the provinces' addiction to the spiral approach. It is also interesting that the unique Alberta study was spearheaded by Dr Joe Freedman, an indefatigable lay person crusading for educational reform. American educators study the programs of their successful international competitors; Canadians do not.

Preparation for Work

Vocational subjects are generally in decline in the secondary schools. Ontario statistics, were they publicly available, would show a significant decrease in enrolments in these subjects from 1970 to the present date. Statistics are available that show the decline from 1970 to the early 1980s, and I have seen local data for the early 1980s indicating that this decline was continuing. There is no reason to believe that there has been any reversal.

New Brunswick officially has a single common program in the senior high school and no vocational programs, and that policy is generally observed in the francophone sector, but less so in the anglophone schools. Across the country, whether by deliberate policy or by benign neglect, vocational programs have not fared well over the last twenty or so years. Quebec is the only province that has provided strong, official support for the vocational sector.

Statistics Canada's annual publication *Education in Canada* shows that full-time enrolment in community colleges increased between 1988–89 and 1992–93 by 34 and 30 per cent in social sciences and services and humanities respectively, and by 26 per cent in engineering and applied sciences. The same pattern is found in the universities, where undergraduate enrolment increased over the same period by 27 and 25 per cent in humanities and education respectively, and by 16 and 10 per cent in engineering and applied sciences and mathematics and science respectively. The university statistics are the more revealing. In the colleges the engineering enrolments are still nearly three times the size of the other two groups combined. In the case of the universities, by 1992–93, enrolments in humanities, education, and social sciences counted for 264 000; those in engineering and applied sciences and mathematics and science for 73 000.

This book is not directly concerned with the postsecondary sector. To a considerable extent, however, enrolment at that level is dependent on previous preparation. Engineering, mathematics, and science require concrete secondary school prerequisites (programs in the arts, humanities, and social sciences effectively assume little prior knowledge for their courses). If credentials are more important than learning, if governments pay most of the cost of postsecondary education, and if arts graduates are much cheaper to produce than scientists and engineers, then the statistics, bizarre in the context of the social and economic conditions described in chapter 2, become comprehensible.

Many young people understandably choose the easiest and cheapest route to a respectable credential, preferably a university degree of some kind. Those degree programs are also sources of profit for the university. Mass programs in social sciences in the university parallel general courses in the high school; they both provide a credential without requiring much personal sacrifice.

It may appear cynical to assert that many students prefer the easy route. I recall taking an advanced seminar as part of my doctoral program at the University of Chicago. The professor was brilliant and stimulating, and his ideas were of particular interest to me. The students were all in doctoral studies in education. Most gave perfunctory presentations of their major term topic, exerting little effort; all passed. At the time I was surprised by my fellow students' laziness, forgetting that I had had the same motives and had been equally lazy, or more so, in my programs at other universities. That course had special meaning for me, but not for everyone else. It is not unusual for human beings to take an easier route if it is made available at no obvious cost.

If we turn to what the schools do directly in the area of job preparation, the avoidance of difficult, hands-on programs becomes more evident. Bear in mind that even with increased postsecondary enrolments (which have stabilized somewhat in recent years and are likely to remain stable or decline as governments pass more costs on to the beneficiaries), a minority of the age cohort continues from secondary to full-time postsecondary education. At the secondary level, between 1987–88 and 1991–92, full-time pre-employment and

vocational enrolment at the secondary level *dropped* from 92 000 to
77 000. Despite the secondary enrolment per year being three times
that of the postsecondary enrolment, more young people register
each year in undergraduate programs in the social sciences alone
than in all the secondary vocational areas combined.

Educators argue that vocational training in the school is obsolete
because of the changing and more varied nature of the job market.
In Ontario, cooperative education in secondary schools is more popular than vocational subjects, and the Conservative government
hopes to increase its enrolment, talking at one time of making it
compulsory (as it is, in more structured form, in British Columbia).
Unfortunately, while there still is a market for certain kinds of vocational graduates, cooperative education is a fuzzy concept that is
expensive to run and its overall effects are unclear.

The original idea of secondary cooperative education in Ontario
was to give high school students an idea of the working world. At
first it was often academic students proceeding to university who
enrolled as a matter of interest (Ontario has long had a five-year
secondary program leading to results similar to other provinces with
four-year programs, despite efforts by the government to reduce it).
In many Ontario districts, the focus has changed, and the emphasis
is now more on having students take a cooperative program in the
industrial area in which they are interested in working. Some school
systems – Scarborough and the city of York are examples – have
developed sophisticated and practical programs.

In general, however, the approach is plagued by problems of inefficiency and lack of focus. It is costly to the school in terms of teacher
supervision, and there is little advantage to the employer, other than
public relations. Some teachers accuse employers of abusing the
system by using students as unpaid replacement workers. Employers respond that students are inadequately prepared or supervised
by the school. The program doubtless helps some students understand the ways of the workplace, but as a model for the movement
from school to work it is both inefficient and ineffective. It was never
designed for that purpose.

The term "new vocationalism" may refer to either of two opposing policy directions, to the idea that every young person should
have school-supervised *work experience* while in high school or to the
concept, supported in this book, that more direct efforts should be
made to make *employable* those young people who are not continuing to postsecondary education. The ends and means of the two
views are quite different. I am sympathetic to the various purposes
of cooperative education, but I believe that they can be more efficiently achieved outside regular school hours and should not be

considered part of an academic or training program. Large numbers of high school students are involved in work or volunteer activities totally independent of the school. What we lack in Canada are ways in which young people who are not going on to postsecondary education can readily find work.

Choice of School

The single most central issue about educational reform to be considered in this book is the basis for choice of school (or program). The question is not whether we should have choice. We already have many options in Canada. As we have seen, they form a patchwork quilt across the provinces. There is also enormous variation within provinces. Some school boards, Edmonton and North York (Toronto) being prime examples, provide genuine choices. Other large boards, among them the Wellington and Waterloo systems in southwestern Ontario, still attempt to supply something like a common school for all. The crucial issues are as follows: which choices should parents be allowed to make? and under which policies and which financial circumstances should schools of choice be allowed to operate?

As I have shown in chapter 1, several provinces already make some conditional financial provision for independent schools, while others do not. Choices within the public system are equally varied. There are two major fully funded options available in large sections of the country in addition to first language of instruction. One is Roman Catholic education, already discussed, which is available on a constitutional basis in Alberta, Saskatchewan, Ontario, and Quebec (at the time of writing, together with nominally Protestant education) and on a local basis in the Maritime provinces.

The other generally available funded public choice, where numbers warrant, is French immersion. Between 1981 and 1990 participation in such programs increased threefold to 6 per cent of total enrolment (*The Canadian Global Almanac 1992*). This option is particularly significant because there is strong evidence that choice of French immersion, apart from a structural division within the public school population, is not randomly distributed among Canadian children; both the original selection and children's continuation with the programs are positively related to social status. This fact is strikingly evident in David Oborne's doctoral findings on secondary school immersion in Manitoba, completed at OISE in 1988. He had to select all the most academically advantaged students in non-immersion programs to find a comparison group of equivalent social and academic standing to those in French immersion. His immersion students were still different from the comparison group in several ways:

they were mainly girls, they were more likely to be planning to take social sciences in university (nearly all of both groups intended to go to university or college), and they were less likely to be interested in engineering, math, or science than the equivalent girls in the comparison group. They were not more likely to be planning courses in French (or the arts and humanities) after high school, and they did not differ in their attitudes with respect to Manitoba's controversial plan (at that time) to translate its statutes into French. There may have been attitudinal effects from being part of a small French-immersion elite, but they did not pertain to language.

Certainly, the choice of French immersion is not simply one of a preference for competence in the second language. If the students who persist with French immersion to the end of high school (outside bilingual or francophone areas) do not plan to use French immediately, it seems unlikely that the many immersion students who transfer into regular programs (usually at or before the beginning of high school) will continue the language in a serious way unless they live in areas where their skills will be an immediate, practical advantage.

Parental choice of French immersion is affected by factors other than love of the language. Ambitious parents often see the alternative program as better than the regular one. Being in a class of hard-working, ambitious students is an academic advantage. French immersion is the one major alternative approved of and funded by the political elites.

These two choices (Roman Catholic education and French immersion) are numerically the most important, but there are others. Occasionally, a choice between francophone and anglophone first-language schools is a reality. Some districts allow a general choice of school at the secondary level. Some offer vocational programs or schools in a variety of specializations. Others have secondary schools of the arts. A few districts, as already mentioned, allow extensive school choices. Ironically, religion, the basis for choice that is in greatest demand (according to enrolments in private schools), is the one that is generally not permitted, except where it is constitutionally required. In addition, the accessibility of independent schools varies greatly from province to province, as shown in chapter 1, with reasonable accessibility in British Columbia, Quebec, Alberta, and Manitoba and a very low degree of access in the other provinces.

Instructional Methodology

Instructional methodology is the main focus of educational debate in the media. The provinces vary greatly in their official approaches to this issue. Practice may of course differ from policy. Saskatchewan and Quebec have a clear policy giving teachers professional freedom. The Saskatchewan department of education's publication *Educational Approaches – A Framework for Professional Practice* provides an overview of various instructional approaches, suggesting that the teacher should apply the best technique for the situation at hand. The document is biased, however. Direct instruction, not favoured by educational experts in Canada, is accompanied by comments about its alleged shortcomings, whereas no such reservations are made about the application of "Inquiry" and the "Co-operative Learning Group," methods for which there is much less support in the instructional literature. An extensive list of references includes none of the many comparative studies showing the superior effectiveness of direct instruction. Nevertheless, the document is to be praised for its recognition of the teacher's professional freedom to choose an appropriate instructional method. A major weakness is its failure to state clearly the teacher's accountability for learning outcomes, the unwritten message being either that what children actually learn is scarcely relevant to the choice of methodology or that it does not really matter what children learn (particularly in matters of substance). If one looks at Canadian schools, both those interpretations of underlying attitude would appear to be valid. Even in those provinces where the department of education applies mandatory assessment of results, the importance of getting good results often fails to permeate to the level of the classroom. The next chapter will show how that situation comes about.

The reader may reasonably ask why one would choose different methodologies except to get better results; but better results imply testing, something that Saskatchewan, like many other provinces, is not very fond of. Imagine having to choose a heating system for one's home and being told that no one has bothered to check which one is most effective or how much each costs.

Analogies like that infuriate Progressive educators, who claim that people such as me who are interested in results believe that children are little jugs into which knowledge can be poured, rather than self-activating, thinking people who will choose how and what to learn for themselves. I do not believe that children's minds are jugs, but I do believe that the purpose of the school is to have positive effects. If it does not have the effects we want, we should investigate how best we can get those desired results, if we can at all. In the same way, if some kinds of surgery or psychiatric treatment have no discernible impact on patients, it is not clear why the public should continue to pay for the service, however much doctors and patients may enjoy the experience. The school is not a sacred undertaking in which educators are trusted to do whatever they feel like on the basis of their own education and personal values.

Quebec, like Saskatchewan, has a policy that "the teacher has the right to manage the students." It has for some time published separate curricular documents, one of goals and objectives, which is policy, and one of instructional teaching units, which is advisory. No other province makes such total recognition of the teacher's responsibility for choosing an appropriate instructional methodology, as distinct from goals and objectives. The Yukon also recognizes the teacher's instructional responsibility, but most provinces are vague and ambiguous on the topic, stating that methods are often implied in their guides (Prince Edward Island and Manitoba) or that they have highly centralized curricula that leave comparatively little room for the individual teacher (Newfoundland.)

Ontario had been at the other extreme from Quebec and Saskatchewan, with curriculum guides that were more intent on laying down how teachers should teach than in listing desired achievements on the part of students. As late as 1996, it was still producing vague documents that were a mixture of child-centred dogma and low-level objectives. However, Ontario's latest (1997) language and mathematics programs for grades one to eight are confined to learning objectives, and teachers are left to choose their own methods. The programs were published following the involvement of the reform organization, the Organization for Quality Education.

At least to the end of grade eight, objectives should be so clear and sensible that any reasonably educated parent would be able to understand exactly what their children are supposed to be able to do at a given grade level. In the high school grades there should be no less clarity and precision, but inevitably parents may be too rusty or insufficiently educated themselves fully to understand all the objectives.

It is fair to say that, overall in Canada, there are strong formal and informal pressures on teachers, particularly elementary ones, from faculties of education, from experts providing in-service training, from the provincial department, from the school district, from the principal, and from the teachers' union. Where there is pressure, it is almost always towards child-centred, individualized, and heterogeneous group instruction and never towards the direct instruction and homogeneous grouping supported by the instructional research. Nova Scotia and Ontario are the two provinces where pressure towards the acceptance of child-centred instruction has been strongest, most consistent, and most universal. Excepting Ontario, pressures have probably been least in the francophone systems. Even in Alberta, British Columbia, and Quebec's Protestant system, child-centred instruction is entrenched in the early grades. In some provinces where there has been occasional pressure either from departments of education (e.g. Alberta, New Brunswick, and Prince Edward Island) or from school boards to focus on results, the effect on the teaching and beliefs of elementary teachers has been minimal. There have already been suggestions in Toronto that schools there will not follow the new provincial program.

One reason for the greater entrenchment in the elementary school (elementary and secondary teachers get the same ideological message from faculties of education) may be that principals in those schools have usually greater influence over their predominantly female staff. Whereas the principal enforces the child-centred ideology in the elementary school, collaborative learning in grade nine is typically spearheaded by teams of lead-teachers, with the support of the administration. Another reason is that the colleges and universities expect some knowledge and skills of students coming from secondary schools, particularly in math and science but also including the ability to read and write.

Child-centred education (resulting from the Progressive world-view) takes on the status of a cult, of religious enthusiasm; non-believers are pictured as ignorant rednecks who disgrace the educational profession. To those who cling to child-centred learning as a religious enthusiasm, any contrary advice or proposal is described as political interference. If teachers are reinforced in their Progressive ideas, then the advice is considered "professional." Lillian Hrabchak developed a thesis at OISE in 1995, to see whether teachers and principals hold an administrative bias, that is, if they tend to believe that the principal is superior even in areas of professional instruction. To her surprise, she found little evidence of such bias. What she did discover was that, in her Toronto-area sample, elementary teachers welcomed the interference of administrators in other teachers' work in the classroom when it reinforced their own beliefs, but objected to such interference where it was inconsistent with those beliefs. The concept of genuine professional authority and responsibility would not seem to be well established in the Toronto suburb under study.

While there are zealots on both sides of the instructional debate (child-centred and direct instruction) who would like all teachers to be forced to do things their way, there is surely some advantage for everyone concerned if teachers accept professional responsibility for their teaching. Once methods are dictated, doing things the "right" way is rewarded, and doing things the "wrong" way is disapproved of, irrespective of children's learning. This is equally true whether it is Madeline Hunter methods in Prince Edward Island (a direct-instruction fad at one time), child-centred methods in elementary schools throughout the country, or collaborative learning, the latest fad to reach the secondary schools. The practical result is that outcomes are ignored, if indeed they are known. As I have been told time and time again by Ontario educators, "If teachers are using child-centred methods appropriately, they must be getting good results because we know those are the best methods." Alice in Wonderland lives.

Such an attitude is very convenient for administrators. They do not have to worry about actually getting good results, which is always difficult and requires consistent hard work from all concerned. It often does not coincide with fun. Instead, administrators can busily implement the latest instructional fads, spending their time exhorting teachers to change, and telling parents about the great new things that they and their schools are doing. At least one major Ontario school board is now introducing calculators in grade one. The idea that one should understand mathematics before using calculators and computers, and words and their construction before dictionaries and spell-checks, does not impede innovation.

STUDENT EVALUATION

There is enormous diversity among the provinces with respect to student evaluation. Quebec, British Columbia, and Alberta have examinations to control movement from secondary to postsecondary education, together with tests at other grade levels for samples of or for all students in selected subjects, usually including the basic skills. In contrast, Ontario and Saskatchewan have no regular testing program of all students at any grade level. Ontario has plans for a comprehensive testing program, but good testing has been an intention in the province for a decade.

In Ontario and Saskatchewan, students still have a good chance of spending twelve years in an expensive school program without ever being accountable in terms of learning to a validated standard outside their school. Canada is probably the only country in the developed world where such could be the case. With external standards, teachers and students have an incentive to do well, working cooperatively for the same ends, and parental pressure is directed at schools that lag and students who fall behind. In England and in the state of New Jersey, to use two examples, the results of schools in external tests are made public; in both places, similar schools are grouped

together so that affluent, upper-class schools are not unfairly compared with inner-city ones.

In schools that do not have to meet external standards, there is the
temptation to raise marks (this practice is referred to as "mark inflation"), so that parents and students imagine the results are better
than they really are. The proportion of "honours" graduates in
Ontario increased by more than two-and-a-half times in the twenty
years following the abolition of university entrance examinations.
Not even the most extreme defender of the system claims there has
been a similar improvement in achievement; the defensive claim is
limited to the almost certainly false one that there has been no deterioration, an argument that is impossible to verify across the curriculum precisely because there is, conveniently, no regular, standard
evaluation. The financial reward for the "honour" grant was can-
celled, its meaninglessness apparent to all. Thought was not apparently given to introducing a real standard worth rewarding.
Universities seem to have been corrupted by the system. They accept
school marks at face value, however debased they may be. The
schools produce large numbers of students with high credentials,
each earning financial support from the government. Admission is
simple (just average the best six marks, including required subjects);
the elite universities (e.g. Queen's and the University of Toronto) can
set higher cut-offs, all without cost. Occasionally, a university looks
at the lowering of its first-year course requirements and considers
entrance examinations, but it soon sees sense when the costs and
students' reluctance to apply to a university that actually requires
them to prepare themselves are taken into account. Universities are
prone to mark inflation themselves.

Evaluation experts tell the public that mark inflation does not
matter because percentage scores from high school are simply sym-
bols with no precise meaning, showing no more than the relative
standing of students. There is some truth to that assertion, but it fails
to address parents' attitudes. Many parents tend to equate a mark of
95 today with a 95 in 1975, when they were in high school. The
argument also ignores the idea that there should be clear standards
built into high school grading, that there should be, for example, a
minimum passing requirement, not just a minimal passing mark, an
idea parents that assume (or used to assume).

Quebec has the most defensible and logical policies in these areas.
It surely makes sense for there to be public determination of the
goals and objectives – certainly, if there is to be a monopolistic public
system – and for a common core of learning if there is not. Similarly,
there should be comparative systems of accountability (in the form

of external tests and examinations), determined centrally. By analogy, other professionals – doctors, dentists, lawyers, engineers, architects – do not determine their clients' goals and objectives or exclusively evaluate their own work. But they do have discretionary choice about the way in which the work is done, for which they have authority and responsibility. (Of course, their clients also have a choice of the individual whom they wish to employ, which, for the most part, is unfortunately not the case when it comes to schooling.)

Most recent efforts to fill the gap in the provinces without sound testing programs have been a waste of money. The most likely reason is that the testing programs have been developed by local educators and academics, almost inevitably imbued with a strong, child-centred, Progressive world-view. There is no implication here that they have irresponsibly tried to sabotage the new programs. The truth is much simpler and more respectable. They are philosophically opposed to traditional testing and want to introduce a form suited to child-centred ideas. Unfortunately, they frequently succeed.

In the 1980s there was considerable pressure within the Toronto Board of Education to introduce external standardized testing. The administrative leadership was horrified at the thought and persuaded the board that it would be much better for the system to have its own testing program to meet the special needs of Toronto students. So the Benchmarks program was developed for use primarily at the grade three level. The idea was that the tests would measure exactly what children individually could and could not do in the classroom in terms of the board's program; it would match the actual classroom experience, instead of exposing children to a set of arbitrary external measures. The result was a complex set of tests that had to be applied individually to children. As the process was very time-consuming, only samples of children could be tested, the intent being that teachers could test other students on a need basis in regular classroom time. The board then collated a list of things that grade three children could and could not do.

I have been told that the program cost over a million dollars to develop, but probably no one really knows the final figure, if the time of all the employees involved were measured and accounted for. Toronto, it will be recalled, is among the biggest educational spenders in the country. The reader may think that the ideas behind the program make sense; obviously, members of the Toronto board thought so at the time. Some of the concepts have superficial appeal. Evaluation is a complex topic that I can only touch on lightly here. Given below are criteria that I believe should be applied to a comprehensive student-testing program. Every test need not meet all the criteria, but the overall program should. Tests that meet very few should be seriously questioned.

1 *The program should test nearly every student in the system.* Most parents want to know how their child is doing, not simply how grade three children in the school or system as a whole are doing. There should be a narrow list of exclusions: those so severely disabled that the test result would be of no value, and students whose knowledge of the test language (normally English) is so limited as to make the result meaningless. This does not mean that a reading test should not be given to a student whose first language is Spanish; likely the parents and the teachers want to know where the child is and how help can be given. It does mean that it is unwise to test a child who has just arrived from Guatemala not knowing any English. Tests of samples, within systems or provinces, rarely produce any direct accountability. International tests are inappropriate for every-student testing because they frequently only assess sections of the curriculum. Their purposes (and structure) are also different from those of national and provincial tests. The Benchmarks program in Toronto did not meet this fundamental criterion.

2 *Tests should assess a good proportion of the school program.* Ideally, a test program would assess achievement and progress on virtually all objectives. In practice, given that enormous numbers of Canadian children are not tested properly at all, that must remain a long-term goal. There is no reason, however, why students cannot be tested immediately in reading, language, and mathematics, areas in which there are Canadian standardized tests from primary levels to grade twelve. The areas tested should gradually be extended to other subjects and objectives. Physical fitness, for example, is easy to test, as are many middle- and secondary school subjects. Contrary to popular opinion among Progressive educators, virtually any worthwhile educational objective can be evaluated with reasonable accuracy. There are a few that should not be tested in the normal way because they invade personal privacy. Most objectives that educators claim cannot be assessed turn out to be ones that are unmeasurable because there is not agreement on what they mean. One cannot test the achievement of goals that do not have clear, agreed meaning.

3 *The program should be applied regularly through the grades.* The basic skills should be tested every year, at least for the first eight or nine grades. All subjects should be tested for high school graduation. Occasional spot tests given every few years or small samples are

of very limited value to parents, students, and teachers, the people who have the most practical use for the data and are interested in performance at the individual, class, and school level. Regular, comprehensive testing programs of every student answer the questions about differences between school systems and schools, as well as giving information to individuals. Accountability means giving information to parents about their child, their child's class, and their child's school, in terms of specific objectives and in terms of other children, classes, and schools. It occasionally makes sense to test a particular area at a specific grade level at four- or five-year intervals, where efficiency makes more frequent testing inappropriate.

4 *Individual results should be made available to parents and teachers and, in nearly all cases, to students. Class, school, provincial, and national data should be made available to the public.* These policies are now normal in the United States and England, and they are beginning to creep into Canada. Calgary, for example, publishes (reluctantly) results by school. There are still systems, forced by public opinion to test, who do their best to minimize the distribution of any information, not giving students' results even to their parents unless they specifically demand to see them. In this context, it is not surprising that Progressive teachers, who do not like tests anyway, ignore the results. They then assert that the tests are useless because the results are left in a cupboard.

5 *The tests should be carefully selected to measure what students of the particular age and grade should generally be expected to know and understand, and what one would expect them to have been taught in school.* This is a complicated criterion that, misapplied, leads to worthless testing. Standardized tests in this country assess the basic skills that Canadians expect young people to learn in school. It is obviously inappropriate for a principal or teacher to say that, because the teacher does not teach some things, those things should not appear in the test. I recall a high school teacher who did not believe in teaching poetry. It was unfair that students suffered from his self-indulgence, but it was not the fault of the examinations. On the other hand, there is no point in giving students physics tests if they have never taken a physics course. The frequently used argument that one should never test anything that has not been taught in a particular classroom leads inadequate teachers, schools, systems, and provinces free to reject tests that do not come down to their low standards. Good tests give information about the individual child and the class as a whole; they

provide helpful data to parents and teachers. National standardized tests provide such outcomes.

6 *Tests should be valid and reliable.* The tests should measure the things that they are supposed to test, and they should be fair and accurate assessments of the students' competence in the area tested. Standardized tests are not perfect. They may contain subtests with little validity, measuring aspects of learning (such as alphabetizing) that a school may legitimately consider of secondary or little importance. Parents should be told if the school pays less attention to some test areas and why. They may decide for themselves whether or not the skill that the school downplays is important to them. Validity and reliability are the qualities most frequently lacking in the newer, more fashionable tests (the words "authentic" and "performance" often being clues to a lack of validity and unreliability).

7 *The testing program should be relatively easy to administer and cost-effective.* The instructional time used for testing should not be excessive: two or three days a year in elementary grades, no more than eight at the secondary level. Scoring should be simplified where possible. Multiple-choice questions are the most valid and reliable technique for many objectives.

8 *The testing program should be used for moderating movement from school to college and university and for high school graduation.*

The Toronto Benchmarks program did not meet the first four criteria or the seventh, and was not intended to. Those involved presumably did not believe in the value of such things. One wonders if the trustees considered those questions when they agreed to the program. We know that the vast majority of people consistently believe in regular standardized testing which substantially meets those criteria.

The recent Ontario tests (in grades three and nine) fail to meet many of the criteria given above, their worst problems being their expense and lack of validity. For example, if students have several occasions to address a question, the effect of intervening discussions with teachers, parents, and friends will obviously influence them in different ways, as will differential access to a variety of authorities. It is also unlikely that the tests will ever form a useful basis for clear standards, either across the province or over time.

One of the important advantages of external tests over school-based marking is that they are comparatively free of direct teacher or parent influence during the testing. Assessments of the Ontario type are described as "performance" and "authentic" testing; in practice, the tests are similar to the daily teaching and learning situation. The terms "performance" and "authentic" imply that other tests do not determine performance and are inauthentic. One must always be cautious of educational jargon. In a sense, all tests and exams, in or out of school, are "inauthentic." By definition, they are not part of normal everyday life, at home or at work. The important question is not whether they are "authentic" (a vague term) or tests of "performance" (all tests are), but whether they measure accurately the things that one wants to measure. Teachers' assessments (of tests, classwork, and homework) and valid, reliable external tests each measure somewhat different things; both are valid and important in some ways.

Developing new tests to measure the same things that teachers normally assess is not an advance. The advantages of external, academic tests should be that they measure knowledge, skills, and analytical ability that persist over time, independent of direct and short-term assistance from friends, teachers, and relatives; they are not subject to bias in marking on the part of teachers who know the students; they call for the bringing together (synthesis) of what students have learned over time; and they may be used as a basis for comparing students with expected standards and with one another, for the granting of credentials based on something substantial and for placement in educational programs and the workplace. Teachers measure some of the same things, but their marks also reflect the perseverance, assiduity, and compliance of the students; students who do not do their homework, appropriately, get poor marks, whether or not they have learned the concepts. Teachers' marks are also affected by the context in which they teach, such as an inner-city or a suburban school.

The School Achievement Indicators Program tests produced by the Council of Ministers Canada are also of limited value in relation to their costs. They do not meet many of the criteria outlined above. The provinces insist that the tests be very close to their own individual curricula, so it is doubtful to what extent they even serve the purpose of providing interprovincial comparisons, their principal practical purpose. It is hardly surprising that the results typically show few differences among provinces; in practice, they may be designed to eliminate differences, provinces being able to limit questions to their own low standards. If Alberta, for example, has objectives well beyond the level of the other provinces, Ontario and Nova Scotia will surely object to any item addressing those advanced objectives. International tests are similarly weakened.

Quebec, Alberta, and British Columbia all have satisfactory, if not ideal, provincial systems of evaluation. It is probably not simple coincidence that they get better academic results than the rest of the country. That is not to assert that all we have to do is institute tough testing programs on a national basis to improve our academic standing. The causes and problems are more complicated. One has to ask what kind of educational environment has existed in Ontario over thirty years to permit the continued absence of any genuine, valid external testing, and with none in sight.

Although more remedial action than simply introducing good tests, accompanied by accountability for results, is needed, that would be a start. One should not expect good academic results from provinces that have consistently displayed little interest in the achievement of any measurable results. The climate of the classroom is not one where specific results are important. In Ontario the immediate difficulty facing reformers is that educators, excessively provincial and inbred, are likely to design tests based on current levels of teaching performance – and this is precisely what has happened. The first essential reform is the widespread application of available national tests of basic skills. In fact, the use of national standardized tests in Ontario is, perversely, actually declining in the late 1990s. Administrators, who have gone on record provincially as being opposed to such testing, are very willing to sacrifice the tests; trustees are assured that they are saving money and that Ontario has its own tests.

Evaluation is one area where even the countries most like us, England and the United States, do a better job. England has gradually developed and improved its traditional examination system, with its GCSE "O" and "A" levels, taken at the ages of sixteen and eighteen respectively. The "O" levels are now taken by the vast majority of students in the country; the result is that most young people are able to leave school with a concrete, external, national assessment of their achievement. In comparison, most Canadian graduation certificates, Quebec's being a significant exception, are meaningless in terms of academic standard. England's "A" levels ensure continuing high standards and competitiveness for admission to the country's universities. (I am not, however, an advocate of the narrow specialization of England's, but not Scotland's, last two years of school leading to "A" levels. Only two or three "A" levels are typically required for university entry, together with "O" levels achieved two or three years earlier.) The traditional "A" and "O" level examinations are now complemented by standardized tests administered regularly and nationally at three age levels. Those who think that I have set impossible criteria for evaluation should note that England's tests and examinations substantially meet the criteria. In Canada, only Quebec comes as close.

The International Baccalaureat program of advanced testing is a model of excellence for strong, academic students, particularly if they wish to meet international standards of university entry. It is used by some Canadian public and independent schools. The excellent Canadian Achievement (standardized) Tests are suited to all students from grades two to twelve. They are threatened by the inferior products created by provinces.

Critics will respond that comprehensive testing cannot be valuable because England's educational performance is no better than ours. That country first developed the child-centred approach to elementary education, and for twenty years it was as fiercely imposed there as in Ontario. Change is still strongly resisted. Many English students continue to perform badly on that country's tests, but at least the failure is acknowledged. Benjy Levin, a specialist in educational policy at the University of Manitoba, wrote informally in the spring 1996 issue of the CASEA Newsletter (a publication representing Canadian professors in educational administration) of his year's experience in England. He congratulated the teachers in his local English school for resisting the efforts to introduce direct instruction, noting that they clung to such child-centred methods as subject integration. Continuous resistance from educators is one of many reasons why comprehensive and radical reform is needed in Canada. It is also a reason why even comprehensive reform will take time to have effect.

The United States, like Canada and unlike England, has an administratively fragmented educational system with an enormous variety of evaluation practices that will not be detailed. There are two national programs. The best-known and longest established is the system of university-entrance tests administered by the private Educational Testing Service in Princeton. Most students seeking admission to a university or college of recognized quality take the ETS tests. The variation in American curricula, compared with those in England, makes the tests more general and less valid in terms of specific knowledge and skills, but nevertheless they do serve to maintain strong, competitive standards in the better high schools. In addition, there is a national program of achievement testing that publishes results by state. Its value is limited by its dependence on samples, so the tests have less interest for teachers, students, and parents. Although the program is more comprehensive and of greater significance than Canada's ineffectual SAIP program, it is not one that I would wish Canada to follow. Tests have little influence if there are few consequences resulting from excellent or poor performance; evaluation and accountability should go together.

Many American states have their own testing programs. Unusually, the New York Board of Regents examinations are somewhat like England's GCSEs. Many states have tests that are required for high school graduation. These are typically assessments of the basic skills, but once again, although limited, they do give some objective and external currency to the graduation certificates. There is strong evidence that they have contributed to the raising of standards in achievement of graduating students in those states, without decreasing the proportion of graduates. Set a standard and most young people will attempt to reach it, and most teachers will help them. If there is no standard, there is nothing for either students or teachers to aim for. New Jersey and Florida are examples of states that have implemented clear requirements for graduation. There is also evidence that states such as Tennessee and Texas, not traditionally strong academically, have improved their schools' performance by rigorous standards in all areas of school life.

On the basis of rapidly declining test results, California has officially changed its method of instruction in beginning reading from Whole Language to a "balanced" approach that emphasizes phonics. As in Ontario, educators there like to blame immigrants for their poor showing; however, when the last national test data were analysed, it was found that white Californians, like the state as a whole, performed second worst in the country (Chester Finn, address on educational reform at the Inter-Continental Hotel, Toronto, 4 December 1996).

While evaluation systems in the United States are quite varied and less nationally comprehensive than in England, it would be unusual for elementary children not to be given standardized tests of the basic skills at three grade levels. Those who wish to attend a good university normally take some form of national test. In most states those intending to graduate from high school have to satisfy clear standards of achievement, often backed up by a test. None of these generalizations can be made of Canada. I used to hear that mobile parents, typically middle-class, who moved to the United States from this country were concerned about the level of education that their children would receive, unless they could live in elite suburbs. Such is no longer the case. Today, Canadians are becoming as concerned as Americans about choosing a home where their children will be able to attend a "good" school, "good" usually being defined in terms of the social class of the parents.

Sound assessment cannot by itself make a good school system. If instruction is poor, discipline is lax, and work expectations from home and school are lacking, the best testing system in the world will not create effective conditions for teaching and learning. The United States, unlike Canada, has a long tradition of mediocre education outside its elite schools and universities, and its social and economic patterns, aggravated by racial problems on a much larger scale than in Canada, are even less supportive of education. On the other hand, without clear sets of objective standards represented in universal tests and examinations, it is highly unlikely that any system of schooling will be able to provide sufficiently powerful incentives to influence the majority of students over the long term. Good academic standards, notably in math and science, have survived by tradition, with little external support, for nearly thirty years in some Ontario high schools, a tradition under fierce attack by those wanting to make high schools more "democratic" and collaborative. As senior teachers retire, often in distress and despair, the tradition gradually dies.

The Ontario educational establishment contends that evaluation of students by teachers is far better than assessment by external tests and examinations. The argument is empty because no advocate of external tests is suggesting that teachers' evaluation is worthless and should cease. On the contrary, it is extreme Progressives who advocate that teacher testing and evaluation in any formal way should also be stopped, along with the hated external tests. There are many primary teachers who believe that it is unprofessional to administer any form of test to all the students in their classes; some are unwilling to test at all in any formal way.

Day-to-day evaluation by teachers, using written tests as well as observation, is vitally important, and parents appropriately rely heavily on such assessment. But the use of both systematic evaluation by teachers and external testing is better than either one alone; it provides more information and is more valid and more reliable. There is no point in arguing about which approach is better on its own. External evaluation is less dependent on day-to-day circumstances, on help from the home with assignments, projects, and homework, and on (inevitable) teacher prejudice. (How could any human teacher not expect more from some students than from others?) Teachers' assessments, on the other hand, take into account the student's ability to complete work (as distinct from simply having a skill) and, if done well, can judge a wider variety of objectives than available external tests. Critics of examinations for university and college entrance argue that teachers' marks predict first-year university grades better than tests do. They are usually correct, if high school teachers mark much the same way as postsecondary instructors. These critics fail to mention that combined tests and teachers' marks predict university outcomes better than either one alone. They also do not mention that the main arguments for entrance tests are to ensure standards, to be fair to students from different schools with varying levels of marking, and to promote an atmosphere of excellence, where teacher and students work together to promote achievement.

The frequently made accusation that external tests depend on memory is totally wrong, as anyone who has taken one of the major external tests from the United States or Europe knows. On the contrary, many Canadian teacher-made tests and examinations unintentionally demand simple recall of what the students have experienced in class. I have seen teachers give their own "fill-in-the-blank" tests at both elementary and high school levels, where the answer demanded was a single word used in class, even though there were other, equally good or better alternatives. Although some teachers prepare excellent tests, most have had little or no training in test composition, because faculties of education demonstrate little interest in effective testing.

A good, comprehensive method of student evaluation is not sufficient in itself to ensure a good system of education, but it is a necessary one in the long run. Examples of effective teachers and schools that do not depend on external exams and tests exist, but all effective – in terms of their economic and social development and educational aspirations – national systems rely on external examinations. In Canada the widening gap between effective and ineffective educational systems – between Alberta and British Columbia, on the one hand, and Ontario and the Maritime provinces, on the other – illustrates the point.

ACADEMIC ACHIEVEMENT

The academic achievement of Canada's schools is a matter of great debate. Useful summaries are to be found in two publications of the Economic Council of Canada (1992 and Newton et al. 1992). I shall make some generalizations at both the international and the interprovincial levels. The reader is cautioned that international, and to a lesser extent interprovincial, data are subject to varying interpretations depending on the assumptions that one is prepared to make.

Despite the excellent overall quality of the ECC documents, they misinterpret the international data in one important way. They claim that at age ten, in mathematics and science, Canadian children "compare favourably with those in most industrialized countries," but the relative position "deteriorates somewhat" by age thirteen or fourteen, and Canada's position by the end of secondary school is "weak." The data in fact suggest that our position is mediocre by age nine, remains so at age fourteen, and is impossible to assess in any legitimate, overall way at the end of secondary school.

That conclusion is based specifically on the 1990–91 International Assessment of Educational Progress study of mathematics published in 1992 (Lapointe et al. 1992). The two IAEP studies, of math and science, carried out by an independent body, the Educational Testing Service of Princeton, New Jersey, under contract, remain the outstanding international assessments. Although the countries involved had considerable input, the two studies have features that make them particularly useful to those interested in international comparisons of performance. The statistics are clearly presented, background characteristics of students are provided, and performance on items of varying difficulty is separately shown. If there is an American slant, I was not aware of it; there is no reason to suspect positive or negative bias towards Canada. Table 8 gives the average score of the samples from nine countries with reasonably representative data for items used on both tests, one for nine-year-olds and the other for thirteen-year-olds. At age nine, Canada ranks sixth out of nine. At age thirteen it is fifth. Incidentally, the table also illustrates the comparatively poor performance of Ontario anglophones (francophones perform even worse).

Barlow and Robertson (1994) interpret the same international data favourably, correctly observing that Canada does better than many other countries. They do not take into account our schools' comparatively favourable social and financial environment. They also fail to comment on the particularly poor academic performance of Ontario, the province where their preferred Progressive philosophy is most ingrained and where there are fewest standards and least external evaluation. In general, comparisons using Canada as a descriptor are heavily influenced by the performance of Alberta and British Columbia, two provinces with high levels of achievement quite unrepresentative of educational conditions elsewhere in the country.

Table 9 provides a more fine-grained analysis of the two sets of data; it also adds France, a country that participated only at the older level. The table shows how Canada's weakest and strongest nine-year-old students perform. Our tenth percentile (i.e. the weak students who rank at the top of the bottom 10 per cent) place fifth out of nine. Note that we are outperformed by the relatively poor Korea, Taiwan, Hungary, and the Russian-speaking sector of the Soviet

Table 8
Mathematics achievement at ages nine and thirteen (percentage correct on items used in both tests, by country, plus Ontario English)

Country	Age 9		Age 13	
	%	Rank	%	Rank
Canada	45.1	6	76.1	5
England	43.9	7	73.7	7
Hungary	54.9	2	79.8	3
Ireland	43.6	8	74.1	6
Korea	60.0	1	82.2	1
Slovenia	40.6	9	72.8	8
USSR[a]	53.8	3	80.8	2
Taiwan	50.6	4	78.2	4
USA	45.6	5	71.0	9
Ontario (English)	42.2		72.4	

SOURCE: Lapointe et al. 1992.
[a] The sample from the Soviet Union was not representative of all the republics.

Table 9
Tenth and ninetieth percentile correct scores in mathematics (by ranked country plus Ontario, ages nine and thirteen)

	10th percentile				90th percentile			
	Age 9		Age 13		Age 9		Age 13	
	%	Rank	%	Rank	%	Rank	%	Rank
Canada	35.7	5	37.3	4	83.6	7	86.7	7
England	32.8	7	34.5	7	86.9	5	89.3	5
France			37.3	4			89.3	5
Hungary	40.7	3	38.7	3	90.2	3	93.3	3
Ireland	31.2	8	33.8	8	85.0	6	86.7	7
Korea	50.8	1	41.3	2	93.4	1	96.0	2
Slovenia	34.0	6	32.0	9	79.3	9	82.7	7
USSR[a]	37.4	4	42.7	1	90.3	3	92.0	4
Taiwan	41.0	2	35.0	6	91.8	2	97.3	1
USA	29.5	9	29.3	10	83.6	7	82.7	10
Ontario (English)	31.2		34.7		81.1		84.0	

SOURCE: Lapointe et al. 1992.
[a] The sample from the Soviet Union was not representative of all the republics.

Union (as it then was), but that we do better than the countries most like us – England and the United States. Both those countries have a more pronounced underclass than we do, consisting primarily of blacks and recent immigrants from the poorest countries. Note also that Ontario scores the lowest of all except the United States with the tenth percentile of nine-year-olds. Yet one of the claims of the Progressive establishment is that its methods cater to the weaker student and that alternative approaches (involving more direct instruction) are elitist in character. Korea, Taiwan, and Hungary all use more direct instruction in the early grades; they are top scorers. Those are the data used by Barlow and Robertson to defend the Progressive status quo.

When one looks at the more able students – those who are in the ninetieth percentile (i.e. those who perform better than 90 per cent of the rest of the national sample) – one sees that Canada's relative performance is poor; England and Ireland, as well as the other four countries, are more successful than we are with the most able students. Note once again the similar standings at the age of thirteen. By the age of nine, Canada's educational problems are firmly established, with no further relative deterioration between that age and thirteen. Its performance is particularly weak with regard to the best students.

It would take a separate chapter to analyse international comparisons at the eighteen-year-old level. A crucial difficulty is that it is impossible to take into account all the factors, particularly those of deliberate educational policy, that influence national performance at the end of high school. What the statistics show is less the superiority of one country over another than that policies, intended or not, influence outcomes.

For example, Hong Kong apparently does very well at this level. Its educational policies, which are competitive, are English in origin. Those policies are matched by a competitive and industrious social context. There is considerable streaming (separation of students by achievement and ability) within schools and among schools. The students taking advanced math and science are relatively few, they specialize in those subjects, and they receive many hours of instruction. In contrast, British Columbia retains a larger proportion of students in school to the age of eighteen, and of that number a relatively large proportion also take "advanced" (in Canadian, rather than Hong Kong, terms) math and science. If the goal is to produce a relatively small number of excellent students in those subjects, Hong Kong is undoubtedly outstanding. If the purpose is to produce a much larger pool of fairly good students, then British Columbia is exemplary (Robitaille and Garden 1989).

Results of the Third International Mathematics and Science Study (circulated by the Ontario Ministry of Education in 1996) supply additional confirmation of the general picture provided by earlier studies. At the age of thirteen, Canadian students perform at about the same level as students in England and the United States, better than less developed countries, and worse than the world's educational leaders. At age nine, the reported average of the five participating Canadian provinces (British Columbia, Alberta, Ontario, New Brunswick, and Newfoundland) is boosted by an outstanding performance by Alberta. The average is also improved by the differences in provincial populations not having been taken into account in the averaging. On this occasion Canada performed better than England and worse than the United States ("Alberta Students Rank High in Science, Math," *Globe and Mail*, 12 June 1997).

There is evidence that Canada's difficulties in mathematics begin at an early age. The evidence concerning performance during high school is more difficult to assess, partly because the data are more limited by province. My judgment is that Canada is quite successful in producing a good-sized proportion of students adequately prepared for university programs in math (and science) within an international context, but we turn out disproportionately few really excellent scholars, probably because our curricula are targeted at a larger segment of the age cohort.

If we consider Canadian achievement in the light of the needs of the economy and society, it can be seen that we are weak at both critical ends of the age cohorts, the strongest and the weakest students. Canada needs more excellence in mathematics, computer applications, and science if it is to continue its success in electronics and telecommunications. The greatest barrier to Northern Telecom's expansion in Canada, for example, is a shortage of skilled people. We also require stronger basic skills at the weaker end of the age group, if we are to avoid having a permanent underclass. Canada's educational experiments have endangered both goals.

Another caveat should be borne in mind in considering the international studies. As noted earlier, the studies of math and science probably underestimate the achievement of the more successful countries, particularly at the higher age levels. Test items are chosen on the basis of their relevance to the curricula of all participating countries. Evidence from Alberta showed that some countries have more advanced curricula than even that province. The advanced items are not included for comparative purposes because the topics they test are not in the curricula of countries such as Canada. The highest achieving German, French, Hong Kong, English, and Hungarian students would almost certainly perform better than the corresponding Canadian students on advanced items not included in the tests.

Even so, my overall sense is that mathematics and science are two of Canada's educational strengths at the secondary level, compared with the other subjects not assessed in rigorous international testing. We could of course do better if students entering secondary school received stronger instruction. The widely held idea that our major academic problems are at the secondary level is wrong.

My assessment of comparative achievement, nationally and internationally, is based primarily on mathematics. It is the most widely tested subject and is the easiest to assess in different languages. Mathematics is a vital skill. It is also a subject where achievement is relatively less affected by home background and more so by school conditions.

Unfortunately, there are almost no international comparisons in reading, writing, and language. The one comparison we can make is discouraging. The Southam study of literacy published in 1987 found that, overall, 8 per cent of university graduates and 17 per cent of high school graduates were illiterate. Although Canadians aged twenty-one to twenty-five who would have gone through elementary school in the early 1970s, just as the child-centred ideas were being successfully implemented, were ahead of their American counterparts in numeracy, they fell behind overall and in language. Taken as a whole, 26 per cent of the Canadians in the age group were illiterate, compared with 22 per cent of Americans. Yet 20 per cent of the Americans tested were black or Hispanic (both groups with performance levels well below the national average), while only 10 per cent of the Canadians were immigrants (*Toronto Star*, 15 September 1987).

Further, since Canadian immigrants in one respect perform better educationally than the native-born (they are more likely to go to university), the average immigrant probably lowers the national literacy rate less than does the average black or Hispanic in the United States, both those groups being depressed economically and educationally. (Canadian immigrants tend to vary more from the average than do the native-born; proportionately more do well, and proportionately more do badly.) The relatively poor Canadian literacy rate should also be considered in the context of the low performance of the United States on virtually all international comparative tests of achievement. The Southam study, like most reports that bring bad news, was subjected to intense methodological criticism by experts defending the establishment. A subsequent study by Statistics Canada, although not international, confirmed the Southam study's basic findings, with 28 per cent of the group aged sixteen to twenty-four below an everyday reading level, rated at below grade six (Newton et al. 1992).

Interprovincial Differences in Achievement

The data on international achievement show that Canada's provincial and official-language samples, effectively classified for research purposes as different countries, vary as much from one another as from many other countries. Table 10 shows that, in mathematics, Korea and Taiwan (and we may safely add from other research, Japan) have a level of achievement well ahead of the Western countries. But one-half of Canada competes well with Hungary and France, the countries in the second tier. One might guess that these provinces, the three most western ones and Quebec, would also compete well with Germany, Austria, and the Scandinavian countries. The Atlantic provinces, Manitoba, and Ontario, on the other hand, fall into a third tier between England and the United States.

The performance of francophone Canada is particularly interesting. Even francophone New Brunswick, with its traditional Acadian economy based on forestry and fishing and one of the most primitive educational systems in Canada less than thirty years ago, when it was not unknown for high school drop-outs to be teaching in the schools, performs better than the less impoverished anglophone part of the province or affluent Ontario.

Overall, it is the poor performance of Ontario that stands out, most remarkably at the nine-year-old level, where the province is 16 percentage points below leading Korea and 2 points below even the trailing United States. Except in Ontario, the francophone population performs better than the anglophone population, even where francophones are less-wealthy minorities (in New Brunswick, Manitoba, and Saskatchewan). If the imposition of Progressive instruction has been most draconian in Ontario, and the effects of it are most harmful to the disadvantaged, one would expect that province's francophones to perform poorly. In contrast, the francophone school systems of New Brunswick and Quebec are little or not at all influenced by their anglophone counterparts.

In the Third International Mathematics and Science Study, among the five provinces with large enough samples for comparative purposes,

Table 10
Canadian provinces in an international context: mathematics achievement at ages nine and thirteen (percentage correct, in order of age thirteen ranking)

Country/Province	Age 9	Age 13
Korea	74.8	73.4
Switzerland		70.8
Taiwan	68.1	72.7
Quebec (French)	64.5	68.7
Hungary	68.2	68.4
Saskatchewan (French)		67.5
British Columbia	61.9	66.2
Quebec (English)	62.5	65.7
France		64.2
Alberta		64.0
Manitoba (French)		63.1
Saskatchewan (English)		62.0
New Brunswick (French)		60.6
England	59.5	60.6
Ireland	60.0	60.5
Nova Scotia		59.7
Newfoundland		58.9
Ontario (English)	56.8	58.3
Manitoba (English)		58.0
New Brunswick (English)	59.8	57.7
Slovenia	55.8	57.1
USA	58.4	55.3
Ontario (French)	54.5	53.5

SOURCE: Lapointe et al. 1992.

the rank order of thirteen-year-olds in math was British Columbia, Alberta, Newfoundland, New Brunswick, and Ontario. At age nine, Ontario performed better in math than five developed countries: Norway, New Zealand, Greece, Iceland, and Portugal; in the case of last-placed Portugal, it was 9 percentage points ahead. It performed worse than twelve developed countries, being 16 or more percentage points below the Pacific Rim countries, Korea, Singapore, Japan, and Hong Kong. Another way of making the point is to state that only one country, Norway, as affluent as Ontario performed worse, while eleven less-affluent countries performed better. Alberta was close behind the Pacific Rim countries in math; it ranked among them in science. Newfoundland and New Brunswick performed at about the same level as Ontario ("Alberta Students Rank High in Science, Math," *Globe and Mail*, 12 June 1997).

Comparisons among the provinces in reading and language are difficult to make, the only published data coming from the questionable SAIP tests, where every participating province attempts to ensure that items match their curricula. Once again, Alberta and Quebec performed comparatively well, but unlike the outcomes in mathematics and science, Ontario did better than British Columbia (in 1994). My sense is that Ontario elementary schools give more emphasis to language than to mathematics. The province's relatively better performance in language weakens its claim that immigrants are to blame for its poor outcome in math. Reading and language are more affected than math by the home, where a significant proportion of language learning, including reading, takes place.

Overall, Alberta, Quebec, and British Columbia are the strong performers, and the Atlantic provinces and Ontario the weak ones. All countries show regional disparities in achievement. The less-developed American South has traditionally achieved at a lower level than the rest of the country; the northern plains states (adjacent to the Canadian prairie provinces) are the highest achievers in that country. I have noted the anomalous California, whose educational standing has fallen considerably. The Canadian anomaly is Ontario, economically affluent, spending more than the west on elementary and secondary education, and yet performing at the level of the most disadvantaged provinces.

Family income is statistically a reliable, if rough measure of the home environment, which in turn consistently predicts individual and school performance in educational research (better than anything else except children's measured intelligence). I examined the relationship between the provinces' wealth (the gross provincial product per capita) and math and science achievement from the IAEP results. The correlation coefficient is a fairly high 0.62, similar to other educational statistics linking home background with mean school performance (usually between 0.4 and 0.6). When a graph of the relationship is drawn, only one province stands out as being well below the level of achievement that one would predict from its wealth; that province is Ontario. The achievement score among the English-speaking population there predicted from the analysis was 125, but the actual score was 116. In contrast, Quebec (French-speaking), with an actual score of 129, was 7 points above its predicted level.

The data raise the question as to whether the Canadian educational problem is essentially an Ontario one. The provinces typically in receipt of federal equalization grants appear not to be performing badly considering their social and economic disadvantage. Notable are the cases of the francophone majority and minority in Quebec and New Brunswick respectively. The difference between the New Brunswick linguistic minority and the Ontario linguistic one – 7 percentage points at age thirteen – is one of the most remarkable findings.

It is possible that provincial differences are changing over time, with Alberta and British Columbia increasing their lead while traditional differences between Ontario and the Atlantic provinces have narrowed or disappeared. One must be cautious about generalizing from different tests administered at various times. If that is the trend, however, it would suggest that differences in provincial policy are having more effect than affluence or spending levels. Ontario, the most affluent province and the biggest spender on formal schooling, is near the bottom of the heap. It also has educational policies and practices that appear to be particularly poor in eliciting excellence.

In all likelihood, Ontario both represents and exaggerates Canada's educational weaknesses. British Columbia, Alberta, and Quebec do not suffer from policy problems to the same degree. But that does not mean that parents are much happier in those provinces. International test scores in the elementary school are not the most important educational criterion for most parents. Nevertheless, it is the case that Alberta and British Columbia are, from most points of view, fortunate in their schools compared with other provinces. It is not that they cannot or should not improve, but that they have less distance to go.

Parents in Quebec, a province that comes out well in the performance data, are far from satisfied with their schools. It may well be the impersonal, unionized, and bureaucratized nature of that province's educational system and its enormous *polyvalent* (comprehensive) secondary "factories" that are most dysfunctional. One can run a well-organized, Technocratic system without engaging people's hearts and minds. The Roman Catholic Church no longer concerns the typical Québécois parent, but no other commitment has replaced it within the school.

I remind the reader at this point that, although I see the need for changes of a Technocratic kind in much of Canada, notably in Ontario, I do not believe that improved technocracy is the principal, still less the final, answer to the country's educational problems, as the case of Quebec amply illustrates. Just as improved evaluation is a necessary, but insufficient requirement, so Technocratic efficiency is necessary if we are to spend our money fairly and effectively; but it does not reach the heart, the real meaning, of education. Mistaken attempts to change Canada's Progressive schools have typically been Technocratic in nature, sometimes literally so in the form of a "computer on every desk." Even if parents are given everything that money can buy (the typical Canadian response to complaints in the past), it will not be what they want. Simply, there is no single thing that all parents want most, including better test scores for their children.

Are We Getting Better or Worse?

Changes in achievement levels over time are as important as comparative data at one time. There will always be differences in achievement levels between national, cultural, and socio-economic groups. All countries and provinces cannot be above average.

Explanations for differences in educational outcomes among groups within the population (based on nature, nurture, or – the media's favourite – prejudice) were considered earlier. If one looks at differences among individuals and schools (instead of between racial, ethnic, or religious groups), then the home background (including both nature and nurture) far exceeds in importance any differences among schools. School effects are examined in chapter 4. To match the Japanese and the Taiwanese, we would probably have to change our whole culture, which we could not do even if we wanted to. Our problem is that we do do not do particularly well compared with even the United States and England.

There will always be winners and losers in interprovincial testing programs. As long as the more educated and affluent move to and live in Ontario, Alberta, or British Columbia, those provinces may be expected to achieve better results than Newfoundland and New Brunswick. A session at an academic conference demonstrated with great local pride that the performance on tests of basic skills of elementary students in the Edmonton public schools had improved remarkably over the period of a few years. The years in question had been an era of heavy immigration during an oil boom. The evidence showed that the average measured intelligence of the student body had actually increased more than its performance in the basic skills!

Interprovincial differences do not matter much if we are improving overall and if we have a solid international standing. The only reasonably valid national data over time come from the Canadian Tests of Basic Skills, one of the two national standardized tests. (The federal government is using the other, the Canadian Achievement Tests, which have been mentioned earlier. These have been translated into French for the purpose, to develop longitudinal measures of achievement across the country.) An analysis by the Economic Council of Canada (1992) of changes in the average achievement level at grades four and eight gives a depressing picture. By the end of grade eight, the median Canadian student (i.e. the student who performs better than half the students in the country and worse than the other half) in 1966 would in 1991 perform better than 70 per cent of the students in reading comprehension and better than 65 per cent in mathematics. Put another way, the student right in the middle of an average class in 1966 would, moved through time to 1991 and performing at the same level, be rated in the top third. Most of this loss has taken place by grade four. The middle student in grade four in 1966 would in 1991 perform better than 61 per cent of students in reading comprehension and better than 72 per cent in mathematics. (These data, incidentally, help to support my argument that Canada's greatest problems are in the earliest grades. It is impossible to teach "critical thinking" and "decision making" to students who are illiterate and innumerate.)

The CTBS data are more likely to underestimate than overestimate the actual decline. The school districts willing to be involved in testing are likely to be those that use standardized tests; that is, districts opposed to testing are more likely to refuse to be included than are supportive districts. Districts (and provinces) concerned about accountability and test results are less likely, I would argue, to undergo decline than are those that are uninterested.

Nelson, the publisher of the CTBS has become distinctly uncomfortable about the use of its tests to show changes in achievement. Critics of testing (and defenders of the status quo) have quoted representatives of the company as stating that the data cannot be used to demonstrate differences over time. Obviously, it is difficult to sell tests to school boards if the results are used to put their schools in a negative light. Newer versions of the tests are so altered that recent changes in performance are impossible to assess. Nevertheless, the CTBS itself published data for many years on test comparability, providing the basis for the ECC calculations. The statements that I have quoted are simple facts. The changes in the CTBS illustrate the problems one faces when one tries to provide clear educational data in Canada. The use of achievement data in Canadian research is rare for the simple reasons that it is usually unavailable, and when it is, it is rarely accessible. I am not being critical of Nelson, the publisher of the CTBS. It is trying to market a product that is a hard sell to a Progressive establishment, which will use any excuse to avoid buying it.

In the late 1980s and early 1990s, public pressure for accountability on the part of school board members led to the increased use of standardized tests in Ontario, by such large systems as North York and even the Region of York and the Metropolitan Toronto Catholic boards, both strongly opposed to testing for many years. It remains to be seen how long the tests will be used when public attention shifts elsewhere and when home-made Ontario tests are trumpeted. The beginning of a decline is already evident.

North York, with strong leadership from its unusual director (who was made Ontario's deputy minister of education in the fall of 1996), is an outstanding example of accountability, making data available by school. Over time, changes in performance at the school and district level may be available. There are school boards in Canada with long records of testing data that show historical changes, but these data are rarely made public.

Many provinces, including British Columbia, Alberta, Quebec, Nova Scotia, Manitoba, and Newfoundland, have regularly or occasionally monitored achievement change within their own boundaries. British Columbia, by means of its own testing program, recorded a small decline in achievement in mathematics between 1985 and 1990 at the grade four level, most noticeable in the area of measurement, and a small improvement in grade seven, particularly in measurement and algebra. Once again, the early grades seem to be the problem. Alberta compared achievement in grade three science, grade six mathematics, and grade nine social studies in 1983, 1987, and 1991 using departmental statistics. Improvement was noted in science and math, but not in social studies.

Newfoundland administered the Canadian Tests of Basic Skills every third year to grade six students and has records from 1976 to 1991. These results were not based on the same test or the same test items but were comparisons with the national average. Overall, the province moved significantly closer to the national average between 1976 and 1985 but did not continued to make relative improvement afterwards. The average Newfoundland student in grade six achieves outcomes at a level above 40 per cent of students across the nation; if performance in that province were the same as the (anglophone) nation's, then that student would perform as well as 50 per cent of other students. (But note the more recent performance of Newfoundland in the international tests: on a par with Ontario.) Prince Edward Island collected CTBS scores for grades three, six, and nine for 1984, 1987, and 1990. They were generally stable and above the national average. The province's educational expenditure is well below the national average.

A few conclusions may be drawin with respect to levels of academic achievement. There seem to be three educational regions within Canada. Alberta and British Columbia consistently do well on external tests. They also have comprehensive programs of their own. They monitor changes in achievement over time and provide regular results to parents for individual children. Quebec has perhaps the most comprehensive testing program in Canada, with annual assessment of the basic skills and testing in all subjects for high school students seeking graduation certificates. That province performs better than any other in relation to its level of wealth.

Manitoba and Saskatchewan probably fall below the first three provinces, but evidence of achievement is scanty. Saskatchewan displays the least interest in achievement testing of any province. Prince Edward Island may fall in this second group.

Ontario and the three remaining Atlantic provinces have poor levels of achievement when compared with other provinces and countries. Ontario is the clear anomaly. If the Atlantic provinces were compared with the poorer regions of other countries – with eastern Germany, the southern United States, or neighbouring Maine, for example – they might well look better. Ontario, on the other hand, is the most favoured province in what is sometimes considered the most favoured country in the world. The academic performance of its anglophone majority is bad enough, and the performance of the francophone minority even worse.

DROP-OUTS

After the results of achievement tests, the question of drop-outs is the topic that features most widely in media discussion of educational issues. At a superficial level, this is understandable. Most Canadians have a strong belief in the value of education, and it is surely one area of life where, other things being equal, most will agree that more is better. I am part of that majority; generally speaking, I would like to see Canadians become more educated; more competent in the basic skills and the disciplines of knowledge, with stronger virtues, improved aesthetic appreciation, and the ability to express themselves in the arts and in writing; more physically fit; with a greater knowledge and understanding of the world around us and our own history and traditions; more accomplished in the skills, attitudes, and habits required for work and civic life; and more able to live harmoniously within the social and natural environments. Even if we restrict the prescription to a few of those things, more is better.

There are, however, three good reasons why drop-out statistics are not a sound basis for public discussion and policy making in the context of those broad educational goals. It is a fundamental mistake to confuse more hours in school with more and better education, just as more patient-hours spent in the hospital or doctor's office are not indicators of rapid or successful recovery from illness.

First, the data we have are of doubtful validity. Generally, the Canadian drop-out rate is estimated at approximately 35 per cent. What this statistic tells us is the proportion of young people of a particular age group who do not graduate from high school in a fairly normal manner. It does not take into account the growing importance of adult and part-time education, or even the fact that some students may take an extra year or two along the way, because of illness, academic weakness, or travel. Many young people change schools, or work part-time and attend school part-time, or drop out of school and return, or drop out and take make-up programs through adult education. The actual proportion of young people in high school in 1998 who will not have achieved high school graduation or its equivalent by 2006 will be considerably lower than the 35 per cent current estimate of drop-outs. In 1991, according to Statistics Canada, fewer than 15 per cent of twenty-five-year-olds had failed to complete high school or its equivalent. Fifteen per cent (as compared with the nominal 35 per cent) is a better indication of inefficiency in moving young people to work than of the need to cajole them into remaining in school against their wishes, and perhaps their best interests. Legislating extended compulsory schooling will serve only to accentuate the negative feelings of many young people towards school. Sixteen may be too old, rather than too young. I suspect that there are a substantial, but hidden number of young people under sixteen who are not registered for school.

Second, the very idea of drop-outs is not a valuable one in a time of near-universal schooling. "Dropping out" is an American expression and is tied to the concept of high school graduation. There is no clear equivalent of a drop-out, or of high school graduation, in most European countries. Historically, graduation was an important and valuable step to make American high school education a universal opportunity, as distinct from one for economically or intellectually favoured minorities. That move was followed in Canada decades ago, but absence of opportunity is not the contemporary problem.

The Germanic educational systems can be seen as having either a very high or a very low drop-out rate depending on how enrolment in formal education is defined. The proportion of Germans going through a regular academic program and qualifying for university entry is far below that of the United States and Canada, yet most young Germans are involved in formal education, at the same time as they are prepared for work. In Canada the alleged high drop-out rate is bemoaned because "you can't get a job without a graduation certificate," thus reinforcing the misleading connection between a general education (as distinct from training and vocational education) and jobs. The Germanic countries most successful in moving young people from school to work do not have our comprehensive high schools and have no real equivalent of the North American graduation certificate. As pointed out earlier, achieving a higher level of paper certification makes sense for the individual because most employers will choose a high school graduate over a grade nine drop-out, or a person with two years of university over a high school graduate. But lowering the high school drop-out rate will not increase the number of available jobs commensurately, and probably not at all if one excludes the teachers required to provide custody for the students still in school while they await their useless credential.

Betty Donaldson, in a 1989 doctoral thesis completed at OISE, researched a group of students (excluding those continuing to post-secondary education) moving from school to work in a suburban high school outside Toronto. She found that those who found employment used many different, but rarely formal school mechanisms; a common route was to progress from school and a part-time job to a full-time job with the same employer, with or without a graduation certificate.

Ironically, one focus of the "drop-out problem" has been the issue of part-time work, which is often said to lead to dropping out. It is inconsistent to advertise that staying in school will get one a job and then complain that students are dropping out because school interferes with their work. Banning part-time work beyond a fixed number of hours has been suggested on the grounds that it interferes with school work. Precisely how this restriction would be monitored is not clear, since strongly motivated young people would probably find two or even three jobs. To the extent that part-time work leads to gainful permanent employment, the young people concerned should be congratulated rather than chastised. The "couch potato" sitting in school all day doing nothing and watching television much of the night is hardly an example to the industrious young person who combines long hours of work with productive attendance at school. Instead of thinking of useful ways to combine two productive activities, education and training, in a manageable way for the young people concerned, school systems try to shape everyone with the same cookie cutter, presumably with the intention of convincing them that they would be better off aiming for university and a degree in sociology or a career in neurosurgery.

In third place, the obsession with drop-outs leads to complex, expensive, and absurd schemes to persuade young people to stay in school without considering what they are staying there for and why they would be better off doing so. Too often, staying in school means simply that – putting in sufficient (generously interpreted) hours to earn a piece of paper, allegedly as the route to a job. The alleged drop-out problem puts additional pressure on school officials to tolerate almost any breach of discipline or failure to work, rather than demand adherence to reasonable standards of effort, progress, and behaviour. As if there were not pressure enough already from within the monopoly of public education to count bodies and hours of instruction, rather than achievement, training, and civic virtue, political and media pressure on the drop-out further aggravates the problem. The only problem solved simply by having more young people stay in school is that of insufficient jobs for teachers, administrators, and those employed to fight the drop-out problem by, for example, publishing expensive advertisements in the *Globe and Mail*, hardly renowned for its wide readership among disadvantaged youth.

As already noted, Quebec is the only province with clearly defined and mandatory measured standards for high school graduation (although British Columbia and Alberta have clear standards for those moving on to postsecondary education). Quebec also has the highest drop-out rate. Thomas Boudreau in *Le Devoir* (19 January 1993) argues that if the province's exceptionally large adult-education sector were taken into account, its drop-out rate would fall to 25 per cent, close to New Brunswick's figure of 22 per cent (the lowest drop-out rate in Canada); that province's achievement levels, he notes, are below Quebec's.

Staying in school is only valuable if either additional education or some other valuable purpose (such as job training or improved work habits) is likely to be achieved. If it means a greater tolerance on the part of the school of poor attendance, poor work habits, undisciplined behaviour, lack of achievement, sloppy appearance, and bad manners, then a reduced drop-out rate is counter-productive. Few people, other than officials of a public service union, would justify a large and growing civil service, accompanied by poorer and poorer service to the public, on the grounds that it was employing so many people. We would hardly applaud the growing use of expensive hospitals if time in hospital did nothing to reduce the duration and severity of illness.

In Canadian schools there is typically little accountability. If one looks at classes and curricula in sequential skill subjects such as math and language at the lower levels of the high school (often described as general or basic levels to distinguish them from the college-preparatory academic level), one finds it virtually impossible to distinguish a grade ten from a grade twelve course. (Unfortunately, this is also sometimes true of academic courses, except in a second language, music, math, and science.) We know that many high school graduates are illiterate and innumerate, in the sense that they cannot achieve the standards reflected in the average achievement level of a Canadian twelve-year-old. My recommendation that there should be a minimum standard for graduation (one that would roughly equal the average grade six level) is considered harmfully radical in Progressive educational circles on the grounds that it would lead to a massive increase in the drop-out rate. That is not the experience in the United States, but the horrified opposition does demonstrate an awareness of the low academic level of many high school graduates, despite claims that all is well. The link between attempts to reduce the drop-out rate and low academic standards is rarely made. One can have both tough standards and low drop-out rates, but it requires a very different regimen from that of the typical North American comprehensive high school.

The federal government funded research by the Conference Board of Canada in 1992 on the economic cost of secondary school drop-outs as part of an expensive stay-in-school campaign. The inane conclusion of the final report was that it was "puzzling as to why any student would drop out of secondary school". It would be puzzling indeed if one were to believe the authors' claims. The private financial rate of return, according to the report, for completing secondary school in 1985 was 65.4 per cent for males and 74.4 per cent for females. As for society, the combined social and private cost of those dropping out in the age group that would have graduated in 1989–90 was $4 billion.

Those assertions are built on a series of assumptions, not the least of which is that the alleged costs would have been essentially unaffected by the recession that arrived shortly after the study was published. To put it mildly, not every economist is convinced that the calculations are valid. My own opinion is that the entire project was a waste of money. The money would have been far better spent developing pilot projects with two parallel purposes: first, to help students move from school to work by combining part-time paid work with part-time schooling (based on a set of clearly written and tested objectives); and second, to develop school programs with clear, sequential content leading to a credential based on measurable and meaningful levels of achievement.

It is well established that, in good times and bad, university and college graduates earn more than high school graduates. There is no doubt that a high school graduation certificate bears a monetary value. Thus, it does make financial sense for the average individual who has a real choice as to whether to complete high school or not to do so, other things being equal. That argument holds at the level of the average individual, but other things are frequently not equal. Some people's jobs at age sixteen do lead to reasonably permanent employment, and that possibility may be predictable. For example, a young person may join a relative or friend in a new and growing small business or on a productive farm. There is no similar expectation for those who graduate with nothing other than a high school graduation certificate if that credential is accompanied by poor skills, poor attitudes, poor attendance records, and poor work habits.

Yet those who are bribed or pushed into staying in school by permissive or naive parents, teachers, administrators, and judges are likely to exhibit exactly those characteristics. There does not have to be a conspiracy favouring weakness; the chain is only as strong as its weakest link. Parents who excuse their adolescents' excesses and failures by writing letters permitting absence because of "sickness" resulting from all-night parties and indulgence in alcohol, sexual activity, and drugs undermine the most conscientious school. Weak-willed administrators who want to keep their enrolment up and drop-out rate down no matter what undermine the many teachers who try to maintain standards of behaviour, dress, and work. Principals often enforce a maximum failure rate for all classes, thereby setting a low standard of achievement, to avoid the appearance of failure, at the same time corrupting teachers. And weak-willed, burnt-out teachers undermine conscientious parents and administrators by subverting real standards if they are set. This is one important reason why the large comprehensive, cafeteria high school cannot work. Inevitably, there are weak links somewhere among uncommitted parents, teachers, and administrators, for whom there is no consensual educational purpose. "How can I demand good work if the student himself, his parents, and the principal are content with benign custody?" asks the teacher. Students quickly understand when they are being warehoused rather than educated, however resistant to education they may be. Being at fault rarely blinds one to the faults of others.

Even at the level of the individual student, the researchers' argument only holds to the extent that, first, most other students do not make the same decision to stay in school (otherwise the pool of those competing for the limited number of available jobs will increase), and second, the individuals who are persuaded to stay in school develop the same characteristics as those now remaining in school and not the traits of those dropping out. Presumably, there is some reason why high school diplomas still have a cash value; it logically lies in the constellation of desired attributes and habits more likely to be found, on average, in graduates than in non-graduates.

At the societal level, the researchers' conclusions change from being sensible (but hardly newsworthy) to at best wishful thinking and at worst culpable stupidity. It is simply not reasonable in the 1990s to imagine that employment in Canada awaits everybody who is suitably qualified (however one defines the term). Thirty or more years ago, some economists did sincerely believe that employment was a direct function of education and training, that is, that investment in education and training provided a direct and profitable return in both the quantity and the quality of jobs created. There is probably no reputable economist in Canada today who believes that. I am not suggesting that deteriorating, mediocre educational systems do not affect the economy; but simply manipulating the credentials of the unemployed is unlikely to have much economic effect, except in those few areas where there are clear labour shortages. There are good high-technology jobs available, but they will not be filled by marginal drop-outs.

There may be some value in targeting spending on education and training. But the investment will only be economically rewarding if it is made in the right place with the right people at the right time, and those are variables that are imperfectly understood and inherently unpredictable. Governments do not have a good track record in this area, partly because their motives are mixed. One cannot tell today's fifteen-year-old with any accuracy what jobs will be readily available ten years from now, and if the young person happens to fall below the average in intellectual skills, useful prediction becomes even more difficult.

The economic effects of education are just part of the overall picture. The miseducation provided to drop-outs persuaded to stay in school is much more harmful in personal and educational terms than in fiscal ones. It is cynically argued *sotto voce* that rebellious young adults are preferably warehoused in secondary schools than on the rampage outside. Miseducation teaches them to play the training game, to place the responsibility for finding work on others, and to separate schooling from personal responsibility. It also promotes bad habits that inhibit gainful employment in the future. And I am not recommending rampage as an alternative. It is dishonest to suggest that the problem of youth unemployment is essentially an individual one: that if young people were not so perverse as to drop out, they would all have good jobs. In current conditions of schools and the labour market, dropping out is sometimes a rational decision. Why stay in school for an empty credential if there is no job available anyway?

There may be a partial solution (in addition to economic growth and gradually declining numbers of young people) to youth unemployment. If there is, it lies in finding effective ways to help young people move from school to work, in other words, to give them a genuine and visible reason to stay in school. Persuading more academically, morally, and socially ill-equipped young people to endure a longer high school experience will not miraculously improve either the quality or the quantity of available work. In chapter 2, I looked at the general problem of school and work in contemporary society. It is one of the greatest challenges facing our social and educational systems. But it probably gets less emphasis in the media than other questions because it tends not to be of direct concern to the middle classes, whose children are likely to attend better secondary schools and continue to postsecondary institutions, and for whom high school graduation with a solid credential is the absolute minimum. In chapter 5, I recommend that we eliminate, rather than expand, the opportunity to occupy physical space in secondary school without productive activity. We should offer more numerous directed programs in the senior years, and we should encourage combined programs of education and training, of school and work. The drop-out rate is a symptom, not a disease.

STUDENT DISCIPLINE

Discipline is one of the greatest concerns of parents, particularly at the secondary level. There is some evidence that the prevailing standards fall not only below the level desired by parents and the public, but also below that desired by secondary principals. Jonathan Black-Branch, as part of a 1993 doctoral dissertation at OISE, interviewed twenty-five secondary principals from across Canada. Most of them, assured anonymity, expressed real concern about the discipline in their own schools, many saying that fear of allegations that might be brought against them in the age of the Charter and the Young Offenders Act deterred them from taking the disciplinary action they felt appropriate.

Legal experts argue that the principals' fears of the courts are unwarranted because the courts have generally defended the right of principals to take strong and reasonable action to maintain order.

Black-Branch points out that the concern expressed by principals is not so much of ultimate conviction by a court as of the smearing of their character by allegations publicized by the media: for example, that the disciplinary action was racist or a denial of fundamental rights. They doubt that the school board would consider them for promotion as long as they were under the cloud of such an accusation. Imagine the fury of a special-interest group if the individual whom it accused of prejudice or physical abuse were promoted before the matter was dealt with, or even after a charge was dropped or settled out of court. Allegations of politically incorrect behaviour are not quickly forgotten or forgiven, however unfounded they may be. And how many school boards or senior administrators have that much courage, or foolhardiness?

One complex area about which there is almost no factual record is that of suspension and expulsion from school. We simply do not know how many young people are expelled, for what period of time, or for what reasons. It is not unusual for schools and systems to fail to collect or maintain data on important questions such as absenteeism and disciplinary action. Parents of wrongdoers increasingly argue that schooling is compulsory and that their child has a right to education, irrespective of what he or she has done. The issue is further complicated because serious breaches of discipline are sometimes dealt with by the courts and sometimes not. If the court sets a sentence, it may be argued that it is unfair for the school to add its own punishment. If the case does not go to court, parents (or their lawyer) may argue that it is unfair for the school to treat a student more harshly than the courts would. Many matters involve misbehaviour outside the school; administrators, who say they look away from infractions inside the school if they can, are not usually more eager to deal with problems that arise when students are on the way to or from school, whatever their legal rights.

Sometimes a court effectively sentences a young miscreant to regular attendance at school; this may be a person the school has good reason not to enrol at all. The sentence constrains the school from taking strong discipline, for fear that the court will intervene, arguing that the school is unreasonably countermanding the court's sentence. For example, good principals sensibly set tight limits around badly performing students, with the result that the actual incident which triggered the suspension or expulsion may seem trivial to a judge looking at a single event in a legal context and unwilling to consider a long string of previous incidents.

I was involved in a court case in which a student sued the school system and individual educators (as well as other parties). The

young man had been viciously assaulted in the school and had allegedly suffered permanent mental injury. My judgment, based on the
various pre-trial sworn statements, is that the vice-principal involved
had failed to take adequate disciplinary action prior to the actual
fight. However, the evidence was clear that his behaviour was
normal for the school and that he had lengthy experience as a vice-
principal in the school district. On the basis of my knowledge of
school discipline in large secondary schools, his behaviour (inadequate though I thought it) was well within normal bounds. In
essence, I believe that the prevailing standard is not a reasonable
one. It is difficult for an individual or school to depart from generally
accepted norms within the district, even if they are over-permissive.
Leadership is required from the province and from the school district; it is conspicuously lacking. Obviously, I would not hold the
vice-principal personally responsible in this case.

A teacher in one of my courses, who asked that she and her large
suburban high school, serving a predominantly middle-class clientele, remain anonymous, reported from a study in her school thus:
"Since the survey was administered [in the fall of 1992], an incident
of aggravated sexual assault has occurred in the school's washroom
and weekly racial fights occur both inside and outside the classroom." This school is in an area that I happened to know well. It did
not have a reputation, as some schools did, for problems of racism
or violence, at least in the press.

High school principals are frequently believed – by students, parents, teachers, and themselves (in confidential moments) – not to be
in control of their schools. The real or imagined barriers to dealing
firmly with students who commit acts of defiance and violence, let
alone refuse to work, are significant. Fear of a high drop-out rate
adds to the reluctance of principals to act firmly; schools, like school
districts, need the body count to justify their budgets. An independent school is under the same (or even stronger) pressure to retain
bodies, but that pressure is balanced by the need to maintain a deco-
rum that will attract and keep clients whose behaviour is not dysfunctional. In contrast, it is almost impossible for the public school,
with its healthy monopoly, to go out of business, however bad it may
be. When schools served communities, there was a balancing pressure from the community as a whole, comparable to that found in
an independent school. A principal who did not deal firmly with
miscreants (everyone knew who they were) would be condemned as
ineffective and would not last very long.

Another problem is that, in an age of rights and individualism,
most cases of discipline are considered in terms of the best interests

of the individual. Too often, the interests of the school, of society, and of other students are simply not taken into account. In 1997 the Supreme Court of Canada ruled that school systems do have the right to remove severely disabled students from the regular class-room, but only if it is evident that doing so is in their own best interests. It does not appear to have occurred to the court that inter-ruptions arising from a severe disability may interfere with the best interests of the rest of the class, or the court may have only been interested in the rights of the individual.

In my research with samples of educated Ontarians and educators (1995), I found that directors of education were the only group not to agree that it is too difficult to suspend or expel students from school; only 21 per cent of directors supported that statement, com-pared with 63 per cent of a broadly based sample of educators. These figures help explain the mindset of educators furthest removed from the problem and the resulting lack of leadership in this area.

Ideally, a traditional school would not need a strong written code of behaviour because all concerned would share common values and agree that, for example, consistent refusal to do school work, an act of violent sexual or physical assault, or repeated disobedience or cheating would lead to legitimate expulsion from the school. Today, when there is no consensus and when assertions of individual rights are commonplace, such codes must be written down. It is absolutely necessary for every school principal to have the right to suspend or, subject to review by a superior or the parent committee, expel stu-dents. To argue against this provision is to suggest that the school should become a form of prison, as well as fulfil other contradictory roles. Young people should have a right of access to education, but that right should not mean access to a school in which their behav-iour has been objectionable.

The question arises as to what should happen to students who are repeatedly suspended or expelled. In most of Canada, there is inad-equate provision for such students, the harmful nonsense being propagated that young people cannot really be bad and that a good school and a good teacher should be able to deal with every student, whatever his or her problems. The extent of violence, disobedience, and total failure to complete work is concealed, denied, and ignored. If high school principals were asked how many students had been expelled for not doing any work, they would probably look puzzled. They would be thinking of the many "more serious" problems which they had to deal with, problems involving violence, theft, drugs, vandalism, and defiant and abusive behaviour. If middle-school and secondary teachers were asked how many students failed on a regular basis to complete their work, most would say there were several in all but the strongest academic classes. One might ask, too, how many students are conveniently absent for tests and other inopportune deadlines. The typical high school routinely condones students' failure to appreciate its supposed central activity – academic work.

Every school should have access to a facility, within the school or nearby, to deal with students who fail to behave in an acceptable way, either by not working adequately or by consistently not complying with reasonable rules. The facility should consist of one or more classrooms with fifteen or fewer students. They should be run on a very strict and consistent regime, with the understanding that failure to comply would lead to expulsion, and consistent good behaviour result in a provisional return to the regular classroom.

The province should also run (or purchase places in) schools, including boarding schools, for students who have been expelled. These would be institutions to which students would be sent, but enrolment would fundamentally be optional, in the sense there would be no cells for solitary confinement for those who rejected the strong discipline and rules. Some young people might be sent to these schools by court order; facilities for young offenders would be the alternative should they fail to conform or should they commit a criminal act. Others would be sent by schools or school districts as a condition for eventual return to another school (different from the one from which they were expelled). These institutions would be a last chance for the student.

Expense is no doubt one reason for neither of these types of facilities being readily available, but it is probably not the only one. Authorities can more easily deny the problem, even though such denial is leading to the corruption and breakdown of many of our high schools. There is no reason to wonder why cynicism, burn-out, desperation, and hopelessness are too often characteristic of secondary school teachers and even some middle-school ones. They are expected to teach many young people who have no interest in learning, indeed, some with a strong determination not to work. Those attitudes are gradually penetrating the lower grades, where they are less visible because little work is actually demanded.

Even if we had data on expulsions, their interpretation would require great care (as is the case with drop-outs). A high rate in one year might mean the school was out of control, or that the principal was cracking down on a bad situation. A low rate might mean an orderly school or one where teachers and administrators ignoreed infractions and made few demands. The true goal is a low rate of suspension and expulsion within an orderly, civil environment.

OTHER EDUCATIONAL OUTCOMES

It is fair to generalize that the most important concerns of the public are academic performance, discipline, behaviour, and values, together with preparation for work or further education. These are reasonable reflections of the Cultural, Traditional, and Technocratic world-views, but not of the Progressive. Even in the case of the minority of parents who favour the Progressive outlook when their children are young, many would not disavow those popular concerns. They assume, as do many teachers, that those things are looked after by magic in a good educational environment. There are other important outcomes that are of some significance to nearly everyone and of crucial concern to a few.

I refer particularly to performance in and appreciation of the arts and to physical education and fitness. Evidence of outcomes in these areas is scanty. Carol Harris, in an OISE doctoral thesis completed in 1990, conducted a detailed study of music education in three Canadian school districts and found a wide variation. One district, which was among the highest spenders in Canada, left music to the elementary classroom teacher to "integrate" with other subjects. ("Integration" of subject matter is an important part of Progressive dogma.) The results were the virtual absence of disciplined teaching of choral and instrumental performance at the elementary level and a heavy dependence by secondary music programs on students who had had private tuition. The other two districts, less affluent but still well funded, had solid music programs from the beginning of elementary school and a good degree of performance and interest at the senior secondary level. Both these districts prided themselves on their exceptional devotion to the music program. They succeeded by resisting the fads of subject integration and the adoption of happiness as the first goal, probably because there were strong traditions of high-quality choirs and bands to uphold.

At best, musical performance in Canada is patchy; the systems I know best (in three provinces) have suffered steady deterioration in this area. Involvement in competitive music festivals has declined over the years, reflecting the Progressive idea that competition is bad and the joy of expression is itself a sufficient reward. Progressivism is antithetical to excellence in all spheres of endeavour because it opposes competition, rigorous discipline, and strong demands. One may assume similar variations in emphasis and quality in art; the deterioration may be even greater if the idea that all appreciation of art is a subjective matter for the individual is more deeply rooted in that field, which it probably is.

According to the Canadian Association for Health, Physical Education and Recreation, only one-third of Canadian students have physical education daily. Statistics on subject enrolment (see Tables 6 and 7) show that by grade twelve, the enrolment in physical education (which in semestered schools is in any case likely to be scheduled for only half the year) is limited to less than half the student body. In Ontario, the *Globe and Mail* reported, "high-school students need only one physical education credit to graduate ... many take a course in Grade 9 and never take another" (15 April 1993). The same article states that obesity is a problem among young people and that aerobic capacity falls drastically as they move into and through adolescence. An unexamined question is the extent to which physical education classes actually demand hard exercise and produce fitness. Emphasis on teaching psychomotor and gymnastic skills may result in students leaving physical education classes without having experienced any aerobic challenge.

There is a tendency for educators to seek out more complex tasks, perhaps because teaching straightforward things such as basic skills, cleanliness, and politeness seems trivial (it is also difficult). Just as academic teachers may talk about self-actualization, decision making, and visual literacy instead of personal responsibility, good behaviour, arithmetical skills, and reading comprehension, so physical education teachers may talk about micro- and macro-psychomotor skills and leadership rather than fitness. The problem is not so much with the jargon as with the change from important, measurable factors to insubstantial, non-measurable ones (usually because they cannot be clearly defined) and from objectives that are achievable within the school to those that depend much more heavily on behaviour outside it. It is possible to teach virtually all young people such things as the basic skills of reading and mathematics, cleanliness, courtesy, general knowledge, the fundamentals of science, geography, history, art, and music and to make them physically fit within the school; but it requires rigour, determination, and effort. How much easier and grander to talk about self-expression, creativity, self-directed learning, developing one's own personal values, critical thinking, "oracy" (speaking ability), and a hundred other things for which the school can never be held to account. It is also easier to claim credit for maturation than effective instruction.

The actual and potential effect of schooling on outcomes in music, art, and physical education (and other non-core objectives) is an insufficiently researched topic; there is virtually no Canadian research. I summarized the state of knowledge about the relationship between achievement in school and later success in life for the

Ontario Ministry of Education in 1985, most of the reported research having been conducted outside Canada.

I have used the term "outcomes" in this chapter with some trepidation. It seems to be a useful piece of educational jargon, referring to changes that take place in young people during their years in school, changes to which formal education may reasonably be believed to have made an important contribution. The expression "results of schooling" implies that schooling is the only cause of the changes, which is hardly ever the case. Unfortunately, "outcome" has fallen into disrepute with many parents because its recent use has often been in the context of obscure objectives, which are difficult enough to comprehend, let alone to assess the contribution of the school, if any. My use of "outcome" does not refer to high-level decision making, creativity, critical thinking, or sensitivity to planetary ecology. (Underneath those terms, there is valuable knowledge, together with important skills, but the terms themselves lack any agreed meaning.) Useful educational outcomes include, among others, academic knowledge and skills; the ability to appreciate music, to express oneself musically, and to understand music; physical fitness, cleanliness, and honesty; and the ability to analyse, synthesize, and evaluate ideas in many branches of knowledge.

ATTITUDES TO EDUCATION

One indicator of the success of the school system is public opinion. No sensible person would argue that the schools should try to react in a knee-jerk fashion to every change in popular opinion. On the other hand, in a democracy one hopes that educational policy is sensitive to deeply held beliefs over a period of time, to established public will. It is paradoxical for defenders of the educational establishment to assert that all is well, if large proportions of parents cannot get the kind of education they want from the system and if there is widespread public dissatisfaction.

One of the most interesting opinion polls was conducted in British Columbia in 1984 and published by that province's Ministry of Education in 1985 as part of its *Let's Talk about Schools* report. Unusually, separate samples of the public and of educators were polled, and dramatic differences emerged. While 94 per cent of the public considered standardized teaching materials to be important, only 20 per cent of the educators agreed. Similarly, 69 per cent of the public thought that standardized methods of evaluation were very important, compared with 3 per cent of the educators. Those discrepancies reflect the differences in world-view that I described earlier. In my own research in Ontario, I found that, while only 11 per cent of directors of education agreed with annual achievement testing of elementary students, the proposal was supported by 59 per cent of a similarly educated comparison group of non-educators. This finding, about the value of external testing, has been well documented for over twenty years, but there are still many school districts and provinces that have no or almost no regular, meaningful standardized testing of students in basic skills.

In the United States, an annual Gallup poll of public opinion is taken and the results published in the fall in the *Phi Delta Kappan* educational magazine. There is considerable continuity of questions over time, a factor that is particularly important because changes in wording frequently alter results. The closest equivalent in Canada is OISE's survey of opinion in Ontario, which has been published continuously since 1979 at approximately two-year intervals. It also confirms public support for the external testing of students, a policy issue that divides the public and educators sharply in those provinces with little or no external testing, including Ontario. The dissatisfaction in that province may indirectly reflect its poor standing in tests of educational achievement, which have been given great play in the media. Such dissatisfaction demonstrates the long-standing differences in preferred educational policy on the part of the public and the professionals, in a context where the three major political parties have, intentionally or more often unintentionally, accepted educators' preferences rather than the public's. It is possible that the slight lessening of public discontent in Ontario is attributable to the public discussion of Technocratic reforms.

Ontario's Progressive framework was introduced deliberately by William Davis when he was minister of education in a Conservative (but not conservative) government. Indeed, a motive for opening the Ontario Institute for Studies in Education was to make an end run around the government Department of Education, which in the late 1960s was opposed to Progressivism. After Davis became premier, the Progressive policies were continued right into the 1970s. Although neither the subsequent Liberal government nor the NDP government supported Progressivism, both were either unable or unwilling to confront the educational establishment.

Newton and his colleagues (1992) looked at national surveys of public opinion and discovered no consistent patterns over time. They did not find overall dissatisfaction, with one notable exception, and that was with the preparation of young people for work. A difficulty with interpreting that discontent is the tendency of parents to think that other people's children should be prepared for work, but not their own. The obvious solution is the principle adopted in the Germanic countries (even in Denmark), where focused programs at the senior high school level are available to all who qualify; programs leading nowhere do not exist. One works towards specific competencies, be they academic or vocational. Putting in the hours (or not even that in some schools where attendance is poor) does not count.

Is there some contradiction here? Am I not arguing that parents should be able to select the education of their choice? It is not parental choice to which I object (and parents in many cases have little influence over the choices of their increasingly independent adolescent children), bur rather to the existence and growth of programs of miseducation in the public schools, of programs that appear to lead to a high school graduation standard when there is no such standard, and of the tolerance of idleness, absenteeism, and unruliness in the secondary school. Few parents will actively make such choices, but they make them unknowingly by default. Often, there is no viable alternative. I favour informed choice, initially on the part of parents and later by older adolescents and their parents together, but the choice should be between genuine educational programs with certified standards. By contrast, parents have a choice of physicians, but provincially approved medical care must meet certain standards.

LAW AND THE EDUCATIONAL EXPERIENCE

It is well known that provincial governments have constitutional jurisdiction over education. Any commentary on education in Canada must accept that central fact. Even so, as noted in chapter 1, there has been a long history of federal involvement in education, particularly at the postsecondary level and less obviously at the elementary and secondary levels. Important areas of federal involvement in the school system include education of the First Peoples, educational "infrastructure" (i.e. new schools with a vocational or technical element) in the 1960s and 1970s, second-language instruction beginning in the 1970s, and many smaller initiatives in the last few years. Reference has already been made to the federal government's financial involvement in terms of grants to provinces and to the drop-out initiative.

Increasingly, given our financial difficulties, there is recognition that greater cooperation and clearer separation between the provincial and federal governments are necessary, in taxing, borrowing, training, health care, and elements of education. Equally obvious is the fact that the Council of Ministers of Education, although it has served many useful managerial and collaborative functions among the various governments involved in education, has not acted as a coordinating and standard-setting body for elementary and secondary education. Because it depends on unanimity among the provinces, and because complete agreement among them is about as imminent as a return visit from Haley's Comet, there is no reason to believe that it could or should fulfil that role.

Realistically, standards should be left to the provinces. Interprovincial coordination and federal involvement, unfortunately, will only lead to further procrastination and to the reduction of standards to the lowest denominator. Quebec, British Columbia, and Alberta have relatively good systems in place, but most provinces have not. If national standards were based on the most stringent policies among provinces, that approach would be valuable. But suppose that they were based on those of Ontario or Nova Scotia? In the case of the smaller and poorer provinces, financial incapacity is an important barrier.

One other important legal factor is the status of teachers. In general, membership in a union is a condition of employment. Similarly, in all the major provinces, teachers have the right to strike, and the strike is in practice the means used to resolve major differences with the employer. Those two conditions, if perpetuated and if the public quasi-monopolies continue, will severely limit and probably frustrate any serious attempts at educational reform. First, the existence of strong monopolistic unions, holding children's custody and education as a powerful hostage, makes fundamental change in the employment conditions of teachers close to impossible, particularly where there are still strong local school boards, many of which are always eager to capitulate. Second, because elementary teachers (at least in the early grades) are committed to Progressivism, with an enthusiasm more appropriate in a religious cult, change by external pressure has almost no chance of success – as witnessed by the failure of successive Liberal, NDP, and, to date, Progressive Conservative governments in Ontario for well over a decade and by the survival of these practices even in Alberta and British Columbia.

If the school systems remain within their current legal frameworks, there can be little prospect for substantial educational improvement. Even if governments are prepared to take strong action (as Alberta, followed by Ontario, has in the fiscal domain), there is little evidence that they can have a profound influence inside the classroom. As long as the unions maintain a closed shop, their power over major educational and curricular policy is enormous. They may not be able to regulate change themselves, as they have done indirectly in the past, but they can still veto it within the classroom.

If it is not feasible even to introduce clear standards throughout the country, it is even more unrealistic to think that monopolies can change their internal workings by means of external or internal pressure. Quebec is a model for the rest of the country in terms of goals, programs, and standards. Its outcomes are relatively good in relation to its economic and social conditions. But there is considerable discontent with the school system among parents. Governments can create policy conditions under which education flourishes, and which are Technocratically sensible; but most have yet to do even that. The combination of strong, mandatory teachers' unions and a virtual monopoly of publicly supported education sets a vise that cannot be loosened.

In the end, successful schools depend on the participation of the people centrally involved – parents, teachers, and students. The active level of participation in policy making of the three partners may vary enormously: contrived committees are far from a complete answer. The crucial point is that parents, teachers, and students must all be committed to and engaged with the educational process.

Students' educational experience should essentially reflect the varying desires of parents. Teachers should be full participators and should have control over the day-to-day classroom instruction (but not the program objectives). Teachers should be able to choose the kind of school in which they teach, not be arbitrarily assigned by central bureaucracies. Students should be able to participate in an educational experience with clear objectives which make practical sense to them. It should have set standards, in terms of which their progress is regularly assessed. If older students above, say, fourteen are to be full participants, they should share with their parents the choice of schooling, but their influence on its day-to-day direction should be relatively minor. Their short-term and long-term interests conflict. The extent of their influence should vary according to the wishes of the local governing body (composed mainly of parents and teachers).

Highly bureaucratized, unionized monopolies stifle participation and make major reform impossible. Chipping away at the educational problem will be of little avail if day-to-day power is left in the complacent hands of unions and school boards. I am pointing here to a division of powers, with centralization of power over spending, standards, and major goals and with local, day-to-day policy in the hands of parents. If schools thrive outside the monopoly, union power will become less important; but Canadian provinces are too feeble to dismantle the existing structure or encourage growth outside it.

CONCLUSION

What follows is a brief summary of the educational situation in Canada in the late 1990s. It is directly related to the final chapter, in which a reform program is proposed. Overall, while Canada's school system can be seen as severely flawed, it would be inaccurate to assert that the educational experience of its young people is inferior to that of the countries most like us, the United States and England. Those educational systems are also in trouble, for similar, but not identical reasons. Their problems – exacerbated like ours by rigid, monopolistic bureaucracies, but less powerful than ours – are significantly a result of their social systems. England suffers from a division between the have-not industrial north and the affluent south, its surviving class system, and the concentrated populations of poorly educated immigrants, notably in London and the major industrial cities of the Midlands and the north. The United States suffers from its underclass in the big cities and rural South and from the associated problem of its concentrations of poorly educated blacks and Hispanics. In comparison, our social problems in the rural and coastal Atlantic regions and the poorly educated immigrants in the greater Toronto and Montreal areas are numerically far less severe. While the educational effects of embedded social problems in those countries will take decades to erase, even with the most enlightened policies, Canada's lesser social problems and their educational counterparts are both more readily addressed.

In Canada the severely disadvantaged underclass probably amounts to only a small proportion of the population; in the other two countries it is significantly higher. I distinguish here between the inevitable relative poverty that exists in all countries and an underclass. The latter is characterized by unemployment, unemployability, and a tradition of family breakdown and abuse from generation to generation. It is as much a caste as the lower end of a spectrum. The United States has an underclass in a way that most Western countries, including Canada, do not yet have. The effects of relative poverty on schooling have long been mitigated in the sense that children from poor families have, in all three countries, been able to progress to the highest levels of postsecondary education. The impact of an underclass is, by definition, more impregnable.

Clearly, the size and challenge of the educational problem depend on its definition. My judgment is that, because our social problems are less severe than those of the United States and England, the issues in our schools, perhaps more serious in relation to our social environment, are less difficult to surmount. Our problems, I am suggesting, although obviously related to the social environment described in chapter 2, are, significantly, a result of bad and inadequate policy poorly executed. Why else should Ontario schools perform so weakly? In chapter 5, the educational problems and non-problems are defined, as I attempt to explain what educational policy can and cannot achieve.

A difference between Canada and the other two countries is that they are both making concerted efforts to address their educational problems, with some signs of success; we are not. Indeed, smug and defensive self-satisfaction still typifies the educational establishment here. Albert Shanker, the best-known unionist in American education of his time, spent his last years demanding tougher standards. His rival, the National Education Association, approves of charter schools, quasi-independent schools within the public system (admittedly only if they are over-regulated). Our educational establishment still fights to prevent any genuine parental influence on school policy and any crack in its monopoly.

Canada's level of academic achievement is similar to that of England and the United States, but below the level in the countries with the most effective systems of education. We do not do well in math, compared with rich countries such as Japan, France, and Switzerland, or even compared with less-affluent Korea, Hong Kong, and Hungary. Ontario performs particularly badly in comparison with other provinces and countries of similar affluence, and its poor showing drags down our national statistics.

The endemic problems of Western, English-speaking societies inevitably affect Canada. At the same time as there are widening gaps in personal values, world-views, and religious beliefs, there is a general decline in young people's commitment to such characteristics of a strong community as truth, industriousness, and belief in the value of the traditional family. Television, popular music, increasing verbal abuse and physical violence in the schools, a growing emphasis on personal freedom and rights, and decreasing deference to authority in the form of teachers, parents, other adults, police, and government make the daily life of the school more difficult.

Canada has no national focus in education. Policy and discussion have traditionally been provincial, metaphorically as well as literally. There is little in the way of national academic competition or standards, equally little in the areas of fitness, art, and music. Sports are a major exception, where competition, both in school-run and even more in parent-run activities, is often excessively strong, dividing children and their parents into addicts and abstainers. Sports are the only sanctioned type of competition for children. Canada and most of the provinces do not have available (readily or even at all) longitudinal statistics of achievement by school through the grades; student attendance; teacher attendance; suspension and expulsion by cause; incidence of violence and crime in and on the way to and from school; enrolment by grade, subject, and level; and destinations after leaving school.

Choice of school and program and the level of financial support vary greatly by province and (in Ontario) school district. Taxes for education are very low in the rich city of Toronto (pre-amalgamation) and much higher in other parts of the country. (It is not clear whether current legislation in Ontario will change this inequity or simply obscure it.) Most parents do not have access to an academically intensive elementary education, despite the fact that it is clear that large numbers would choose that option; the least-advantaged suffer most because it is they who depend on the school system to overcome their poor start in life.

Discrimination by religion is widespread, with only British Columbia and Manitoba being entirely free. Two provinces have actually acted to increase discrimination. Ontario extended Roman Catholic schooling and increased its funding without providing any support for other religious options. The province later banned even out-of-hours involvement in religious education in the public schools. Roman Catholic schooling is not freely available to all Christians. Newfoundland, on the basis of a strong majority in a plebiscite, proposes, with the assistance of the federal government, to eliminate the constitutionally established educational authority of Roman Catholic and Pentecostal minorities despite their strong opposition.

In terms of the overall educational product, we have strengths and weaknesses when compared with England and the United States. One strength is that we have few really low-quality schools, compared with many in the inner-city areas of those countries. On the other hand, we have large numbers of mediocre schools, even in middle-class areas. Probably as a result of Progressive "learn at your own rate" schooling, we do a poor job with the weakest, as well as the strongest, students. Canada's unemployment record for young people is a major disgrace. At the same time, secondary programs to help young people move from school to work are few, widely dispersed, and often unfocused and ineffective.

This country has a comparatively high proportion of students completing reasonably strong high school math and science programs, thus producing a large pool of young people prepared to do adequate, if not excellent, academic work in the university. Our schools are generously supplied with teachers and with good physical conditions, buildings, and instructional materials. The young teachers entering the profession are among the most able in their peer group, which is often not the case in other countries, notably the United States. Overall, we have reached a high level of equal opportunity; our schools and universities are available to all, and a determined young person from any household can reach the highest academic rung with intelligence, hard work, and perseverance.

One significant weakness is that we get poor value for money: we spend more than most other countries, with similar or worse results. An explanation for our financial inefficiency is the unfair distribution of educational moneys among the provinces and between different groups. We have less-challenging social problems to deal with than either England or the United States, yet our results are about the same. Our elementary schools are a particular problem, with generally mediocre and declining standards. We have the poorest systems of accountability and student evaluation in the developed world. There is little spirit of excellence in our schools, and our best academic institutions do not provide the challenge of the best public schools in the United States and England, as evidenced by the comparative performance of the top 1 and 10 per cent of the age cohort. The United States varies more than we do in terms of per-pupil spending, but we are probably second in this respect in the developed world. As a level of spending above a reasonable minimum has little effect on results, it leads less to inequality of opportunity (young people in Nova Scotia have about the same chance of going to university as those in British Columbia or Alberta) than to general inefficiency and waste of scarce funds.

Compared with schools in the other English-speaking democracies, Canadian schools are firmly under the control of the educational establishment – provincial bureaucracies, the bureaucracies of large school districts, teachers' unions, and the faculties of education. It is too often impossible for parents who do not like the standard fare ordained by the establishment – and their numbers are growing – either to change the local school or to choose an alternative, unless they can afford an independent school. The result is that the available alternatives are increasingly selected for a variety of reasons. Roman Catholic schools are chosen, where the establishment permits it, by non-Catholic parents, and French-immersion schools are selected for their more-challenging programs and more-able student body. American school systems are generally smaller and closer to the people than Canadian ones. New Zealand has strong parental control at the level of the school. Australia and England provide more genuine choice.

It is not surprising that those involved in the educational system are upset and defensive over the widespread criticism that they have received in recent years. Much of the criticism has been unfair, particularly that directed at teachers as a whole. They are the system's messenger. Partly as a result of overblown claims by leading educators, schools are blamed for social problems and deviant young people, over which they can have little control.

Two important facts remain. First, the public school system is a part of the problem, reflecting and condoning many societal problems and creating some of its own. The system is not entirely responsible: it does not legislate provincial policy. But most aspects of schooling are under its control or strong influence. Second, the educational establishment consistently opposes any attempt to bring about genuine reform, whether it be accountability for student achievement, clearer and more-demanding curricula, salaries based on more than credentials and time served, increased authority by parents over schools, greater variety in instructional methodology, or more-genuine and less-discriminatory choice of schools.

Theory and Practice
in Canadian Schools:
Research and Teachers

The last chapter provided a sketch of the purposes, programs, and outcomes of Canadian schools. Some readers will conclude that the school is simply a reflection of Canadian society, and there is truth in that view, as chapters 2 and 3 taken together attest. One could equally observe that if Canada is the best country in the world in which to live, it is not the best one in which to be schooled. Certainly, there are many Canadians who are poorly or not at all served by the public system. Irrespective of the overall quality of Canadian schools, which reasonable people may dispute, there are many areas in need of improvement.

Furthermore, there are countries whose educational systems appear to outperform their economic and social systems; Hungary, Korea, and Switzerland are examples. There are also countries whose educational systems underperform their economic and social systems. Canada falls into the second category. Defenders of its schools will point to the fact that the United Nations gives this country a top spot in terms of education. However, the United Nations measures schooling simply in terms of quantity. If quantity is all that matters, then Canada is indeed a world leader. But is quantity enough? The UN categories are defensible internationally; obviously, a country that has all its children in school for ten years is doing better than one that has only half its children in school for that period. But whether Canada is doing a better job than Switzerland, Germany, or Denmark is an issue requiring other criteria than quantity.

This book, however, is not about other countries; it is about educational policy in Canada's provinces and the extent to which it capitalizes on our potential to produce the best possible educational results with the substantial amount of money that Canadians are willing to devote to elementary and secondary schooling.

Two additional factors help an understanding of the status quo and the prospect for reform. Research may assist us in identifying avenues for change, and understanding the teacher's role in education today is essential for determining the kinds of change that will and will not work. There is an abundance of educational research; surely, most people will assume, we can learn something from it. But great care must be taken in interpreting it. There are many questions, including the most important ones, that research cannot answer. It is also fair to say that there is no other field of study with such a high proportion of inadequate and inconsequential work.

Whatever the policies chosen by politicians, school boards, and administrators, however well the relevant research is applied, parents and research agree that the teacher in the classroom remains the single most important factor in a child's school experience. The average parent has a relatively limited choice in schools and is sometimes unaware of the options available. Even the most active parents have little chance of changing school and district policies in the face of the normal establishment intransigence. This chapter looks at what research can and cannot tell us in the context of educational policy and at some characteristics of Canada's teachers. Among other things, it will give parents an idea of what to look for in a good teacher and a good school and some indicators of mediocrity.

THEORY: THE RESEARCH CONTEXT

Research cannot answer the most important question in education: Which knowledge and wisdom are of most worth? Analogies with the delivery of health care are sometimes useful when one looks at education, but there are important differences between the two fields. The most crucial one concerns purposes. There is virtual unanimity about the purposes of health care. They are two: the prolongation of life and the improvement or maintenance of its quality. There are many differences about means (for example, on the priorities of prevention and treatment and with regard to aggressive treatment and palliative care), but the ends are agreed on. There is, as chapter 3 has shown, no such consensus about the purposes – the philosophies or world-views – of education, and none concerning the means. The reader is warned that educational research is usually based on assumptions about purpose that are not always obvious, particularly if they are ones that the reader agrees with. The research summarized in this chapter is no exception and those who are opposed to my judgment concerning the importance of academic achievement as a goal are unlikely to share either my assumptions or my conclusions.

Even some apparently straightforward, practical questions are not easily answered, because the research has not been attempted, because most of it is of poor quality, or because the (often hidden) assumptions are so important that research findings depend entirely on how the questions are asked. For example, concerned parents ask about the effects of split or combined grades: of combining students from, say, grades five and eight or of "streaming" students in different ways, so that the more able ones in a grade are taught together. There are no simple, factual answers to either of those questions.

The greatest single difficulty is that sound research is supposed to examine just the one factor being addressed, such as streaming in middle grades, while keeping everything else the same, on the grounds that if other factors are changed too, it is impossible to tell which one makes the difference. In education, it is quite rare for everything else to remain the same, so the results are usually inconclusive (or worse, incorrectly attributed to a single cause).

In the case of streaming, it makes little sense to separate students by ability and then to instruct them in exactly the same curriculum as if they were in unstreamed classes. So "good" research that keeps everything else the same is meaningless in some circumstances because it is educationally invalid. Most intelligent, honest, and sound educational research (research that might pass muster with scientists) finds that the factor being considered, whatever it is, does not make any difference. Repeating grades and combining grades three and four tend not to make a difference, if everything else is kept the same.

If grades five and eight are combined, there will likely be more individualized and small-group learning; the overall results will therefore probably be negative, not because of the split but because of the changed instruction. Ontario destreamed grade nine by abolishing the old advanced, general, and basic levels. International evidence suggests that streaming or not makes no difference to overall achievement (it may benefit the best or hurt the poorest students). But in Ontario, destreaming was combined with a heavy involvement in unstructured forms of collaborative learning. (The research suggests that collaborative learning can be effective if it is highly structured.) The province did not measure changes in achievement, even among ethnic groups who were supposed to be helped by destreaming, but it did assess the degree to which teachers were resisting collaborative learning methods to see how they could be better implemented! The general perception among teachers and parents has been that the emphasis on academic achievement was reduced, and the effect has likely been harmful in large comprehensive schools with sizeable, pre-existing general and basic programs. There are plans to reintroduce streaming, a sensible decision in the current, anti-intellectual context (but only because of that context).

This does not mean that none of these policies is important. It does mean that they should be examined in the context of what one is trying to do, broadly defined. Middle schools, irrelevant in themselves, are likely to lower academic achievement if they are combined with an expansion of elementary methodology into higher grades, just as destreaming grade nine in Ontario was effectively an attempt to leapfrog primary methods into the secondary school. Split (consecutive) grades are of no account if the same teacher continues to instruct the students in the same way; there is a problem only if the change is accompanied by pressure to move to child-centred methods, as is often the case; indeed, such an emphasis may be the real rationale for the split grade in the first place.

The research on which the following comments and conclusions are based is empirical, most of it scientific (statistical) in nature. The level of statistically significant findings in educational research is much lower than is the case in physics or even in medicine. To say a finding is statistically significant is only to state that it is real – that the finding is probably not a matter of chance. The magnitude of such findings in educational research is generally not great. What is true overall of schools or of teachers is not true of numerous individual cases.

Some academics reject all large-scale educational research for these reasons. But many of those who do so still put inordinate faith in small-scale case studies and in their own research, inferences, and observations. When I asked a colleague who is a strong supporter of child-centred learning if he could point to large-scale research supporting his ideas, he invited me to watch a video of students learning his way or visit a classroom.

The value of large-scale statistical research is not that it should in itself prescribe action for anybody, but that it should be a guide to policy makers, teachers, and parents, always within the limits of an assumed and public world-view. Most parents and employers are interested in the most efficient and effective ways to achieve good standards in the basic skills of numbers, reading, and writing, on which most of the research that I consider relevant to educational reform is based. As I have already pointed out, this assumption is not readily compatible with a Progressive world-view.

Effective Instruction

Most of the large-scale research on instruction has focused on the teaching of skills – mathematics, reading, language, and writing – and it is to those important areas that my comments are confined here. Of this research, most has taken place in the last twenty years. In 1975 there was scarcely a single generalization that could safely be made abouteffectiveinstruction,exceptintheareaofbeginningreading.

A useful summary of the instructional research is one by Patrick O'Neill of Brock University in St Catharines (*Canadian Journal of Education* 8 [1988]). He concludes that effective teachers are well organized, with a constructive series of structured activities; have high, but not unrealistic expectations of pupils; maintain a warm, supportive, firm, and fair classroom climate; minimize disruptions; provide opportunities for success; favour large-group or whole-class instruction; use direct instruction (which means that the teacher teaches the ideas or skills to be learned, as distinct from giving students individually or in small groups the opportunity to find them out for themselves); emphasize individual responsibility from the beginning of the year; regulate and monitor; maintain focus on the task at hand; provide rapid feedback; give relevant, genuine, credible praise; and avoid scorn, rejection, disgust, or disdain.

Those acquainted with the typical Canadian elementary school, notably in the primary grades, will see how strongly the research findings conflict with prevailing practice. Progressive, child-centred ideology provides a very different picture of the ideal classroom. The Progressive teacher believes that children should be given opportunities to learn, rather than have instruction imposed on them; that high self-concept is a prerequisite to learning; that children require constant praise irrespective of the quality of their work; that they best learn to read naturally, just as they learn to walk, without focused, sequential teaching; that they should be encouraged to work cooperatively in small groups; that talk and movement should not be greatly curtailed; that they should read, write, and spell freely with little guidance or correction; and that their work should not be formally tested, marked, or criticized. Those beliefs are so rigidly followed in the primary grades that parents often find it difficult to locate an alternative, even in independent schools, whose staffs have typically come through the same faculties of education as public school teachers.

A document published by the Toronto Board of Education in 1990 entitled *Some Basic Principles of Language Learning* concludes (partially quoting Frank Whitehead), "'the main business of the English teacher is not instruction in any direct sense, nor even teaching in the sense which may be applicable in some other subjects. It is the provision of abundant opportunity for the child to use English under the conditions that will most conduce to improvement.' The process of language is itself the process of learning." An extensive bibliography supplied with the document contains no reference to any of the major empirical studies. For example, there is no mention of the second edition (1983) of Jeanne Chall's established classic on reading, an area where phonics has been shown for many years to be the single best approach.

Because it is structured, sequential, and teacher-centred, phonics is disapproved of by Progressive educators and is only used in most primary grades when the child-centred approach has demonstrably failed, sometimes not until grade three or four, when the child is assigned to special education as being "learning disabled." Some educational psychologists refer to this syndrome, with intended irony, as being "instructionally disabled," because the problem is really one of the quality (or lack) of instruction. If a teacher believes unquestioningly that so-called balanced, child-centred instruction is the only way to teach, it follows that there is a problem with children who do not learn, of whom there are many. One has to be wary of the word "balance." The same term is used in California, where phonics is being reintroduced, and in Ontario, where lip-service is given to phonics "on a need basis" and where the Whole Language approach still prevails. In California the policy intent is that phonics should be the basic starter for all children and that alternatives will be used with those who fail to learn. All children would have, in addition to phonics instruction, plentiful reading on their own once the code is mastered, and would also be read to. In Canada, balanced instruction in the Progressive classroom means using phonics in one of two ways: either on a need basis where children fail to learn naturally or incidentally with all children as they explore reading by themselves or in groups. Neither of these two approaches is supported by the research.

Perhaps the most comprehensive assessment of research in reading is found in a book by Marilyn Jager Adams (1991), who shows clearly why phonics is the single best starting point for structured teaching to all young children (which is not to deny that other approaches have a role). In a paper detailing the consistency of contemporary knowledge on reading instruction, Keith Stanovich, a professor at OISE, writes, "An adherence to a subjective, personalized view of knowledge is what continually leads to educational fads [he is referring here to language process and Whole Language] that could easily be avoided by grounding teachers and other practitioners in the importance of scientific thinking for solving educational problems." He should have written "instructional" problems, which science can address, not "educational" ones, which it usually cannot (*The Reading Teacher* 47 [1993]).

The Follow Through Project (see Carl Bereiter's and M. Kurland's article in *Interchange* 12 [1981]), one of the largest research projects ever undertaken, evaluated a number of experimental approaches to helping the disadvantaged in the primary years and found that direct instruction was the best. The child-centred models were among the poorest performers. Another large-scale American project, the Instructional Dimensions Study (William Cooley and Gaeia Leinhardt, *Educational Evaluation and Policy Analysis* [1980]) examined four hundred classrooms in five states. The classrooms, unlike those in the Follow Through study, were measured according to individual characteristics (as distinct from classifying them under one major heading). Against the fashion of the times, which favoured strong individualization, the study's "most pronounced" finding was that the best thing for students with underdeveloped math and reading skills was more direct instruction.

The American National Institute for Child Health and Development has made available on the Internet a summary paper entitled *30 Years of NICHD Research: What We Now Know about How Children Learn to Read* (http://www.ksagroup.com/thecenter/). The paper emphasizes both the fundamental importance of phonics and the prescription to balance but not mix instruction. Mixing (or integration) is, unfortunately, a founding belief of Progressives, who like to combine language with science, physics with math, vocational education with general instruction, fifth grade with eighth grade, the disabled with the brilliant, and advanced students with beginners.

What holds in the primary grades applies equally at the secondary level, where there are sequential skills. George Hillocks (*American Journal of Education* 93 [1984]) looked at all the major empirical studies on the teaching of written expression and found that the most successful approach was again direct instruction. The required skills should be sequentially taught, practised, and integrated into writing. The language-process approach, still most widely used in Canada and advocated by Kenneth Goodman, Donald Graves, and Frank Smith among others, was determined to be much inferior.

Very little research has been conducted in this field in Canada, perhaps because the Progressive ideology was well entrenched before the major breakthroughs in research were made in the late 1970s and early 1980s. Brian Usher and Mary Ann Evans of the research department of the Etobicoke Board of Education (in Metropolitan Toronto) did carry out an excellent and rare small study of traditional and newly introduced Progressive approaches to primary instruction as long ago as 1976, at a time when both researchers and educational leaders in Canada were for the most part sure that the Progressive ideas would prove superior in all ways, including empirical research. (Today they disapprove of empirical, scientific research.) Demographically equivalent classrooms were matched, and the declared objectives of both programs were evaluated in each set of ten classrooms. The researchers also observed the classrooms and measured specific factors so that they could analyse different characteristics across all the classrooms, as well as the comparative performance of the two sets. They found no difference in the specific outcomes nominated by the Progressive teachers (which one may assume were largely the result of family and maturation), but discovered the "traditional" classrooms to be superior in mathematical concepts and reading. The characteristics of the successful classrooms in both groups were word analysis activities, printing activities, minimal exploratory-repetitive play activities, and low levels of fantasy or role playing activities (*The Early Childhood Study Project Evaluation*).

The research was not made available to the public by the board at that time, and only emerged when Brian Usher left its employ many years later and a few reform school trustees, led by Ruth Weir, demanded to see the study. Administrators, no doubt in good faith, at first denied the existence of the research; it had been well and truly buried by their predecessors. The board then hired a retired director of education to write a report on the instructional controversy that erupted. His report incorrectly stated that the board was compelled by provincial policy to adopt Progressive methodology, quoting an Ontario advisory document of 1975 that at no time had policy status. With the suppression of the research, the Etobicoke system continued its implementation of the Progressive approach, and only in the last few years have there been a few cracks in the ironclad monopoly of child-centred instruction in beginning reading. Today elementary schools in the Etobicoke system are daring to "experiment" with phonics, thanks to the dedication and determination of Ruth Weir. She was once a renegade teacher with the Toronto board, where she successfully taught students using direct instructional methods despite intense pressure.

Although less well established, there is good research to suggest that using well-constructed homogeneous groups is the most successful way to teach many middle-grade classes. Research has generally suggested simply that whole-class instruction is superior to both individualized and small-group teaching. In Canada individualized instruction in reading is widely used in the early and middle grades, children frequently choosing most of their own reading material. Robert Dreeben and Rebecca Barr (*American Journal of Education* 97 [1988]), in a piece of meticulous research, found homogeneous groups to be superior provided that children are placed in groups based on objective achievement and aptitude (not on teachers' observations of effort); the work is carefully structured and sequenced; grouping is flexible; and there is a genuine need for grouping, evidenced by very different levels of performance within the classroom. Most research on grouping does not measure those important criteria. It is not the grouping that matters so much as the instruction that follows: taking children on from where they are in a challenging manner. One may infer that the central problems with individualization and small groups is the absence of instruction; even with only twenty-five students, an efficient teacher cannot manage two minutes of instruction per hour. Instruction to small, mixed-ability groups is likely to be ineffective, as well as brief, in sequential courses. Teaching the entire class gives many instructional minutes; teaching a few large homogeneous groups provides fewer minutes per group but more focused instruction.

The individualized nature of primary education in Canada leads to large variations in achievement level by the middle grades because achievement depends even more on home background and individual motivation, which, as I showed in chapter 2, are also increasingly differentiated. The more the school avoids sound, sequential instruction in the basic skills, the more that knowledgeable parents compensate by teaching their children at home or by purchasing additional instruction outside regular school hours. This outcome simply widens the gap between educational haves and have-nots.

The reader unacquainted with contemporary schools may well wonder how it is that provincial departments of education and school districts promote Progressive methods in light of the one-sided nature of large-scale research. One reason, already mentioned, is the claim that large-scale research is irrelevant because it does not measure what the self-styled "experts" (sometimes playing more of the role of cult leader) are interested in. Test results are less important to Progressives than observations by teachers in the classroom. It is true that children in Progressive classrooms are often happily engaged in what they are doing; unfortunately, what they are doing is rarely instructionally focused. There is little confrontation between teacher and student in the Progressive primary classroom, precisely because little is demanded of the student. As young children become ignorant adolescents, confrontation is more difficult to avoid, and they are sometimes frustrated because they cannot learn. Even in high school classrooms, however, the level of confrontation can be lowered if little is demanded, students collaborate, and the teacher is tolerant.

Later in this chapter, evidence of what teachers say they particularly look for when assessing children's learning will be provided; it is not primarily skill improvement. Progressives argue that skills are less important than enjoyment and the love of learning. Satisfaction gained from reading is without question extremely important, and it is an infrequently assessed outcome. However, enjoyment of reading in the long run depends on being able to read easily; there is no reason why the teaching of basic reading skills cannot be combined (but not mixed) with the enjoyment of challenging and interesting books. One of the reasons that Progressive classrooms are not very successful in promoting skills is that they leave reading matter mainly to individual choice, and children often do not know what they will enjoy in advance and do not realize that more-challenging books eventually provide greater satisfaction. The fact, repeated by Progressive academics, that some children choose to challenge themselves in no way proves that most will. No one doubts that Progressive methods often work perfectly well with highly motivated self-starters. Academic supporters of Progressive ideas base their ideology on theories of how children learn. If children learn from experience, by doing and by natural practice arising from spontaneous interest, then forced learning is of little avail.

In the past, advocates of direct instruction defended their arguments pragmatically, demonstrating that the approach works in practice, in the same way that doctors knew for years that acetylsalicylic acid reduced pain, without knowing how. Recent research on early reading suggests that Progressive learning theories are simply wrong. For example, it has long been asserted by Progressives that good readers predict what is happening in the text; they do not read word by word. Those good readers also guess the meaning of words that they do not know, Progressives claim. These hypotheses (repeated as facts) led to the idea that precise verbal knowledge and spelling are irrelevant to good reading. I knew such was not the case with me; I rarely if ever predict sentences, paragraphs, or an entire book (even a mystery story). I rarely guess words that I do not know, and they delay my reading either for a moment or until I have checked the dictionary.

Research summarized by Frank Vellutino (*Journal of Educational Psychology* 83 [1991]) suggests that the Progressive theories are wrong. Guessing is a characteristic of bad, not good, readers. Good, highly skilled readers scan every word and stop or hesitate when they encounter an unfamiliar one, which they typically investigate and add to their vocabulary. Thus it is possible that the poor reading skills found among large numbers of Canada's young people stem in part from their failure to learn to read carefully and accurately. They scan quickly, omitting or guessing at unfamiliar words or ideas, and therefore have poor levels of comprehension. Their lack of word knowledge also prevents them from recognizing a new word (which, if pronounced, they might know) simply because they cannot tackle phonetic structure. There are children, mainly girls, who do learn well without a strong phonetic system, but knowledge of phonics hurts no one and provides word-attack skills. I have noticed that young children frequently guess unknown words from the context of a story, as they have been instructed to do, sometimes using a word that fits reasonably but that misses the connotative meaning.

Not being an educational psychologist, I am more interested in what works than in exactly why it does. Progressive methodologies do not work well overall, although they are successful with individuals and a few gifted teachers. I suspect the reasons are complex, one of the most important being that the entire Progressive philosophy is ill-conceived, based as it is on a false and harmful understanding of human nature. It glorifies self at a time when children should be combining awareness of others with respect for themselves and a good dose of humility. It assumes that they will naturally prefer good quality over bad if left to choose. Relativist world-views have problems in defining the difference between good and bad, since it usually becomes a matter for individual determination. There is then a reluctance on the part of truly Progressive teachers to impose their opinions on their students; middle-class children are more likely to get messages of good and bad quality in books provided by their parents.

It is wrong to jump to the conclusion that faulty instructional methodology is all that ails Canadian schools. It is worse to take the next step and assume that the cure is to demand that teachers base their instruction on over-interpretation of the proven research; this is the implicit message of many cries for educational reform. It is also the direction that was often adopted in the United States in the 1980s following the publication of the reform document *A Nation at Risk*, a document that spoke eloquently of unilateral educational disarmament. Readers may be surprised by that rejection of the regulated adoption of direct instruction, particularly if they have heard the educational establishment's version of what reformers want in education:

all schools regimented like those (allegedly) of the 1930s, desks always in rows, rote memorization, and so on.

A few years ago, TV Ontario staff members asked me to suggest some ideas for programs on schools. I proposed that they film good examples of direct instruction and child-centred learning. I suggested a rare direct-instruction classroom in Mississauga; child-centred classrooms were abundant. The TVO team visited the classroom and talked to the teacher, but they regretfully rejected the proposal because the teacher did not fit the Dickensian stereotype that they held: the classroom was not all in rows, the teacher did not lecture and shout all the time, and the children sometimes worked in groups. There was a friendly, supportive atmosphere.

There are good reasons why even well-established research findings should not simply be imposed on the public school as a panacea. First, research is based on averages. There are highly effective teachers who use methods different from the effective ones outlined above. There are also ineffective teachers who employ the methods supported by research. It is possible to abuse any method of instruction. For example, simply putting children in homogeneous groups and then teaching them all the same things at the same rate is the worst of both worlds – instruction low in both quantity and quality.

Second, compelling highly educated professionals to change their methods contrary to their deeply held philosophical convictions is most unlikely to bring about improvement. Some thoughtful, professional teachers are not happy about being forced to use methods of which they generally approve; consider the degree of their antagonism if they are compelled to employ methods of which they disapprove. Going through the motions of good teaching practice is not enough; involvement in and commitment to improved teaching, learning, and testing is required.

A third reason is that, if one takes into account my conclusion that educational leaders are more deeply committed to the Progressive idea than are many teachers (after all, they have been promoted on the basis of their commitment to the concept), one must wonder who would enforce the changes, and with how much integrity. Consider it from their point of view; would it not be "professional" to sabotage what they regard as bad, politically inspired education?

Fourth, although the public is generally unsympathetic to Progressive ideas, there are many parents and vocal others who support it. I have talked to hundred of parents over the last fifteen years while I have been involved in educational reform, and my guess would be that the parents generally most sympathetic to the Progressive idea are ones with primary-age children; some of them do not believe in

imposing external standards of behaviour on their children at home
and do not want teachers to impose universal standards at school.
These parents are a minority, even among the middle class, where
they are mainly found, but they exist and have strong voice. They
are often those most involved with the school and with home and
school organizations, where they are welcomed, praised, and encouraged by teachers and principals who understandably prefer supporters to critics.

A fifth consideration is that instructional methodology is not the
most important factor in predicting success in school. The most
important elements lie in the home. Also, there are other factors at
the school level besides instructional methodology. No one should
imagine that schools serving disadvantaged communities with poor
levels of skills will reach the standard of middle-class schools once
improved instruction is introduced (partly because most middle-
class parents soon demand reform too when they recognize the
advantages of direct skill development).

Sixth, there are other, deep-rooted problems that affect students'
learning: the failure to evaluate outcomes, the unfair and wasteful
allocation of money among provinces, districts, and schools, and in
many schools, particularly for the disadvantaged, a low emphasis on
academic achievement as a goal. A seventh reason why research
findings cannot simply be imposed is that instructional reform has
been the major focus of reform in Schools in the United States for
nearly fifteen years; and while there is some, but mixed, evidence of
improvement among the most disadvantaged, the changes have generally been seen as failures. The American school system, like the
English one, remains a model that we would do well not to use as
our general standard. That conclusion does not mean that neither
system has any exemplary practices or policies. There has been a
tendency for Canadian policy to ape the American approach. Progressivism in Canada during the late 1960s and 1970s was a more
virulent strain of the outbreak in the United States ten or so years
earlier. The Technocratic reforms attempted more recently in New
Brunswick are similar to American ones introduced during the
Reagan era. We make enough mistakes of our own without import-
ing others' for no good reason. Policy should be based first on what
we want to accomplish, a question that research cannot answer.

Those are mainly practical reasons why research cannot be seen as
a panacea for the Canadian school system. Most fundamentally, I
have already emphasized the importance of professionalism in
teachers. Most young teachers are intelligent and highly, if inappro-
priately, educated. They should be encouraged to take professional

responsibility for their teaching, to be accountable, and not be regulated into any particular methodology. Some will be excellent teachers while using unorthodox approaches. Canada needs excellent teachers, orthodox or unorthodox. There are few things that will drive good teachers out of teaching faster than standardization.

Effective Schools

The effective school, in the context of educational research, is defined as one that gives significant "added value" to students in the area of academics, mainly the basic skills and, in a few studies, other outcomes such as behaviour and citizenship. It is based on measurable outcomes that may reasonably be determined to result from differences among schools, as distinct from intellectual and cultural characteristics that come from outside the school, notably from the home background. That the influence is from the school rather than the home is determined statistically in various ways, for example, by comparing results from matched groups of students (e.g. on the basis of students' measured intelligence or aptitude and the income, employment, and educational level of parents).

Some readers may not like that definition. They may, for instance, decide that academics and behaviour are not what schools should be about; in that case, the section that follows will not be of interest. Many Progressives discount effective school research, just as they downplay the research on effective instruction. If education is primarily about natural growth, pleasant experiences, raising self-concept, moral autonomy and individual choices, and stimulating creativity and critical thinking, then a set of desired outcomes determined in advance by adults may well be considered irrelevant. I have many times been told by teachers and other educators that, if effective schools research is about what tests measure – it is to a significant degree – they are not interested. Most parents do not agree with them, but some do.

It is easy to be dismissive about the Progressive argument because the people who make it often become interested in achievement when their own children are concerned, perhaps half apologizing that it is what universities want. A more subtle and confusing point is that many parents may reasonably be just as interested in the school's level of academic *achievement* as in its level of academic *effectiveness*.

They are not the same thing. Schools with a middle- and upper-class clientele nearly always have higher levels of achievement than those with children who come from less-affluent families; not because the schools are better, but because the children have qualities (the nature of which is debated) better suited to academic instruction. An often hidden assumption of most effective school research is that parents ought to be interested in the "added value" of the effective school; the argument is that they should want a school that *adds* to their own contribution rather than one that *reflects* it. Against that view, it can be argued that a high achievement level in the school is more important than added value, because the former implies a good climate for one's own child (provided that he or she is capable of achieving the high level expected in the school), whereas the effective school may excel with children very different from one's own. No school is effective for everyone. For example, an ambitious, upper-middle-class parent might not unreasonably say, "For heaven's sake, I don't want a school that compensates for other parents' negligence and incompetence, I want one that will further challenge my son in the way we challenge him at home."

This subtle, but important distinction, entirely lost in the media's hunt for white and black hats, prejudice and favouritism, can be illustrated in practical terms. Jim and Maria Burgess are trying to choose the best secondary school for their daughter, now finishing grade eight. Fortunately, they live in North York, so a great deal of information about the schools and their achievement is available. The neighbourhood school, Don Valley Collegiate Institute, is known as an academic institution serving students from middle- and upper-class backgrounds. It seems a bit dull to them, however, and the program appears unexciting considering the able student body. Over 80 per cent of graduates go directly to university, but the school does not participate in academic, musical, or dramatic competitions. Football is the high-profile sport, and girls vie to become cheerleaders. This school is a high-achieving school, but not a highly effective one. It coasts on its advantaged clientele. The principal is good at public relations and avoids trouble and confrontations. He is an excellent mediator, and the school rarely gets bad press in the local newspaper.

A nearby school (both are fictitious), Patmore Heights Secondary School, has a vigorous principal who is promoting, with apparent success, the kind of things that Jim and Maria want in educational policy: a strong and enforced code of behaviour and dress, excellent academics based on consistent effort and regular homework, a part-time work/part-time school program, and broad participation by both sexes in competitive activities in the arts and in sports. The student body is much more mixed, in terms of both ethnicity and social class. Thirty per cent of graduates continue to university, and the ninth grade CAT scores in the basic skills are above average but below those of Don Valley. This school is more effective, but lower achieving than the other. It is particularly effective with disadvantaged students (of which Don Valley has very few) and with average students who develop high aspirations. The principal shows particular commitment to the least advantaged, and friends of Jim and Maria say that she takes little interest or pride in the success of students who win university scholarships, unless they come from minority or disadvantaged groups.

The choice is a difficult one to make, and giving all the information to the student and allowing her to choose may be the best way to go. Jim and Maria like the richer, more vigorous climate of Patmore Heights, but they fear that it will also be easier to get into the wrong set in that school. Don Valley seems a safer, if uninspiring bet. University entrance, which they want for their daughter, is assumed there, not an exception.

I recommend a school that is both effective and high achieving, but the two do not necessarily or even normally go together. It is sometimes difficult to find even a high-achieving school, and accurate identification of an effective school is well-nigh impossible in most of Canada. In England and in some American states, where schools with similar demographic characteristics are grouped together for the publication of annual test or examination results, the interested parent can see which are the high achieving – they have the best academic outcomes – and which are the more effective – they are the ones that get the best results among a group of schools with similar kinds of students.

Sensible parents will still have different preferences, depending on the nature of their child, and will give varying levels of choice to the student involved, according to age, maturity, and their own personal philosophy of upbringing. Some may aim simply for the highest-achieving school, hoping to give their child the strongest challenge and environment. Others may choose a school where their child will feel at home with other young people like him or her, but which is or appears to be above the average for its group in effectiveness. Still others may look for social or ethnic diversity.

Genuine, knowledgeable choice is usually impossible, however, and the interested parent has to decide more on impressions and guesses – of the behaviour and character of the student body and of the apparent success of its graduates. He or she should always visit possible schools while they are in operation, including before and after classes and at lunch time. Careful observation of students in different contexts may provide as much information as an interview with the principal or teachers.

I visited one prominent private school, where several teachers assured me that they were actually more Progressive than their classrooms appeared; they had to be careful not to move ahead of the parents. Knowing that I was an academic from OISE, they assumed that I must be an enthusiastic Progressive and critic of any traditional practice! I was saddened; these teachers appeared to be moving in the wrong direction. The school was undoubtedly high in achievement, but its effectiveness was more doubtful. Upper Canada College, Toronto's most famous independent school, has a fine reputation, one that, based mostly on informal and unpublished evidence, is well earned. There is no doubt that it is high achieving, but it is also effective. Unfortunately, reputation is generally a better guide to achievement than to effectiveness. If one does not have an exceptionally able child and plenty of money, the best advice is to look for the qualities of effective schools shown in the research.

The effective-school research had its origin in the late 1960s when James Coleman led a group of American researchers in a large-scale project intended to find the educational causes of inequality among groups, particularly between blacks and whites (*Equality of Educational Opportunity* [U.S. Department of Health, Education, and Welfare, 1966]. The research was largely ineffective in that the endeavour and its techniques and findings were extraordinarily controversial. It did, however, develop several conclusions that have stood the test of time: school effects are far less influential than are those of the home; differences in effectiveness between schools (in the developed West) are not explained by their material qualities or by material differences in their teachers (qualifications and experience); the black minority did not differ from the white majority in its level of self-concept, but it did diverge in having less sense of control over its destiny (understandable in a population at that time still heavily concentrated in the inner cities and the rural south).

The next two decades saw a flurry of research, mainly in the United States and England, but also in Canada, Australia, New Zealand, the Netherlands, and the Bahamas, which was mainly designed to disprove Coleman's findings that school factors were irrelevant, that school effectiveness did not exist as an important factor, and that schools were essentially mirrors of the students they enrolled. The research was substantially successful and reached similar conclusions in different Western countries. My own early doctoral research in Canada had tentative and small-scale findings consistent with the later, more substantial research (*Interchange* 2 [1971]).

The most consistent finding of that body of research is that schools with strong academic climates are the most academically effective. The academic climate is not an organizational or structural element,

but a matter of attitude and will (Coleman had originally concentrated on material factors). In brief, schools where teachers and students place a high emphasis on academic success, where there are
strong demands and clear standards, are the most effective.

A particularly famous study is one by Michael Rutter and colleagues (1979), carried out in London, England. They found that secondary schools with positive climates were not only more successful
on that country's external examinations but had better attendance
and more positive patterns of student behaviour. Instruction in the
successful schools was focussed on task. One finding was of considerable interest, given the enormous influence of home background
on achievement. The most effective school found by Rutter and his
colleagues achieved better academic results with students from the
lowest social class than the least effective did with the highest (the
bands were defined by the same criteria for all schools). That finding,
although interesting, is often over-interpreted; the schools surveyed
all had fairly similar or homogeneous groups of students. The
researchers did not find that the most effective schools were more
successful with low-class children than the worst were with high-
class ones (which would have been an astounding finding) because
neither group was represented in the small sample of lower-middle-
and working-class schools.

The most recent major project is the Louisiana School Effectiveness
Study, which, by using large numbers of schools and exemplary
methodology, has solidified and elaborated its central findings (Teddlie and Stringfield 1993). Two of its many interesting findings are
that external projects do not make schools more effective (the decision to change comes from the school) and that effective middle-class
schools involve parents, but effective low-social-status ones do not.

The central conclusions of the research are that the effective school
has the following characteristics (often referred to as the effective-
school correlates to emphasize that the research is based on relationships, as distinct from identified cause and effect): a strong sense of
educational commitment and purpose, high expectations for both
academic work and behaviour, regular assessment of achievement,
an orderly and pleasant school climate, strong instructional emphasis, and consistent efforts by home and school. The factors do not all
have equally strong empirical support. The two with the most universally consistent support are the academic climate of high expectations and the strong instructional emphasis, that is, the effective
instructional activities described earlier.

Many educators believe that the appropriate strong home-school
relationship can be brought about by means of public relations, that
is, by persuading parents to come to the school and listen to tales

about all the good things the school is doing. This is an appealing solution to a benign, bureaucratic monopoly; it is also fallacious. There is no evidence that good public relations helps children learn, although they do make life easier for administrators and teachers. In a school, like charm in an attractive person, good public relations may conceal a lack of substance.

Since the early 1980s, three lines of research have emerged from the effective-schools movement, none with as clearly established findings as the correlates listed above. First, the claim by some advocates, notably Larry Lezotte, that effective-schools ideas can overcome the impact of children's social background, has led to school improvement efforts based on ideas intended to help low socioeconomic schools reach normal levels of achievement. Second, there have been generalized school improvement efforts that have often departed in substance from the core ideas of the research. Third, there have been further important advances in the area of home-school relationships and community.

The first two lines of research can be reasonably and briefly dealt with together. Despite the enormous efforts in the United States to base school reform on effective-school research, the overall success has been minimal. Although intensive, small-scale projects have shown improvements, large-scale efforts have not been objectively evaluated, have not used appropriate controls, or have proved unsuccessful.

I was the external evaluator of a statewide school improvement project carried out between 1986 and 1989 in New Jersey. Seventeen schools volunteered to attempt to improve themselves on the basis of the effective-school correlates. They were given additional state funding in return for agreeing to be externally evaluated. My 1990 report to the state department of education documented the enormous difficulties and complications of such an attempt. For each school in the project I selected twelve comparison schools with similar social status, demographics, size, and achievement scores. The evaluation was complicated by changes of principal just before and during the project, vigorous and apparently successful efforts to become more effective made by two of the schools before the project began, a lack of genuine commitment on the part of several schools that had been "volunteered" by the principal or senior administrators, a change of achievement test in some schools during the project (making comparisons over time less helpful), and the decision of two (unsuccessful) schools to use-child centred, rather than effective-instruction reforms. Of the seventeen schools, I could conclude that only one had definitely improved as a direct consequence of the project. Several showed improvement, but there were other factors besides the project that may have partially or completely explained that outcome.

One important finding did emerge from an analysis of the project and comparison schools at the three grade levels tested (grades three, six, and nine). Quite crude indicators of social background, together with proportions of students of minority status (in New Jersey, essentially blacks and Hispanics), predicted school performance extremely well. The larger the school and the higher the grades served, the better these background characteristics predicted the level of achievement. When past performance was included, the three factors of ethnic composition, poverty, and previous achievement together explained over 80 per cent of the difference in achievement among schools at grade nine, but considerably less at grade three. Clearly, there was little room for interschool changes in effectiveness at the high school level. The point is that home background factors are so important that, by high school, differing levels of educational practice are unlikely to have a major effect, given existing school structures. The high schools in the sample were large (between 1000 and 2500 students.) There is more flexibility in small elementary schools, and the improved schools were at that level.

Before leaving the mainstream effective-schools research, I should mention one interesting factor that became evident during my New Jersey evaluation. The state was, during those three years, implementing a plan whereby all students would have to pass a high school competency exam in order to graduate. Most students (by 1989) passed the exam when it was first taken in grade nine. Those who failed took it annually until they passed. The pass rate increased phenomenally after the state made it mandatory; most of the schools improved their scores substantially. At first sight, this statement appears inconsistent with the previous conclusion that large high schools are insensitive to improvement efforts, but there is no necessary contradiction.

Consider the following three statements. First, there is very clear international research showing that the schools which are most effective in giving their students (particularly those most disadvantaged) added value in achievement and behaviour generally have a set of characteristics known as the school-effectiveness factors or correlates listen earlier. Second, both "top-down" (managed by administrators) and "bottom-up" (managed by teams of teachers) efforts to implement a given set of factors usually fail, sometimes because the factors are not implemented and sometimes because, when they are, they do not carry with them the hoped for gains in achievement. The third observation to be made is that, paradoxically, even large high schools respond to external "high stakes" tests in which students must reach certain standards or fail to graduate.

Successful change requiring sustained effort appears most likely when there is general, spontaneous, and genuine support for it from both students and teachers (together with, very likely, parents). The issues are high for all three parties in high-stakes tests. If that explanation is correct, then the claims that Coleman and Hoffer put forward as a result of their more recent, brilliant, large-scale research study (1987) make real sense. The importance of external tests and standards can be crucial if the stakes (e.g. graduating or failing to graduate from high school) are high enough. There is a negative side effect of high-stakes tests, however; they may become so dominant that other goals are given low priority or neglected. If teachers place most of their attention on getting everyone over the hurdle of a graduation test, then there is little time left to push for excellence in the minority. My sense is that in the late 1980s in New Jersey, there was, throughout the state, immense pressure from teachers, students, and parents to achieve a pass on the High School Proficiency Tests in grade nine. Bright students, who would have passed anyway, were little affected, but the tests were the major focus for the marginal students.

Coleman and Hoffer conclude from their final study of American high schools that they can be divided roughly into three categories. The most effective in terms of academic and civic behaviour owe their success to shared commitment by parents, teachers, and students who live in community. The second most effective have shared values but no real sense of community besides a common vision of schooling. The least-effective schools are the non-communities: large high schools serving varied purposes without any sense of common direction, purposes, or values. The New Jersey high schools in my sample fall into the last category; only a powerful external threat to teachers, parents, and above all, the students themselves – failure to graduate from high school – apparently galvanized the students into some meaningful activity.

In Canadian terms, the first, most successful category of school – "functional communities," according to Coleman and Hoffer – is represented by small, independent, religious schools serving a strong local community and by the few remaining rural schools that also serve genuine communities. The second, intermediary category, that of "value communities," is represented by public and independent schools of choice – elite schools, French-immersion schools, public academies, and schools of the arts. The final category represents Canada's typical urban, suburban, and comprehensive school, with a host of conflicting visions, cultures, and purposes, and with teachers and parents divided from each other as well as among themselves.

It seems likely that the idea of the functional community can be applied to elementary schools on the Pacific Rim. In Japan, Taiwan, South Korea, Singapore, and Hong Kong, parents and teachers have a single vision of education and it comprises both civilized, restrained behaviour and hard work. Society and elders hold precedence over youth, free choice, and individualism (less so as these countries are Westernized). All parties also agree on and are able to enforce the use of effective instructional and school practices.

Pandora Johnson, in a doctoral dissertation completed at OISE in 1988, examined Bahamian high schools; she adds a caution to the interpretation of Coleman's thesis. Generally, she found, as one would expect, that the most effective schools were to be found among the small public schools on Family Islands and the independent schools, none of the large public schools on the two major islands being above average in effectiveness. (Her purpose was not to compare achievement levels but effectiveness, defined as the added value of the school beyond home background characteristics.) But she also found some anomalies: several small community schools were among the least effective. Her explanation is that the rich, modern fishing communities (rich from fishing and drug running) may have shared values, but if so, education is not one of them. It is not enough to have a community school; the community's values must include the results one is looking for if the school is to be effective. Therefore, as obvious examples, one should not expect a school of the arts to excel in physics, or a fundamentalist school to shine in biology or contemporary literature.

In sum, schools are most effective when they have practices consistent with the goals to which they aspire, strong, clear standards for which they are externally accountable, and a sense of community. Chester Finn, who is extremely knowledgeable about educational reform in the United States over the last two decades, puts it this way: "Successful schools are small, have a clear mission and are places where those concerned want to be."

Parents and the School

The Coleman research leads us back to where education should begin, with parents. It has long been known that the home background, broadly defined, is the most important factor predicting young people's achievement. This does not mean that schools do not vary or that parents can easily manage without them. What it does mean is that schools in countries such as ours are all fairly well equipped and have educated teachers; some are excellent, some not so good, and a few incompetent. Different children get different things out of similar conditions; similar children get much the same from different schools. Those are generalizations; they do not hold either for extremes or for numerous individual cases.

Consider this analogy. A random sample of adults agree to improve their fitness by taking physically demanding exercise for thirty minutes three times a week. One randomly assigned group jogs, another runs, a third works out on equipment at home, and a fourth group goes to an exercise class. A slight difference may be found among the effects of different types of activity, but the greatest difference would be attributable to the various individuals. Some skip or cut sessions short or drop out; others put in additional sessions. Some eat more fats and drink more sugary beverages than others; some plan a complementary diet. Some were healthy to start, and others begin as couch potatoes, and so on. The magnitude of the effect of individual differences in comparison with the effect of the different activities does not mean either that activity is not really helpful or that there are no important differences among various activities (although there may not be). It is just that the previously and continuously occurring differences among the people involved overwhelm the other factors.

Schools and researchers have often attempted to set parents aside, as a kind of unfortunate given. They have been told not to teach their children to read before they come to school and not to help them with their work. Within the culture of the school, parents who are "too" pushy, "too" aggressive, and "too" demanding of their children are feared and disparaged. Teachers would do well to divert their attention to the children whose parents place insufficient academic demands on them. But those parents do not create waves. When parents are brought into the picture, it is too often to gain their support for the school through public relations exercises. If parents or parent committees try to become involved with the educational substance of the school, they are quickly told that this area is a professional reserve.

In educational research, parents have been excluded as background factors. When they are included, it is in terms of "parental involvement," usually with regard to the school's public relations, or as potential helpers for the teacher, at home or at school. Recently, however, the prevailing wisdom of the parent as potential nuisance (requiring some form of harness) has been increasingly questioned. The idea of community in the school has, since Coleman and Hoffer, become a matter for discussion and research.

Over the last three decades, community in Canada has been systematically destroyed, usually unintentionally. School districts in every province have become larger, to the point that very few still represent anything remotely like a community. Schools have also increased in size, with the establishment pitted against parents when small schools are closed on the grounds of supposed inefficiency. The obvious solution is never considered by large bureaucracies, because it would break their rules and regulations. If a small rural community wanted to keep the school that was crucial to its vitality, it could be given the choice of opting out of the school district (and its rules and regulations) and running its school independently at the average per-capita expense of the other schools in the district. Increasing the size of schools is not the only (and often not a good) answer to inefficiency. Another possibility would be to cut costs, by reducing services from outside the school, by increasing the pupil-teacher ratio, or by paying teachers less. Special treatment like this is anathema to both school boards and unions.

In rural areas, added choice, such as French-immersion and French-language schools, destroys the old community school, which was, in some cases in Ontario and New Brunswick, a bilingual one, a type now extinct. Choices may also introduce a new form of value community school where there was none before, when parents holding similar ideologies choose French immersion. The recent decision in Newfoundland, which will destroy the strong Pentecostal and Roman Catholic communities in small settlements, continues the tradition of defining community as the enemy of schooling. And it is the enemy if schooling is defined in terms of rules, regulations, centralization, and union rights rather than in educational terms. The small geographical community that may initially become the focus of a combined school is soon destroyed by the march of progress, as ever larger and allegedly more efficient central schools are constructed ("central" being defined in terms of bus routes).

Jiemei Li, in a doctoral dissertation completed at OISE in 1996, looked at the issue of community in education. Li argued that to the extent possible, society should be taking advantage of community, rather than destroying it. Parents in a community can be a very powerful force to maintain standards – the standards that they want. Put their children in a comprehensive cafeteria-style school, and they will merely act as individuals trying to get the best for their child from a limited menu. Students, freer to make their own choices within such a school and influenced more by peers than by their parents, sometimes take a shorter-term view, with the object of obtaining a credential with the least effort. On balance, the community school is more successful, not only in meeting the wishes of parents, but academically as well.

In New Jersey, Li found evidence that Hispanics (generally low achievers compared with the majority white population) actually perform better when concentrated in strongly Hispanic schools, although conventional opinion has been that minorities are better separated from their fellows so as to be more influenced by the more successful groups. There is a little evidence that community may have the same effect with blacks where they form a community in a small school (but not in a 2000-student comprehensive one); in recent years, blacks in some communities have preferred black schools in the belief that they can focus more on their own specific needs. Put simply, based on significant, but not conclusive evidence, the prevailing liberal claim that large, centralized, secularized, comprehensive cafeteria-style schools are best for everyone, particularly for minorities, has been challenged. Such schools are also often described as "democratic," despite the irony that this form of democracy involves taking control over children from their parents and handing it to bureaucratic organizations.

Li concluded that there are four ways in which schools may relate to parents. In one arrangement, parents are simply not considered seriously as educational agents. Educators define the task, with the result that there is apathy, perhaps suspicion and unease, among parents. This is typically the case in large urban and suburban secondary schools where discipline is poor and academic standards low. In a second category, parents, with or without intent, effectively delegate authority to the school. It provides positive public relations, and some parents are involved in volunteer activities and fundraising. This is the model to which public elementary and secondary schools aspire. It avoids overt hostility, but parents are essentially separated from the instructional task, from school life, and from program goals. Parents who teach their children at home typically tell the younger ones (there is no need to tell older children, who understand school culture) not to mention the fact at school: let the teacher take the credit and avoid hostility.

There are also two categories of community school, roughly reflecting Coleman's "value" and "functional" communities. Two different factors are at work here. First, there is the matter of parents having hands-on control of the daily life of the school. In many religious schools they not only choose the principal and teachers but determine specific instructional and disciplinary policies and even practices. Second, there is the question of the extent to which the parents live their lives within a natural community or whether they simply come together with other parents as a result of shared educational choices.

The "functional" community is defined as being a natural one; the examples in Canada include some religious communities and a few isolated rural areas with a single public school. Hands-on parental management is more likely to be found in the "functional" community, but it may also be found in the "values" community. Such involvement is not superior to delegated authority; it probably works best when the community is close-knit and highly consensual, and where the danger of powerful cliques is lessened. The key point is that community, which may arise in many different forms, can be an integral part of education rather than its enemy.

In this section I have gone beyond the rather preliminary and tentative empirical research. The value of community is more a matter of belief than of science; nevertheless, it is interesting that science may actually support the concept of community, that our worst schools in terms of engagement, discipline, and outcomes are those with least community. This issue lies close to the heart of school choice, the major policy question facing Canadian education today. It is becoming clearer that large schools and large school districts are not an adequate answer to our educational difficulties; there is persuasive, but not conclusive evidence that communities can best bring about the common values they share, and it is easier to develop community in smaller schools than in large ones.

On the other hand, the educational establishment is not being irrational in fiercely opposing the recognition of community in policy. Educators have reason to fear the loss of power, the loss of security (although they have already experienced some of that in many provinces), and the erosion of the bureaucratic rules and regulations from provinces, school systems, and collective agreements that both protect and restrict them. (The more regulation, the less responsibility; the less responsibility, the less accountability.)

The fundamental question is the extent to which schools should be run by the educational establishment, supported by vocal minorities outside education. My argument is that authority should be tilted more towards parents. This is not to say that community is the answer for everyone and that all schools should be compelled to construct some artificial community. Doing so would be neither possible nor desirable. Community is not for everyone. Children should not be forced to join communities against their parents' will. But to many people, their community membership is extremely important, and its advantage to their children should not be overridden by domineering agents of the state.

Community should not be summarily dismissed as an obsolete distraction. Young people, for the most part, like the security of community. If they are not part of one, they usually form their own subcommunities, frequently with values at odds with those their parents would like them to develop. These subcultures may include drugs, alcohol, shoplifting, violence, and contests in sexual prowess. Those who refuse to join the subcommunities (cliques, gangs, and perhaps more often changing patterns of alliance) and those who are expelled from them may be ostracized and alienated. It is true that exclusion from communities officially supported by parents and teachers can be equally or more vicious; my point is that some form of community, however bastardized, is a part of human relationships, and its problems do not disappear in the secular and nihilist modern world.

Some students, in a time of individualization, undoubtedly prefer large, anonymous, individually scheduled schools totally lacking in official community, precisely because they can go their own way and make their own choices without feeling pressure from peers or adults. But that is no reason to impose the industrial model of a cafeteria-style high school on everyone and, ironically, to permit groups of peers to impose alien values by default on those who seek comfort in some form of belonging.

Effective Schools in Summation

The research on effective instruction and effective schools at first sight appears to provide a ready explanation and a remedy for Canada's mediocre educational standards. It is rather as if a patient who loves to eat red meat, cheese, ice cream, butter, and baked goods is found to have hardening of the arteries and a high level of cholesterol. One is tempted to recommend a radical change in diet and a drug to bring about a rapid reduction of the cholesterol. The problem is that even those who quickly reduce their levels by following the regimen may have no better life expectancy than those who do not, although the causes of death are less likely to stem from cholesterol. So, although it is bizarre that so many Canadian educators and schools should ignore the research on effective instruction and effective schools, one cannot point to research showing how marvellous the results will be the instant that they change. There may be some moderate gain at the elementary level for the most disadvantaged, but simply putting enormous pressure on teachers to change is unlikely to have much positive effect. Further, I have argued that teachers' professionalism inheres in their instructional freedom, within reasonable limits. And effectiveness, like community and like professionalism, cannot be ordered in as if it were pizza.

It is not possible to discern the precise contributions of social culture, family background, and school. Defenders of the public

monopoly are apt to exaggerate the contribution of external influences to poor performance, but are quick to claim credit for any
positive evidence, such as the decline in the drop-out rate over the
last thirty years. Its critics, of whom I am one, are often too eager to
blame the monopolistic establishment for any and every school problem. Educational reformers should recognize the nature of our society; we cannot turn our schools into Japanese or German clones. At
the same time, that fact in no way implies, as defenders of the system
assume, that the status quo is therefore desirable; that our schools
reflect us, so everything must be all right. Educational policy should
be developed to bring about the right things. It is a matter of values,
of politics. Our schools should make us more what we Canadians, in
our better moments, want to be; but there is no single answer.

There do appear to be two positive lines of action. First, we should
develop programs containing sequential objectives, with accompanying tests and examinations. Even here, caution should be exercised.
If the stakes of external tests are raised too high, negative, rather
than positive, behaviour will be induced. Experience from the United
States suggests that placing too much emphasis on external tests
leads students to work only for those goals, coming to value performance on a test as more important than the comprehension and
appreciation that should underlie it. Furthermore, teaching is sometimes directed solely at getting everyone to pass the hurdle of the
test, with the result that the students who would pass easily in any
case may receive little teaching or challenge. Worst of all, some educators may even be corrupted (particularly if school finances are
dependent on test scores), so that they teach test items rather than
the underlying skills, ignore areas not to be tested, and encourage
those unlikely to pass the test to be absent on the testing day. Despite
those real dangers, schools should have strong external standards
towards which collective efforts should be directed. In the majority
of provinces in Canada the idea of a high-stakes test is not even
being considered.

Second, we should abandon the idea that every school should try
to embrace every possible belief and value. This does not mean the
opposite, that none should; many parents and young adults like secular, generally low-doctrine, cafeteria-style schools. But obviously,
many do not. Although size in itself may not be the most important
negative factor, the most incoherent and divided schools usually
happen to be of large size, particularly at the secondary level. We
should be looking at ways to develop a variety of schools with a
strong sense of direction for those who want them. At the same time,
the neighbourhood public school attended by most students should

have its own clear sense of direction, a requirement that is impossible if there are no available alternatives for dissenters.

It is fundamentally wrong for school systems to persist in enforcing instructional and school practices known to be related to poor academic achievement. But we should not forget that there are explanations for such foolishness. The Progressive idea has become a religious enthusiasm among some educators. They could no more, in good conscience, promote direct instruction and high standards than a Seventh-Day Adventist could promote Islam. In the reality of many secondary schools today, where the ambition of administrators and teachers is to get to the end of the day without violence or disruption, the imposition of a code of hard work, high standards, emphasis on results, and attention to courtesy, citizenship, and dress is a fantasy. Furthermore, the evidence is that simply putting pressure on existing institutions to change will have only marginal results, for a variety of complex reasons.

The research on effective instruction and schools reflects, for the most part, one set of important educational goals, the basic skills. Just because it is one of the few areas where research can guide us, we cannot assume that reform should be based purely on that research. The reader is reminded that even here, an essentially Technocratic domain, the objectives are not value-free. Most people will certainly endorse them, but their priority is greater for parents and the public than for educational leaders.

The implications of the tentative research on community will have less universal support. They run counter both to continued Progressive control and to Technocratic reform. The strongest advocates of support for community will base their arguments more on the importance of freedom of choice than on research evidence of stronger academic outcomes. Indeed, making choice dependent on evidence of superior academic performance is a Technocratic imposition on parents, whose disposition may well be Traditional or Cultural. More simply, the priority of community and choice is much lower than Technocrats' love for computers.

Readers who, like me, are not members of a strong community should not be too quick to dismiss community members as simply special-interest groups on the sidelines of the major debate; there is no consensual educational majority in Canada today. Furthermore, the problem is deeper than simply funding religious schools. It is not only that different people want various religious, spiritual, and moral beliefs taught in the school (that is itself far from a trivial question affecting only a few minorities), but also that people do not have the same goals for their children in other areas as well.

Our schools are governed by the expectation that everyone should try to go to university or college. That expectation immediately condemns most of the population to failure and the substantial minority that do not graduate from high school on time to disgrace. Lost in the constant repetition of the mantra that "you're toast" if you do not go to university is the value of purposeful work and the dignity of the person who accomplishes it well, whether it is cleaning a building or raising children. I am far from alone in believing that a person's success in life has ultimately far more to do with who he or she is than what an individual becomes in material terms; at the least, that viewpoint should not be trivialized and set aside. What is a man profited if he shall gain a PhD in computer science and lose his own soul?

Reformers are faced with a fairly clear choice. They may push for moderate reform within the system. They may work, for example, for a change of policy on teaching from child-centred to direct instruction and for changes in the programs in faculties of education. At the same time, they may press for parent committees at the school level to advise the principal. They may also demand more testing. I believe that approach to be both ineffectual and wrong. It is ineffectual because the child-centred idea is firmly embedded in the elementary school and is even making inroads (under the guise of subject integration and collaborative learning) in the secondary school. The approach is also ineffectual because the problems with Canadian schooling run deeper than inadequate instructional techniques. It is wrong because one cannot expect to help teachers become more professional in terms of devoting themselves more to children's learning by telling them how they must teach. It is also wrong because moderate reform ignores the gross discrimination that has become an integral part of the school structure in most of Canada, where the system favours some groups and ideologies and ignores or trivializes others. Canadian education has been captured by a liberal, secular, low-doctrine, and permissive mindset that does not represent the Canadian people as a whole. The educational establishment believes that, if it is not a perfect representation of Canada, then it is a reflection of a consensual compromise, with extremist, special-interest groups on either side. But it is not. The establishment is itself a special-interest group. It quickly embraces moderate reform, and it appears to be tolerant, to be open to change, and to be moving in step with the public. In reality, little change is made, new proposals replace the old ones, and the establishment maintains its control and central beliefs.

One option is to swing the pendulum "our" way for a change, on the false assumption there are only a "we" and a "they." To obtain even limited success, "we" (whoever we are) would have to be as authoritarian and ruthless as "they" have been. A better one is to accept pluralism; parents should be able to choose the kind of education they want for their children, but only within carefully defined limits representing the spirit of a pluralist Western democracy.

Those policy issues form the focus of chapter 5. Before turning to them, we must understand the position of the teacher in the classroom. Canada's teachers understandably believe that they are under attack. Somehow, educational reform must be brought about in a way that will give them their rightful place at the heart of education, without letting them or their unions determine the fundamental goals and policies of elementary and secondary education. A brief examination of teachers' attitudes will illustrate clearly why moderate reform cannot be the answer. The influence of the well-established research on effective instruction and schools is scarcely visible in Canadian schools, but the ideas are regularly attacked and rejected. As for community and choice, these are matters not even worthy of discussion.

PRACTICE: THE CLASSROOM TEACHER

Classroom teachers are important because they represent the system to students and parents. The classroom experience, as influenced by the hierarchy, effectively defines formal education. I have emphasized the problems caused by unjustified faith in Progressivism and the excessive powers of teachers' unions. Those problems are not abstract entities within a distant system; they are part of what goes on in the classroom.

Teaching Methods

The most comprehensive survey of teachers' opinions is to be found in a report prepared for the Canadian Teachers' Federation by A.J.C. King and M.J. Peart (1992). Unfortunately, their questions were not phrased to capture the proportions of individualized work and direct instruction and the level of student choice. The authors nevertheless feel able to assert, "Small group work appears to be particularly *effective* in the early years of elementary school" (my emphasis). This conclusion is based simply on statements by teachers about what they do, a triumph of ideology over empirical research. The quotation shows the probably unconscious bias of the experts. Groups in the primary grades tend to be heterogeneous, that is, of mixed ability, as they increasingly are in the upper elementary and middle grades. Heterogeneous groups make efficient, direct instruction in sequential skills impossible.

King and Peart do not directly address the question of the teacher's professional "right to teach." My own more limited Ontario sample (1995) shows an important discrepancy between teachers and principals. Whereas only 35 per cent of principals believed that teachers should have the greatest say about pedagogy, 61 per cent of teachers felt that way, the only surprise being that 39 per cent of teachers did not.

That theme is picked up by a 1993 publication of the Alberta Teachers' Association, which expresses the frustration of teachers with the ever-changing educational scene, for which teachers seem to get an unfair share of the blame. It quotes a Department of Education discussion paper as asserting, "We are quite sure, for example, that the practice of grouping students homogeneously for an entire year … is more harmful than beneficial. We also know that the development and use of Individualized Program Plans based on clearly specified intended outcomes facilitates student attainment." The teachers' reasonable response to mandated individualization of instruction, according to the report, was that it was a "ridiculous expectation." Instructional research, I have shown, supports the use of whole-class instruction and intelligently organized homogeneous grouping, not individualization. The mandating of an inappropriate methodology is not only ridiculous but unprofessional. The ATA document has a recurring theme of the erosion of professionalism. Shortly after its publication, the province's policy of individualization and continuous progress was abandoned, as arbitrarily as it had been begun. One wonders if someone in the department actually read the instructional research or simply heard the union's voice.

Student Behaviour

The view of the problems of student behaviour that I outlined earlier is shared, according to King and Peart, by teachers. The proportion of teachers who feel "almost always" or "frequently" (as compared with "sometimes") worried about being "physically injured" by students varies by province, from a high of 20 per cent in Ontario and Manitoba to 10 per cent. Individual teachers talk of sitting "face to face with kids who have committed murder"; of student rights with no responsibilities, of a lack of protection from authorities, and of constantly being told what they cannot do. They attach particular blame to the Young Offenders Act and the Charter of Rights and Freedoms.

Student Evaluation

As one might expect, student evaluation is the area where teachers' views are most troubling to the outsider looking for some assurance of accountability. According to teachers, the most important factor in their evaluation of students is not achievement but effort, that is, their opinion as to how hard the student is trying. But trying and succeeding are two entirely different things.

Formal tests, according to teachers, only become important after grade nine. At the grade five level, effort and behaviour are by far the most important factors, followed by social skills, attendance and homework, class assignments, and notebooks. King and Peart observe that in the primary (kindergarten to grade three) grades, "there is as much emphasis on teaching appropriate behaviour and social skills as on teaching specific skills." They quote a grade one teacher as saying, "I never give a test in anything"; a grade three and four teacher, "I have a little kid-watching scribbler ... I just make a note on the person who has a little bit of a problem"; and another grade one teacher, "On the one hand, I think they [parents] have a right to know how their child is doing comparatively, but on the other hand that goes against my emphasis on each individual child."

Even in the middle grades, actual level of performance is not a major factor in students' evaluation. According to the report, "Teachers ... attempted to evaluate each student in relation to both other students and the student's own ability." Precisely how the parents and students are supposed to figure out how much of the grade comes from each source is not discussed; neither is the basis of their information about students' ability. Aptitude tests are hated more and are even less frequently used than achievement tests. Primary teachers are notoriously bad at identifying bright children (they tend to pick the oldest). Analysis of the statement itself shows the emptiness of educational discussion of evaluation; it is not at all clear what measuring a student's ability without the context of others means. One reports that a six-year-old can read precisely because some others cannot; one does not report that a twelve-year-old is toilet-trained (unless he is in a context where some are not), or that a high school graduate going to university can read.

The statement also ignores the authors' own finding that effort rather than achievement is the most important factor. The reader is not told how effort is judged. Is it based on comparison with others? Or is it judged by how much change in effort there has been? It is small wonder that parents are frustrated by misleading reports from school. Mindless contradictions are a key part of practice in student evaluation in most Canadian elementary schools.

School Effectiveness

King and Peart's definition of school effectiveness departs in very important ways from the literature on the subject discussed in the previous chapter. King and Peart do not define effectiveness as the add-on value of the school, measured by objective tests and taking into account the character of the student body. They define effects in terms of successful course completion rather than by external, objective measures of achievement related to ability or background. We have no way of knowing whether the course credit in the various schools they surveyed is based on similar or completely different standards of achievement. Several small-scale research projects in Ontario have all found discrepancies in standards among secondary schools, some as great as 10 percentage points; that is, a 75 per cent average in one school may be equivalent to 85 per cent in another. Yet single percentage points determine scholarships and admission to competitive university programs. If the importance of course completion is combined with an undue determination to prevent dropouts, then it is not surprising that academic standards are falling. Further, suburban schools inevitably have more course completions than inner-city schools, but as we have seen in the literature, that does not make them more effective.

The King and Peart survey of teachers' impressions of whether their school was a good one is based on an unusual and inappropriate measure of effects; thus the characteristics considered desirable are those related to invalid measures of effect, perpetuating the false idea that important indicators of school effectiveness include (as well as some valid factors) working conditions, student support services, and warm, supportive administrators. It is obviously tempting to emphasize the soft, imaginary factors rather than the hard, real ones. Canadian teachers and citizens are thus encouraged to make two false assumptions about school effectiveness: first, that course completion is a valid measure of academic effect; and second, that any factors related to these invalid measures are themselves evaluations of effectiveness. Thus "effective" administration comes to be defined as the provision of such things as good material working conditions, warm and supportive leadership, strong collegial relationships among teachers, and the provision of good social services to students within an empathetic and caring environment. None of those factors actually proves to be significant in the well-documented international research on school effectiveness already described. I am not saying that they are necessarily trivial or negative matters for teachers and others in the school; but they are outside the mainstream research on academic effectiveness.

Omissions from the King and Peart Report

One of the most important influences on teachers' daily lives was not addressed in the study carried out for the Canadian Teachers' Federation. Their legal status as unionized employees determines their daily behaviour, working conditions, and salaries, which are detailed in lengthy collective agreements. The reason for this important exclusion may be that neither the CTF nor King and Peart could imagine life outside a unionized closed shop, just as goldfish cannot envisage a life outside their bowl. Teachers' opinions of their collective agreements, salary scales, right to strike, and compulsory union membership are therefore irrelevant.

Most teachers in public systems in Canada are employed subject to mandatory membership of a particular union – even where there is more than one union operating, as in Ontario's elementary schools, they may not choose which one to join – and are paid by a contract that determines salary on the basis of two criteria: experience and credentials. Typically they teach in circumstances (i.e. maximum class size, number of preparation hours, number of different courses taught) determined by a district or provincial agreement, rather than by some authority at the level of the school. And they are collectively limited (in nearly all provinces) to a single final mechanism for settling irresolvable differences in contractual negotiations, the strike.

There certainly appears to be no widespread dissatisfaction with this arrangement on the part of teachers, although a strong minority are against the right to strike. British Columbia has a small, formal teachers' association that opposes the British Columbia Teachers' Federation and the unionization and deprofessionalization that its power brings. The province, the only major one where teachers could not strike, granted this right a few years ago in response to court action taken by the British Columbia Teachers' Federation. Teachers throughout the province overwhelmingly chose the union route.

On the other hand, there is strong public opposition to the effects of teachers' unionization, in particular the right to strike. I am not aware of a single reputable poll showing a majority of the public in favour of teachers having that right. It is also anomalous that a profession should be so strongly unionized, particularly that the right to teach in a public school should be limited by law to those who agree to join a union. Dependence on formal qualifications and experience for salary purposes is also controversial, especially in times of teacher surplus when lay-offs follow the last-in/first-out principle established in the manufacturing industry. One principal told me how he agonized when he had to tell parents that the two most popular and, according to reputation and his opinion, most effective teachers in the school were to be laid off on grounds of least seniority.

One thing is clear: the legally enforced unionization of Canadian teachers (a situation not found in the countries most like us, England and the United States) leads to enormous rigidity and is one of the greatest barriers to reform in the schools. Indeed, it is fair to say that radical reforms to education, even on a limited basis, will prove incompatible with the virtual union monopoly of education and will therefore be strongly opposed by teachers' leaders.

What follows is an example of a reform – differentiated staffing – that might well be advantageous to students, but is blocked by union agreements. The unions of course will say they have no objection to the hiring of teachers' aides, one form of differentiated staffing, provided that they are in addition to the full complement of teachers. Such hiring, often accompanying the so-called integration of severely disabled children into the regular classroom, explains some of the increased cost of education over the last twenty-five years. Differentiated staffing would reduce costs in the long run because of its greater efficiency, but the most important benefit would be a greater commitment to students. One of the greatest drags on school performance is not the totally incompetent teacher; there are relatively few teachers in that category. A greater problem is the number of mediocre ones who have settled into a comfortable, unstimulating routine.

To begin with, differentiated staffing could see teachers promoted in a way similar to university professors. They would be hired as interns, not necessarily with teaching qualifications. Those without qualifications might have a beginning salary of $25 000; those with qualifications, say, $28 000. Interns would take a full teaching load but would be under the supervision of a "senior teacher," who would be paid an additional sum for each intern ($3000 a year). Unqualified interns would take courses (primarily at their own expense) during evenings, weekends, and school vacations; qualified interns would also attend seminars dealing with the practical life of the teacher. Internships would normally be for two years, but would be renewable annually by the school to a legislated maximum of five years. Interns who met the school's standards (which would be based on a provincewide guide to professional standards for teachers) would be promoted to tenured positions, with a salary scale running from $30 000 to $50 000 at the elementary level (grades one to five), $30 000 to $55 000 at the middle-school level (grades six to eight), and $32 000 to $60 000 at the high school level. Teachers would be eligible for promotion to the senior rank, with possible increases in the maximum salary of up to $10 000. These would be based on experience (up to five years), qualifications (but only subject qualifications relevant to the actual teaching task), and merit. In addition, reward for merit would be payable both in lump sums (not affecting the base salary) and as merit increments. The maximum salary would be attainable by a combination of merit and exceptional, relevant qualifications or by merit alone.

The prime authority for allocating merit and promotion would be the principal, but he or she would be limited by a provincial guide to merit pay and teacher promotion that would describe ethical and unethical practice and by an advisory committee of teachers and parents that would set out policies. For example, the sharing of merit funds among all teachers nearly equally would be unethical. The salary figures given above are simply illustrative; in practice, there should be provincewide guides, which could be negotiable with teachers' unions; but some flexibility at the level of the school would be essential, and would be greater for charter and direct-grant schools operating outside the district's public-school rules.

In the same way, tenure would be based on five factors: merit, age, experience, rank, and qualifications. Merit would be defined as merit pay earned over the previous five years. Senior teachers would be formally assessed by the principal, or by a third party agreed to by the principal and the teacher, every five years to ensure that they still maintained the standards expected of the position.

In assessing the professionalism of candidates for tenure, promotion to senior teacher, and merit pay, attention would be given first to the teacher's competence in and commitment to teaching and students, as distinct from his or her loyalty to colleagues and the union, which figures so prominently in union definitions of "professionalism." Elements in such an assessment would include teaching competence in the classroom, as evidenced by students' academic progress (compared with progress of similar students in other schools and classrooms); knowledge of the subject matter being taught; the ability to plan and deliver coherent programs; the ability to establish a classroom environment where students are courteous, hard-working, and pleasant, in relation to a clear, schoolwide moral code; use of professionally competent instruments of student evaluation, including the regular assignment and speedy marking of homework; full, friendly, and accurate communication to parents; cooperation in extra-curricular activities on a voluntary, but willing basis; professional support of the principal and other teachers; and openness to ideas concerning professional development. I assume throughout this discussion that incompetent teachers should be dismissed for cause.

I have emphasized that the major benefit of differentiated staffing should be more-effective teaching rather than cost-saving. Although there can and should be some economy from reforming teachers' salary schedules, if saving is made the only priority, any improvement in instruction will be lost. Generally speaking, in my view, Canadian teachers are not overpaid when compared with other professional employees. The problem is that mediocre teachers, even a few incompetent ones, are employed in large numbers at high salaries, giving the public a false impression of the nature of teachers' pay. Even competent teachers in the primary grades receive salaries greater than those which they would be able to command in other fields. It is irrelevant to contend that educating a five-year-old or an eight-year-old is as "important" as teaching a seventeen-year-old. One could as reasonably argue that a stay-at-home parent is worth as much as a childcare worker, or that a garbage collector is as valuable as a professional hockey player. We have to live within the real economic and social context, not an imaginary one where the benevolent state, with infinite wisdom, decides exactly what every individual is genuinely worth. The reality is that primary teachers could be readily replaced in a few years at a lower cost without any loss to students; the same cannot be said of twelfth grade, or even eighth grade, teachers. In terms of employment, a good physics teacher is worth more than a good third grade one, which is not to say that the former is a better person. Priests are paid less than bankers.

The use of teachers' aides is another possibility if flexible, differentiated staffing is introduced. In the primary grades, I visualize, for example, a school where focused instruction is confined to three hours per day, with the rest of the day devoted to physical, aesthetic, and expressive activities. The second part would not necessarily be best staffed simply by qualified teachers with a pupil-teacher ratio of 25:1.

Some of the salary savings achieved by reducing the level of primary teachers' salaries over time would be offset by the higher salaries of senior teachers and by merit payments. I envisage a career ladder that encourages excellent teachers to remain in teaching by paying them as much as or more than vice-principals and junior school-district administrators. Principals will have to be well paid for their added responsibilities if those of the school district are cut back. As teaching is made more manageable by the requirement of high standards of behaviour and work and by the exclusion of the most-disruptive students, class size should rise, the easiest way to save money in schools.

I recognize that the relatively high salaries of Canadian teachers, in comparison with those in England and the United States, are in part attributable to our strong unions. However, the value of high salaries in attracting able young people and making teaching a respected profession is offset by the mediocrity of many classrooms, for which dispirited teachers are partly to blame. We should keep high salaries for those who merit them, without retaining the bureaucratic regulations and rules that result from large school districts and unionization.

An alternative to the strike as a means of settling disputes over salaries and working conditions is a mediation system based on final-offer selection. This approach means that both sides (whether bargaining at the provincial or the local level) put forward a final offer on all matters to be agreed upon, and the mediators choose one side's offer. The incentive is for both sides to produce a reasonable package overall. Two things are necessary for this process to work on a large scale. First, there must be clear criteria established in advance; otherwise, educational policy will be set by the arbitrators. While there should be consultation, the province has the responsibility of establishing the framework for public spending on education and, directly or indirectly, on the largest component: teachers' salaries. For example, an index of other professional salaries (such as those for lawyers, doctors, dentists, and engineers) could be used as a guide, with maximum, minimum, and median salaries pegged at a selected percentage of some combined figure.

Second, because the province should not delegate its absolute authority to arbitrators who are not responsible for the consequences of their decisions, however tightly their mandate is prescribed, there must be an emergency clause for the province to intervene in the case of a major financial crisis. But if that loophole is abused by government, the process will soon break down; if education in Canada is to regain solid public support, there must be an atmosphere of trust and reasonable security. That means that a teacher who is doing a good job and getting good results should know that he or she is not going to be arbitrarily fired at the next round of budget cuts. Security is not intended for the incompetent, or comfort for the mediocre.

Some will see a prejudice in favour of secondary schools. In chapter 3, I argued that academic rot sets in at the beginning of school, and our relatively mediocre standard is then maintained. My own experience has been at all levels of schooling, and I am not suggesting that secondary schools are problem-free. Quite the opposite: it is very clear that the typical large urban or suburban comprehensive secondary school is beset by problems of purpose and practice that are irresolvable in the current policy and administrative framework. The average secondary principal does not place a high priority on looking for strong academic teachers to make tough demands in the disciplines of knowledge. The desired teacher is one who can "reach" the students and maintain order. Instruction is, at best, of less importance. The secondary school faces an impossible challenge; the elementary school faces a lesser one and attacks it weakly. The problems, some resulting from bad practice in the early grades, are inevitably more obvious among unruly adolescents.

Elementary and secondary schools both have their problems, but they are not identical. The central issue in the primary grades of the elementary school is the child-centred mindset, which puts less emphasis on academic progress and the values on which success depends. The central problem of the secondary school is that it too often settles for benign custody of adolescents, in the hope of shepherding them through the required hours in order to give them a credential as a high school graduate, a credential that vaguely measures the level to which they have been tamed rather than a standard of achievement or work habits. Neither problem is going to be solved by external exhortation; surely, there has been enough sniping over the last decade by parents, critics, and the media to establish that fact. In both cases, teachers may be a part of the problem; they are certainly essential to the solution.

CONCLUSION

In the section on teachers, differentiated staffing was used as an example of a reform made impossible by powerful teachers' unions. It is an important example, but still only that. If legislation overrode the teachers' authority and established differentiated staffing by central fiat, little would be gained by such a measure alone. Administrators and unions would use their influence to try to keep things as much the same as possible under the new regime. If this book has one message about the means to bring about reform, it is that passing legislation about what teachers are supposed to be doing in classrooms will have no lasting effect. In the late twentieth century, schools in individualistic, pluralist democracies can no longer be operated from a central office.

Governments are not therefore powerless, but their authority must be targeted carefully, not used as a bludgeon. The educational situation can be seen as analogous to the economic context. The more that governments try to run the economy, by developing make-work projects in the name of infrastructure, by setting up hopelessly ineffective, patronage-riven regional agencies to promote employment in the poorer provinces, by devising complex schemes to promote Canadian culture, and by establishing expensive training programs to pay people not to work, the more helpless they seem in the face of global competition. But what they can do is to create a social and economic framework where good work is valued rather than simply taxed, and where quality education, transport, and health-care programs are targeted, supported, and stimulated, rather than run by and for a monopoly. In health care we have the bizarre result that patients can and do see several doctors within a matter of hours or days for a sore throat or a headache, but are usually put on a waiting list for months if they need serious, but not obviously life-threatening treatment. The only way to get fast treatment, unless one is a member of a privileged government elite, is to pay for it outside Canada. In education, parents may pay for private instruction, if they can afford it, but they have to submit to the officials' determination of what service their children receive in the public system. If you want health care, you have choice, but face a long wait if your condition is serious. If you want schooling, you can get it immediately, but have limited choice over what you get.

Within the school system, governments have little chance of improving the fundamentals simply by decreeing new credit requirements, demanding a computer on every desk, or increasing the hours in the school day, particularly if, at the same time, they are laying off teachers according to criteria unrelated to quality and closing schools irrespective of their support from parents. That is not to say that all regulations are without merit; but most simply do not address the core problem or are ineffectual. Unfortunately, politicians in Canada sometimes seem to be divided between those who believe the existing monopolies should be maintained or enhanced at any cost (on the grounds that these inefficient monopolies make us Canadian) and those who believe in cuts and more regulation (on the grounds that government is too expensive and too inefficient). Both needed and possible in education are programs chosen by parents at prices that governments, the economy, and taxpayers can afford. The responsibility of the provincial government in the school system is to set up a framework through which schools can compete to provide the conditions that parents want for their children, within the limits of what is acceptable in a free, democratic, pluralist society and congruent with its fundamental values.

All schools should be publicly accountable both for their spending and for their students' achievement, broadly defined. Because the two largest provincial governments spend (or allow school districts to spend) money so lavishly and unwisely, Canada as a whole is in a position to make some savings and at the same time reform and improve the school system. The combination of lay-offs and exhortation to do better on the part of central administrations is not going to lead to educational improvement, even if it does save money. I usually cringe when I hear the platitude that "crisis" is another word for "opportunity," but in Canadian education it happens to be true.

Although it is clear that there is an important difference between the overall world-view of educators and that of parents and the public, a more detailed examination shows that there is enormous diversity both among educators (between secondary teachers and senior administrators, for example) and among groups within the public. Indeed, teachers share some of the concerns of parents, such as that poorly conceived changes are imposed in an authoritarian manner from the top and teachers are left with the responsibility for their effective implementation. Teachers often feel that ambitious principals wish to make their mark by implementing a fashionable innovation such as integrated subject matter, cross-grade groupings (whereby classes are formed from a combination of, say, grade five and grade eight students), or mainstreaming severely disabled students. Principals may then be promoted to senior administration – and freedom from the day-to-day stress of life in a school, as well as the consequences of their ill-considered innovations. There is no evidence, by the way, that any of those three innovations will lead to improved learning. Parents, in contrast to senior administrators, increasingly demand improved performance in the basic skills. There is inconsistency between the demands made by the bureaucracy, which is most removed from parental and public influence, and those made by the public. The teacher is on the front line and gets fired on from at least two directions.

In many parts of Canada teachers are being deprofessionalized. They are not given responsibility for choosing the most effective teaching methods for their clients and are, in turn, not held responsible for their students' learning outcomes. This unhappy combination makes Canadian schools a ready prey for any passing fad that may be chosen by leaders in the educational establishment. A research officer who interviewed teachers in newly destreamed Ontario grade nines told me of one teacher's *cri de cœur*: "I find it so hard to get used to not having to worry about what students actually learn."

The intense bureaucratization of Canadian education and its lack of accountability to the public make educational fads increasingly pervasive. If teaching method rather than what is learned is important, it is easy to see why aspiring principals vie to be the first to introduce the latest faddish method. There is no negative consequence for introducing a fad that lowers levels of achievement and behaviour; parents may sense the impact, but no one really knows what it is. Most schools do not even maintain longitudinal records of achievement, attendance, and behaviour, let alone make them available to the parents they "serve."

There are two areas where educational research can provide some straightforward evidence about educational efficiency and effectiveness: those of instructional and school effectiveness. Canadian educational leaders have generally ignored the research, or denied it, or have changed its stern message into something warmer and fuzzier that they can endorse; for example, positive principal-teacher relations are often claimed to be an indicator of an effective school. Such is not the case. Research shows that positive relations sometimes hide mediocrity; tension, not complacent self-satisfaction, characterizes a good school striving for excellence. That is not to say that one should promote bad relations; but self-satisfaction is no substitute for clear standards and effective teaching.

The effectiveness of instruction and the special qualifications required for the particular teaching task, for example, senior mathematics or music, are not related to the teacher's salary in any way. Indeed, promotion is more likely to be based on conformity to the bureaucracies' current views than on evidence of effective learning on the part of students, which is frequently not collected. It is apparent from the King and Peart report that external evidence of the level of learning actually achieved is frequently not considered relevant to the evaluation of students.

The legally imposed monopolies of public schools and teachers' unions provide a dual barrier to meaningful educational change. The two for the most part live in harmonious symbiosis with each other. This statement may appear to contradict the evidence that teachers are unhappy with the innovations flowing from above, some of which originate with or are given force by the local district. Although the innovations may indeed be irritants to the classroom teacher, one should bear in mind that some of them have significant support from the teachers' leaders. The child-centred reforms implemented in

British Columbia were generally supported by the British Columbia Teachers' Federation and by most primary teachers. Even in Ontario, where the mode (though not necessarily the principle) of implementating the destreaming of grade nine was opposed by the secondary teachers' union, the approach itself is strongly endorsed by elementary teachers; they see it, correctly, as a mechanism to make high schools more like elementary ones. Where governments mandate reforms that are unpopular with union leaders, such as testing and financial support for independent schools, school boards typically either remain silent or oppose them.

There is of course tension between the two powers, usually of financial origin. In most of Canada, only one means of final solution exists: the strike. Most teachers' strikes focus on money and control. Unfortunately, the interests of learners and their parents are not represented at the bargaining table, and neither party to the process is at comparable risk with disputants in the private sector. There the owners could lose market share and face possible bankruptcy, and the workers risk losing their jobs if their excessive pay scales make the products uncompetitive. In a dispute in the educational sector, government officials, school board members, and administrators have no fear of losing business and a much diminished risk of personal job loss. The result has been a general strengthening of union control over the schools. There have been efforts by governments, notably in Quebec and New Brunswick, to regain some control, but even in those provinces the dispute is between two central agencies; parents are not represented. Even if they were, they would disagree among themselves.

Parents thus have less and less chance of influencing their children's formal education. I have spoken to many parents individually, at meetings, and on open-line radio programs. Again and again, I heard concerned and knowledgeable people tell me or ask me about the research on the teaching of basic skills and about how schools could be improved. Many of these people are angry that educational leaders are still propagating discredited ideas based on values not shared by a majority of parents. They tell me about teachers who are sympathetic, only to discover that they teach phonics secretly behind a closed door, or perhaps are discounted by their colleagues and principals as unprofessional relics resistant to change who like to teach the way they themselves were taught. Above all, parents feel powerless. The classroom is protected by the bureaucracy, and the bureaucracy by the layers between it and the school board, which is led by its officials in instructional matters.

The concept of community has been under attack for over thirty years. Small schools, small school districts, and direct involvement by parents in educational policy and financial matters are all anathema to public monopolies. Community is destroyed and replaced by apathy and alienation, first among parents, then among students, and in the end among teachers. Union leaders may have given teachers what they asked for and more, but it has not brought them satisfaction, except for those so besotted with Progressivism that they can see no problem.

Genuine educational reform cannot be achieved through the existing instruments or with the existing power structure. None of the interest groups – not faculties of education, not governmental bureaucracies, not teachers' unions, not administrators, and not school trustees – has a stake in divesting itself of authority and letting parents have a real say in the education of their children. Doing so would go against their nature; these groups are composed of experts or elected leaders who know best. The only hope for education in Canada is that a democratic government will listen to the people.

– 5 –

Problems and Solutions

A picture has been drawn of elementary and secondary education in Canada within its social context; it is not factually comprehensive. The purpose of this book is the advocacy of educational reform, not a bland, non-judgmental prescription that everyone will accept. While I have tried to be fair to Canadian schools, which have been a major part of my life, I am convinced that the system is out of kilter. There is too much dissatisfaction, not only on the part of parents, the public, and employers, but also among teachers, and it is substantially warranted. I have tried to avoid allocating blame, although readers will infer that some groups – politicians, senior administrators, unions, and school boards – bear greater responsibility than do, for example, parents and teachers.

In a real sense, the central problem is the system. One can retort that there is no such thing as a system, only people, but that is true only from one perspective. Suppose that you are a keen, ambitious, intelligent young teacher just beginning your career with a strong sense of professional dedication to helping students to develop in academics, aesthetics, and physical competence as well as to become contributing, moral members of society. How long are those qualities likely to survive in the average public school? Ethical doctors can and do shut out much of the controversy in health care and concentrate on their practice behind closed doors. The classroom door is more permeable.

Although one can point a finger at individual educators who have failed to put the interests of students first, who have given up, who have sold out, who have never bothered to read educational research, who have avoided, rather than confronted problems, or who have denied, rather than invited responsibility and accountability, the reality is that no easily identifiable collectivity of people is responsible for the problems. They have developed, sometimes for good reasons or with the best motives. The task is not to lay blame but to develop a framework in which a young teacher, and thousands of professional teachers already in the system, will be able to participate with enthusiasm. In this chapter the major problems are summarized before ideas for reform are discussed.

Dissatisfaction   As the preceding chapters have indicated, there is considerable public discontent, for which there are many causes. One is dissatisfaction with the dominant Progressive world-view and methodology. Another is recognition that the academic outcomes of Canadian schools are not competitive with those in many other industrialized countries. There is also a considerable feeling that we do not get good value for money. As well, unhappiness exists that even the successful high school graduates are often unready for work in the contemporary world

Fundamentally, however, today's public school cannot satisfy everyone for the simple reason that people want different things. It is not possible for an educational monopoly to please all its clients, unless it is prepared to diversify its offerings and allow free competition among them. Such an approach policy goes against the grain of a monopoly, many of whose employees believe that one size does or should fit all. If it appears not to fit, then either the child is diagnosed as disabled or it is the fault of the parents.

Some parents want their school to be a cross-section of society, a public and common school; they also necessarily want everyone else to want the same thing (or at least get it). Many others want something distinctive – a gifted program, French immersion, religion, or the arts. By definition, those two major desires, one for uniformity and the other for diversity, are logically incompatible.

Too often, public school supporters refuse to confront that reality, one moment extolling the virtues of the common school, as they reject, on the grounds of alleged elitism, a request from a group of parents who want an academically intensive school, and at the next, boasting of the success of their French-immersion program or their school of the arts, or their flexibility in meeting the needs of the individual child. Even when some choice is assumed, there is reluctance to discuss the criteria for this acceptance or denial. I have known people who, when pressed, try to square the circle by defending both. I was told by one thoughtful and long-term trustee how important the common school is, representing the whole population with differing social and ethnic backgrounds. That idea, I agree, is compelling. "But I thought your children went to French immersion," I replied. "Oh, yes, but French immersion is open to anyone, without any charge" was the answer. Should a religious choice be available to everyone too? "Of course not. A religious choice would be divisive." Very few people really believe in the common school when it means the sacrifice of choices that they want to make for their own children.

Inequitable funding of education   The financing of education is unfair to a much greater extent than is the case with any other public service. Educational spending varies from province to province and in Ontario from district to district. It is easy enough to provide equitable funding in a centralized, homogeneous country such as Japan, but more difficult in a country with ten different provincial jurisdictions (in addition to the territories and the federal schools for the First Nations). Even so, federal governments have contributed to the problem by continuing to use unhelpful formulas for provincial grants, guaranteed to create interprovincial animosity. As with other policies in Canada, there is no public debate; all political parties quietly go along with an unconsidered plan.

Failure to understand, appreciate, and act upon research concerning effective instruction and effective schools   Over the last twenty-five years there has been considerable growth in the Western world in understanding of the characteristics associated with effective instruction and effective schools. Little of this understanding seems to have penetrated Canadian faculties of education, which are for the most part still stuck in the ideology (and thus the methodologies) of the late 1960s, perhaps because that is when so many faculty members were hired or educated. Their ideology has in turn been passed on to generations of teachers. As well, faculty members have chosen their successors, often their own students.

Administrators understandably show a similar lack of knowledge and understanding; many of them have been educated and promoted on the basis of their adherence to the dominant ideology. Teachers who dare to question the approved dogma are understandably afraid of peer disapproval and of negative evaluations by administrators, since their chances of promotion would be minimized.

Lack of accountability for student achievement   As external evaluation of every student and every school is not regularly carried out at all in some provinces and is often so downplayed that information is not readily available to parents even when it is collected, there is often no check on continuing mediocre performance in classrooms and schools. Many teachers whose students perform poorly have no idea that they and their students are doing so; parents are not the only ones without external standards to guide their understanding.

Lack of clear exit standards from secondary school   Most provinces have no clearly stated standards for graduation from high school, and six provinces have no objective standards for admission to college or university. In those provinces colleges and universities rely on school marks for admission. This practice not is only unfair, because school standards vary greatly, but it sends the message to secondary schools that actual achievement does not matter. All that matters is the mark the student is given, an example of credentialism gone crazy.

Mediocre academic achievement   The level of academic outcomes from Canada's elementary schools is unsatisfactory. Korea, a developing country with very large classes, performs better than Canada in mathematics. At the secondary level, Canada does relatively well in producing a comparatively large number of potential mathematicians and scientists, but within this large group there is insufficient excellence. Even those fairly good programs are threatened by "integrated subjects" and "collaborative learning." Our most demanding programs in elementary and secondary schools are generally less rigorous than in other developed countries outside North America.

At a time when our best brains are vitally important in making scientific and technical advances, our neglect of excellence is a problem. The lack of competitive tests and of academic pressure in most schools, combined with mark inflation in some provinces, promotes mediocrity. We are fortunate that there is still excellence in some of our university departments of science, engineering, mathematics, and computer science.

In language, our level of literacy, at best equivalent (among recent high school graduates) to our American neighbour's, should be a matter of real concern. We do not know how well we perform in other subjects, but there is no reason to believe that achievement in history, literature, biology, music, fitness, and geography is unaffected by the trends that undermine achievement in the basic skills. Many informal tests (of history, current affairs, and general knowledge, for example) suggest that most subjects have suffered erosion.

Failure to prepare young people for work   Canada's pattern of movement from school to work is disorganized and inadequate. No province is strong in this regard, and our comparative level of youth unemployment is a disgrace in a wealthy country. There can be no worse preparation for work than unemployment, unless it is pretendwork in an undisciplined, non-academic, disengaged class in high school.

Lack of equal access to available schools   Even when parents sense that their school is not doing a good job, they are usually prevented from transferring their children to a neighbouring school or one in another system. School districts may claim open access to their schools but set up hidden barriers by not counting (for funding and staffing) students from out of zone and by putting arbitrary limits on school capacity. In some districts, a student who is a strong Christian may be refused admission to a publicly funded Catholic school if he or she has, say, an Anglican, instead of a Roman Catholic, baptismal certificate.

Failure to provide parents with reasonable, non-discriminatory choices   It is ironic that a country which boasts of its Charter of Rights and Freedoms should practise gross discrimination in education by religion to a greater extent than England, the country from which the Charter is supposed to differentiate us and one still possessing an established church. Roman Catholic, Church of England, and Muslim schools are funded equally in that country, where most state schools are de facto secular.

In Canada there is religious discrimination in all provinces except British Columbia and Manitoba, but it is particularly odious in Canada's largest province, Ontario, where numerous minorities, both large and small, are denied schools at the same time as the expenditure of money on Roman Catholic schools has steadily increased under governments of all three political parties. Equally objectionable, the religion of the province's Protestant population, which was for over one hundred years prescribed teaching in the public elementary schools, is now forbidden, even as a voluntary lunch-time activity. Rarely in democratic history has a legal obligation turned so quickly to legal prohibition, and in a country where the majority still claim to be Christian. Such an outcome is a triumph for secularism, but a sad day for the influence of parents over their children's education and a disgrace in a society that prides itself on its tolerance and multiculturalism. I recognize the legitimacy of secularizing the local area public school, but only if reasonable provision is made for dissenters in other schools.

Where they have been introduced, academically intensive schools have been outstandingly popular, with parents even lining up over night to enrol their children. Most school boards, willing to supply many other options, steadfastly refuse to provide or increase this one, probably because it would be too popular. The philosophy of the academically intensive school is totally opposed to the prevailing Progressive view. Similarly, most provinces have refused to consider charter schools, whereby parents gain independence from school-district regulations and develop and administer their own policies. The success of charter schools in Alberta is itself limited by excessive bureaucratic regulations and a legislated numerical limit.

Legislated unionization of schools   Most Canadian school systems are closed shops. No teacher may be employed in the system without joining the union. Most systems (in some cases, the province itself) have lengthy collective agreements with teachers that prescribe salaries unrelated to performance, limit flexibility in class size for different teaching purposes, and prohibit flexible staffing. Lay-offs are essentially on the basis of last in, first out. The public school is a virtual monopoly, and unions have indirect control over much of the spending and the key instructional policies of that monopoly, partly through the collective agreement and partly through informal influence over administrators, who are promoted from (and occasionally return to) unionized positions. Parents have no input to policy and are unrepresented at the bargaining table.

Impossibility of compromise where fundamental values clash   In many value areas, there is no possibility of a consensual compromise that would leave all parents reasonably happy. The areas where fundamental conflict is inevitable include health, sex and family life education, literature, and training for work.

In the area of family life, values, and sex education, many parents want their children to be taught that the family (with mother, father, and children) is the best environment for child upbringing and that sexual activity should be postponed until adulthood or marriage. They believe that the emphasis should be placed on honesty, justice, courage, personal responsibility, and consideration of the other person. A vocal minority, with strong support in the media, academia, and government, believe that children should be brought up to make autonomous choices within a much broader definition of the family: a single-parent family, same-sex parents, or different-sex parents, married or unmarried, blended or biological, are all of equal quality. For that minority, the values of independence, individual fulfilment, and high self-concept typically have priority over the traditional virtues and the associated marriage vows.

Some parents want adolescents to be introduced to an appreciation of good, traditional literature. Others believe that reading should promote an egalitarian, anti-racist agenda that would liberate individuals from their Eurocentrism. Still others want literature that will not be disturbing to any belief system. The program in most public secondary schools ends up being an unhappy compromise.

In the case of training for work, most establishment educators – and they are joined in this case by many members of the social elites – believe that all job training should be postponed until after high school graduation. This view creates a problem because many young people do not graduate in the normal fashion. Further, the secondary programs for the majority of young people who do not continue to postsecondary education are generally mediocre, if not miseducative.

Monopolistic control of education by powerful bureaucracies   The educational quasi-monopoly has become too powerful, too expensive, too inflexible, and too bureaucratic. Too much money for education is spent outside the classroom. While Canada's out-of-school bureaucracy has been an educational growth area in the last two decades (consider the administrative palaces in greater Toronto, two across the street from each other in Mississauga and those of Scarborough and North York), New Zealand has eliminated the entire bureaucracy between the central government and the schools.

The problem is not just one of waste. Equally important, large bureaucracies become barriers to public will. School board members are made over by the bureaucracies, and kept busy on matters of finance, school organization, negotiations, and personnel. Administrators perpetuate themselves by promoting people like themselves, so that officials speak with one mind, not because they are submissive, but because they agree. (My research in 1991 on Ontario's directors showed a pronounced similarity of personal background in, for example, religion, politics, and policy issues). Such camaraderie is not unusual and not necessarily harmful, but it is objectionable in a public monopoly supposedly representing the public. The problem is not with the behaviour of bureaucracies, but with their unwarranted authority.

Required promotion through and appointment by the bureaucracy bring about a similarity of point of view; that is arguably a strength

in some public and private bureaucracies and may once have been
so in education. In a diversified, pluralist society it is unacceptable,
unless the national goal is to homogenize the nation – in which case
we must first agree, by strong consensus, on the basis on which we
wish to be homogenized. There is no such basis in Canada, and most
certainly not in education.

There are two parallel problems, both of which should be
addressed by reform. First, the world-view of the educational leaders
is very different from that of the largest groups within the public.
Second, the establishment's liberal, Progressive, and permissive view
of education signally fails to represent significant minorities of parents, to whom these views are abhorrent. It is important to note that
even if the first of those two problems of unrepresentativeness (i.e.
the difference between educators and the public majority) were
addressed, fundamental reform would still be necessary. While it is
objectionable that an elite minority should impose its educational
beliefs on people, it would be almost as bad if the beliefs of a majority (more likely in Canada a plurality) were imposed on every minority, unless we had decided that we wanted to be a homogeneous
melting pot with one national culture.

Administrators are in a quandary. If they follow their own philosophy, probably close to the educators' middle of the road, they do
not represent the numerous minorities. If they do not follow a consistent philosophy, they can be seen as unprofessional within the
context of a one-size-fits-all system. No wonder that minorities are
not represented among the leaders in public education. How could
they represent and implement a low-doctrine, one-size-fits-all program that was fundamentally inconsistent with their own educational world-view? In those terms, the exclusion of minorities (I refer
here of course to ideological and spiritual minorities – of relevance
to education – not to those who are physically different) is politically
legitimate. Members of those minorities are forced to pay if they
wish to exclude their children from an education of which they want
no part, in order to place place them within a convivial environment.

Parental exclusion from educational policy   The exclusion of parents
from their children's schooling is a theme running through many of
the problems faced by the schools today. The increasing size of
schools and districts and the growth of bureaucracies and unions
leave parents powerless. This situation would matter less if there
was consensual agreement on what schools should and should not
do, but there is not. A positive side effect of this problem is that more
Canadians are directly involved in their children's formal education

than ever before. They want to be able to determine their education, and many actively demand genuine choice. They are ready and eager for choice, probably more so than in any countries other than England and Australia. Unfortunately, unless parents are members of strong local, usually religious, communities, this enthusiastic involvement is channelled by default into individualistic efforts.

Changing social norms   The effect of changing demography is by no means limited to increased diversity of educational expectations. There have been, over the last thirty years, a variety of changes in the quality of family life. Increasingly, the professional upper class intermarries. The two-professional-parent family has genetic, psychic, material, and educational resources that provide the children with enormous advantage, in terms of intelligence, educational expectations, quality care beginning at birth, early childhood education, educational visits and travel, and after-schooling in music, sports, and academics.

In contrast, the typical single-parent family, also far more common than it once was, is likely to be relatively lacking in many of those areas. The two trends, of increasing numbers of both strong and weak families, lead to greater differences among children, including separation by residence and school. Increased mobility augments this trend. As the extended family and a close network of friends become more rare, greater weight is placed on the nuclear family. It is either strengthened to bear that weight or collapses under it, with diverse effects on the children.

Students' ignorance of English or French is an obstacle faced by teachers of new immigrants. This problem is often exaggerated; many immigrant groups are more successful than native-born Canadians. The use of immigrants as an excuse for poor levels of attainment is partially spurious. Nevertheless, immigrant children are on the average more likely to leave school early than are the native-born. Some do pose special problems in the classrooms and may well make it difficult for teachers to retain high expectations for those students in the same classroom who speak its official language. Immigrant children who cannot cope with English are frequently not recommended or offered special second-language programs, thus exacerbating the problem for the immigrants and the English-speaking children in their classrooms.

The practice of "mainstreaming" (putting children with extreme physical and behavioural problems in the regular classroom on the grounds that they should have the same educational experience as others) makes good instruction difficult or impossible, and reduces the possibility of maintaining clearly recognizable standards of discipline. This problem is compounded by the difficulty faced by the school in removing non-conforming students. It is made a jail in all but name, but one where the guards are officially supposed to be loving, caring, and effective.

Widespread youth unemployment makes the educational enterprise more difficult, quite apart from its insidious effect on the young adults who experience it directly. Educated young people with general degrees in social sciences and the arts assert that no one can get a job, excusing themselves from looking very hard and persuading permissive parents to support them at home. The reality is that the proportion of the population of working age that is employed is almost as high as it has ever been, and the vast majority of young people, particularly educated ones, are employed. In the late 1990s there are many parts of Canada where an industrious, courteous, well-groomed, and literate young person can readily find a job; indeed, many who lack some of those qualities do so. But there are still far too many unemployed young people, and the fear of unemployment, real or not, is disabling.

Many schools (mainly at the elementary level) react to these various phenomena by taking on a therapeutic role. They provide a caring, friendly, supportive haven from the outside world. They try to look after children's nutritional, medical, social, and nurturing needs. Within a child-centred context, academics become just one focus – and not the most important – most likely only for those whose parents insist on it. The result is that the educational gap widens still further, without any conscious decision or choice by parent, child, or school, in part because of an insistence that everyone should have *common*, but *individualized* schooling (like the construction company with custom-built homes ready for buyers to move into).

Finally, there is evidence of growing alienation that is not simply a result of unemployment and recession. The rates of crime and suicide among young people have been increasing steadily through boom and recession years. Emile Durkheim's remains the single best explanation for anomie (disconnectedness) and suicide. He argued that it resulted from major stress and disorganization in society. Poverty and unemployment in themselves do not cause the problems, but rather the breakdown in established beliefs, structures, and expectations. When the norms in society are confused, changing, and varied, it is impossible for a school reflecting that social maelstrom to impose a high doctrine of any kind. Such a school rarely causes alienation, whose seed lies deeper, but it provides a fertile, morally unstructured environment for its growth.

Disrespect for education; conflict with the media and the modern age   The single most powerful and universally held (if not acknowledged) educational philosophy in Western society is the one I term Techno-cratic – the idea that schooling should provide a base for future success, defined in material terms. Although the practical purposes of schooling should be recognized, the emphasis on material ends to the exclusion of others helps to develop an anti-educational climate in society and in the schools. The Egalitarian aim to provide a good academic background to everyone has been debauched as academics becomes a sign of the modern sin of elitism.

Although Progressivism is not substantively materialistic, its lack of a grounding in virtue provides a vacuum later that is inevitably occupied by individualistic materialism. The happy seven-year-olds who receive praise unrelated to achievement, who are given freedom of choice at school and at home, who are rarely held to account for their level of achievement, behaviour, or service, whose self-concept is constantly nurtured, and for whom immediate self-gratification is generally the rule easily become those disgruntled adolescents who want sex, alcohol, cigarettes, and drugs right now, and a car tomor-row. They resent any assignment that requires hard effort, and their definition of the future lies in fulfilment of their passing wishes, which reflect a continuing need for money and a transcendent belief in more. The elementary school does not cause such disaffiliation, but it does not help to provide an alternative world-view that does not focus on self.

Reading is the very basis of education. Access to computers and databases is no substitute for books, and the best computer data require complex reading or mathematical skills. Long periods of time spent watching commercial television and listening to popular music are not only harmful in themselves because of the trivialization by these media of what is most beautiful and worthwhile in human life. They are also harmful because the bad currency drives out the good; time spent on the passive media of television and vulgar (sometimes obscenely degrading) music is not applied to the more interactive medium of a good book, which engages the reader and demands thoughtful response.

Violence is often the expected answer to disagreement. The serial marriage is normal in the media (to the extent that marriage features in relationships at all). Children may be abused, cute, clever, preco-cious, pert, rebellious, sexy, abandoned, or funny, but they are rarely an important or integral part of a dignified, strong, loving, and united traditional family. Many schools (as well as many homes) are simply not friendly environments for education. They are either therapeutic welfare centres (at the elementary level) or places where credentials can be obtained by putting in time (at the secondary level). The credentials are chips to be cashed in for material rewards. I am not suggesting, as have some romantic idealists, that we should abolish them. My point is that credentials should be tied to publicly defined, worthwhile educational and training objectives, not to meaningless activity. Genuine achievement symbolizes what is worthwhile in our civilization; meaningless activity represents the self-destructive nihilism of modernity.

In some schools of choice, education implies such things as ideas, books, intellectual challenge, standards, constructive scepticism, aesthetic appreciation and expression, physical fitness, and the reinforcement of strong moral standards by which the conflicting ideas one meets in history, literature, and current affairs can be judged. Many, possibly most, educators and parents find this idea quaint, narrow, or, in the current idiom, bigoted and elitist, but such schools have waiting lists, and teachers are well represented in their parent body.

EDUCATIONAL REFORM IN THE PROVINCES

The basic criteria used here for judging the performance of provincial elementary and secondary school systems are quality, efficiency, and equal opportunity. To those I add reform effort: are they trying to move in sensible directions? The criteria themselves are probably less controversial than their interpretation and application. As will be clear from the earlier chapters of this book, everyone will agree that they want quality education; the difficulty lies in finding a consensus about what represents quality in a school system.

The objective information about quality available for the ten provinces is inadequate, so I have to add a fair dose of personal knowledge and judgment. Readers will probably not be surprised by the factors that I include in my informal ratings of the systems in the provinces: achievement, notably academic; programs to move students from school to work; and an effective system of student evaluation. Efficiency is interpreted as quality in relation to spending, together with low levels of outlay on services outside the school; it is "bang for the buck." Effort is a measure of the extent to which the provinces are moving in directions that address the educational problems identified earlier.

There are two factors within equality of educational opportunity. The first is similar levels of spending on schools across the province and non-discriminatory access to one's choice of school, with similar schools being available to all, irrespective of wealth or status. The second is that choices reasonably represent the range desired by parents. It is an assessment of availability and accessibility, not a measure of output. Differences of success rates among cultural, ethnic, or religious groups are not a criterion of opportunity but a reflection of multi-causal results.

Alberta, British Columbia, and Quebec

When I applied the four criteria, giving each equal weight, the provinces fell roughly into three groups. In the first, highest-scoring group are three provinces: Alberta, British Columbia, and Quebec. Alberta and British Columbia are the two that can take reasonable pride in their systems; in any international or interprovincial assessment their schools come out relatively well. They achieve the highest standards of quality while spending less than some other provinces. They also provide the highest levels of equality of opportunity. Both provinces have moved relatively recently to eliminate disparities in inter district spending, and both provide a reasonable level of choice. Alberta is the only province to have legislated provision for charter schools. As well, Alberta and British Columbia have some of the strongest student testing programs in the country, including examinations to determine access to university.

Alberta is generally moving in the right direction, but is not without problems. All ten provinces, including it, are fundamentally sticking to the model of the public, centralized monopoly. The result is that financial and program rigidities remain; teachers are all unionized, and their terms of employment remain part of rigid collective agreements. While there is greater equality of educational opportunity in Alberta than in other provinces, Roman Catholic schools are still advantaged financially over other minority institutions. Their constitutional situation is unique, and negotiations with the other minority schools might lead to an agreement whereby these schools would still have a lower level of funding, compensated for by greater administrative freedom. The fact remains that, even here, choice is provided under sufferance.

Calgary, the largest urban centre, still bears the stigma of having abolished its Protestant-minority (Logos) schools because of their success. The minority has no protection against a majority vote in favour of discrimination. Imagine the media uproar if Alberta, or Calgary, held a vote to determine the future of French-language schools, or even French-immersion schools. Despite the charter-school legislation, power still effectively lies with the school-district bureaucracies. Not only religious minorities are disadvantaged; it is very difficult for parents to gain access to academically intensive elementary schools, which are resisted equally by school-board administration and by teachers' unions.

Calgary's Catholic board had the distinction of supporting a publicly funded Jewish school after it was abandoned by the public board; the school is now independent. The same board runs a secondary school of choice, of over twenty years' standing, that provides a genuinely different, individualized program for students who do not like the traditional model (one teacher and thirty students). The Calgary Catholic board has been a national leader in actively encouraging parental involvement in choice, unlike the public board, which continues to try to resist choice, even charter-school applications. On the other hand, Edmonton was the first major public school board to offer a wide range of choice in schools and one of a very few to permit Christian schools.

British Columbia, like Alberta, scores high on quality and efficiency, and highest of all on equality of opportunity. It is the only province with a clearly thought out plan to provide categories of funding to independent schools based on carefully elaborated criteria, one of which is the level of the school's own financial base. There is no discrimination between Roman Catholic and other religions, and the proportion of students in independent schools is among the highest in the country; the high level results as much from accessibility as from dissatisfaction with the public system, although both are doubtless factors. Unfortunately, the NDP government under Premier Michael Harcourt took a backward step in reducing funding to the fundamentalist schools, to which his supporters among the teachers' unions took strong exception.

It is in the area of ongoing effort that British Columbia is weakest. Although local school districts have taken the initiative to open – to popular acclaim – academically intensive schools, at the provincial level – the direction of education is unclear. The top-down, Progressive Sullivan report has been set aside because of strong negative reaction from the public, but if the province has a different direction, it is not apparent. The Progressive hold on the primary years now seems unchallenged. If the rest of Canada is an indication, the educational establishment will move, assuming that it can get away with it, to push Progressive ideas into the senior elementary years: that is, integrated subjects, combined grades, and the erosion of testing.

The Quebec educational system is an enigma. In terms of public policy and levels of achievement, it is one with a lesser need for reform. The francophone majority scores particularly well on international tests, despite the historically undeveloped nature of the system and the financially disadvantaged character of the province. Quebec is the only province with a comprehensive evaluation system; individual achievement tests are given in the basic skills, and examinations for both graduation and admission to the postsecondary sector.

Like New Brunswick, a province that scores close to it overall, Quebec has a relatively large minority system. In both provinces the francophone population has been traditionally disadvantaged, but today performs better than the anglophone. In Quebec the programs, evaluation, and administration are identical for both sectors, but the anglophone cultural tradition is very different and is more open to external anglophone influence. The francophone performance is outstanding, considering its traditional cultural disadvantage.

Quebec scores low on efficiency, being a high-spending province with large district and provincial bureaucracies. Its system is the most tightly unionized in Canada, and a work-to-rule mentality probably adds to the high degree of public dissatisfaction. There is complete financial equality of opportunity among school districts, but minorities do not fare as well in practice, as the very high enrolment in independent schools would suggest.

Like British Columbia, Quebec does not score well on its effort to reform; there appears to be little genuine will to confront the unions, an action that is required if their bureaucratic hold on schools is to be weakened. Quebec was the first province to establish parent committees, but they still lack authority. It is currently attempting to change its constitutional base from one of religion (Protestant and Roman Catholic) to a system based on language. The move is more defensible than in Newfoundland, where strong Roman Catholic and Pentecostal minorities are losing ground. Most public schools in Quebec, officially Protestant or Catholic, are neither in spirit; they are more like Newfoundland's nominally Protestant Integrated schools. It remains to be seen whether the new regime in Quebec will permit minority religious schools for those parents who want them, or whether, like Ontario, the province will move from prescription to proscription.

New Brunswick, Manitoba, Saskatchewan, and Prince Edward Island

These four provinces comprise the second tier. New Brunswick is quite different educationally from the other three. While they represent an undistinguished middle, with passable, but mediocre systems, New Brunswick is the scene of real reform. Manitoba, Saskatchewan, and Prince Edward Island are similar in several ways.

All have relatively homogeneous populations, with few recent immigrants. Each has a small francophone minority. None is in the vanguard of educational reform. There are few indicators to judge these provinces in terms of quality, none of them being enthusiastic about evaluating students; but the limited available data suggest that they lie in the middle.

All three provinces provide a high degree of equal opportunity in financial terms; their schools are probably more similar intraprovincially than are those of the more populous provinces. Saskatchewan discriminates in favour of Roman Catholics, with a fully supported separate system. Discrimination is much more limited in PEI: only Charlottetown has de facto Roman Catholic elementary education, while the substantial Catholic population is distributed throughout the island. Manitoba is one of the two provinces without religious discrimination. It also is the most generous in its policy towards independent schools. Unlike British Columbia, it treats all independent schools alike, so that private schools for the Winnipeg elite receive the same funding as small religious ones. Roman Catholic schools are supported on the same basis as those of other denominations and sects. This is Manitoba's only notable educational reform. In PEI, reform means larger school systems, now also proposed in Saskatchewan. Too often in Canada, reform is interpreted in terms of shuffling the cards in the pack, changing the administrative organization. Increasing the size of school boards and school units does nothing for the student in the classroom and serves to dilute any lingering sense of community, either in the villages that lose their schools or within the schools themselves.

There is little overt discontent about education in these provinces. Saskatchewan is matched only by Ontario in the degree to which its system is managed in the interests of the educational establishment. In the long term, choice may improve Manitoba's level of achievement. In the short run, it may serve to remove active reform-minded parents from the public school. In contrast with those bland faces, New Brunswick could justifiably be placed in the front rank on the basis of efficiency and reform. It has led Canada in attempting to reduce out-of-school costs and is the first province to eliminate, in 1996, school boards entirely.

Pressed by Frank McKenna, the province is now well into its second wave of reform. His hand seems to have been behind the major thrusts. The first massive reform in New Brunswick took place under Louis Robichaud in 1967, at a time when other provinces were experiencing the first bloom of their love affair with Progressivism. Robichaud's earlier reforms and the later autonomy of the francophone system have probably been the major factors in the success of the largely Acadian francophone population. The initial McKenna reform wave was, like Robichaud's, highly Technocratic, intending to ensure more-efficient governance by means of larger school systems, a long school year of actual teaching days, more student evaluation, and a tighter common curriculum. The government's later reform efforts included the abolition of school boards, larger administrative units under the direct control of the provincial department, and three layers of parental advisory committees. Computerization has also become a high priority.

The most important innovation by far is the tilt towards parental control. Although Quebec has had mandatory school and district parent committees for over twenty years, their role has typically been minimal compared with the power of elected school boards, the teachers' unions, and a massive and exceptionally competent (among Canadian provinces) central ministry. In the absence of school boards and with a small administrative presence outside the school, it is possible that New Brunswick's parent committees will come to play an important role. No other province has made such consistent and determined efforts to reform the schools in a manner generally consistent with parental wishes. Major reform initiatives over the last thirty years in other provinces, such as Ontario, British Columbia, and Nova Scotia, have been less consistent and have all but ignored the wishes of parents.

Unfortunately, I cannot confidently predict success for New Brunswick's Technocratic, American-style reforms, even though I see a glimmer of light. Most of the reforms are top-down, yet parents and students depend mainly on local agents – teachers and principals – for the quality of the education. Even though the New Brunswick teachers' unions (anglophone and francophone) have been faced down by the government to a stronger degree than in most other provinces, they remain a legislated closed shop and thus have a great deal of control at the level of the school. The new parent committees are simply advisory, lacking authority to develop school policy or select teachers and principals. School staffs may quietly ignore uncongenial advice, arguing that it is "political" interference, the usual charge raised against any outside idea that educators do not like. Of the three levels of parent committees (provincial, administrative unit, and school), the first two are likely to develop policies that will further bureaucratize the system.

Even if there were to be true parental control of school policy, it should not be seen as a panacea. In areas where parent authority is real, such as New Zealand and Chicago, the experience has been mixed. (I should note that my commentary on New Zealand is based on visitors' observations, particularly those of Professor Stephen Lawton, and media reports; I am not aware of any large-scale research on the effects of reforms in that country.) The actual level of parent authority varies greatly in practice, with principals often becoming de facto rulers. This is not necessarily harmful; many parents are only too happy to delegate the schooling of their children to competent professionals who reflect their own educational wishes. The crux is that principals should represent and act on behalf of parents, whether they are controlled tightly or not.

Parent control can of course be abused. For example, a special-interest group may gain control and administer policy and practice that reflect a narrow set of purposes. Or a group representing the majority may ignore or reject legitimate educational interests of minorities. Although I favour giving parents control over key policies at the school level, that change should be conditional on free choice of school throughout the province (as it is in New Zealand), if one form of tyranny is not to be replaced by another. Parent committees must also feel free to delegate as much or as little as they wish to the principal and staff of the school. Choice is entirely lacking in New Brunswick's highly centralized reform program.

That province is in some ways the most interesting from the perspective of reform. It is a good test case to see if central, Technocratic direction can really bring about genuine improvement in program delivery and in parental satisfaction. If it does not work in New Brunswick, a province with two fairly homogeneous populations, each with its own school system, then there is little hope for the process to work in the larger, more demographically diverse provinces. My guess is that, even in New Brunswick, the educational establishment will outlast the strong leadership Frank McKenna, who has now left office.

The Technocratic reforms appear to have made little, if any, impact so far on achievement. The emphasis on student evaluation has mainly been diverted to low-stakes tests with little or no effect on the students' educational future. There is no overall testing program for high school graduation or for movement to university, and test results are not published by school. While there is no denying the importance of material improvement in a disadvantaged province such as New Brunswick, in the end it will prove insufficient, particularly because it is administered in a top-down manner that is readily interpreted by those further down the line.

Newfoundland, Nova Scotia, and Ontario

These three educationally distinct provinces form the third tier. Newfoundland earns its place as a result of its economic and cultural lack of development. Although for a time after the province joined Confederation, Newfoundland's school system improved steadily in terms of quality, that progress seems to have levelled off. Equality of opportunity is hampered by the province's sparse population. Even so, it is remarkable that in the latest international tests, Newfoundland should perform as well as or better than Ontario. In terms of achievement related to wealth, Newfoundland deserves to rank much higher.

The province has taken a harmful turn in the area of educational reform, however. Financial problems inevitably play a major role in driving educational policy. Unfortunately, they have led to efforts to build larger, supposedly more efficient educational units. It is not all clear how much more efficient the Newfoundland system can become; it needs more money from a changed program of federal-provincial grants. About the worst way to bring about efficiency is to hold a plebiscite to determine, in effect, if support for Roman Catholic and Pentecostal schools should be limited. I have already criticized the principle of determining minority entitlements on the basis of a majority vote. It is generally inappropriate for a central bureaucracy to decide that a school should close because it does not meet certain criteria of size. Newfoundland is following the mistakes of other provinces at a time when the fact that that bigger district bureaucracies do not necessarily make for better or more efficient education should be known (better to abolish them altogether). Larger administrative units only make sense where most authority is passed to the parents' committees at the school level, in other words, when the central unit has little left to do. The secularization of schools and the elimination of community will lead to a vacuum in the school, one likely to be quickly filled by negative aspects of our culture: bureaucratization, alienation, poor work habits, and disorder. In the long run, those problems may even hinder efficiency, let alone effectiveness.

A way to reduce expenditures, if further cuts are unavoidable, would be to free up the schools by making union membership optional for teachers and by permitting non-union schools. Catholic, Pentecostal, and other schools (or their representative boards) could be allocated a set sum per pupil based on the programs in which students are enrolled, plus a transportation allowance. If a school decides that the amount provided makes its continued operation impossible, it can examine other options, such as raising additional funds, the sharing of services with other schools, closure, or amalgamation. There should be free choice of schools throughout the province. If they stay together under governing boards, that should be their decision. The constitutionally established religious rights should be respected. That does not prevent secular schools from being operated, either independently or under the wing of the Integrated (Protestant) schools, which tend to be secular in practice, as Austin Harte's study, completed at OISE in 1989, shows. Clearly, Newfoundland performs poorly in terms of reform.

Nova Scotia has been a leader in embracing Progressivism in the classroom and a laggard in developing a meaningful testing program. For example, although students take the province's own tests in grades nine and twelve, these tests meet few of the desired criteria; almost nothing hangs on low or high performance, for students, teachers, or schools. A recent reform commission headed by Derrick Kimball, a member of the legislature, produced some sensible, if insufficient recommendations. However, he failed to receive his party's nomination in the next election (the Conservatives were defeated), and the report languishes on the shelves. Nova Scotia performs poorly on quality and reform effort. It has had a probably undeserved reputation for good education; but if performance takes into account social advantage and disadvantage, the province probably vies with Ontario for last place.

Ontario has emerged in this book as the major educational problem in Canada. It exhibits almost every educational problem to be found in the country and is only saved from disgrace by its affluent, highly educated, and ambitious people and by the individual quality and professionalism of many of its teachers. The level of student achievement is about the same as that of the Maritime provinces, falling well below what one would expect from Canada's most prosperous province. Its system is the most "provincial" in the country, with its inbred educational establishment singing in unison that Ontario is the only system that is in step, all other countries and provinces being out of step wherever they differ from it. If a school system decided to bring in a director from Alberta who had some understanding of tests and standards, it would be prohibited from doing so by the Ministry of Education; no such person could meet Ontario's inward-looking standards.

Despite the stated intentions of the three political parties to reform education, the province still lacks any coherent plan for student evaluation that meets the criteria attained by Quebec, British Columbia, and Alberta and by almost all countries in the developed world. Not only is the elementary system up to grade six run on narrow, child-centred lines, but the Progressive idea is now being extended to the middle grades and the secondary school. Efforts being made to improve the dismal school-to-work record (an undertaking that should be easiest to implement in this highly industrialized and urbanized province) are inefficient and poorly conceived. Ontario scores badly on all four criteria – quality, efficiency (with its profligate waste of money in Metropolitan Toronto and Ottawa and its fat bureaucracies in the urban and suburban school boards), equality of opportunity, and reform effort. It is the only province to do so on financial equality of opportunity. In 1996–97 the Hastings–Prince Edward County Catholic Board faced provincial cuts, while Metropolitan Toronto, which spends more than half as much again per elementary pupil, successfully resisted even limited equalization of commercial and business school taxes. It is difficult to see how the government can meet its financial targets in education without either eviscerating the poor boards or trimming the fat off the wealthy.

The province's religious discrimination is the most egregious in Canada. Although technically, one can argue that Saskatchewan is as discriminatory, that province is more homogeneous; its school system is less urbanized and very likely less secularized and politically polarized (in terms of left-wing and neo-conservative dogma). I doubt that Saskatoon has a gay-education program for its elementary schools and probably not even condom machines in its high school washrooms. There is less demand and arguably less need for minority schools in that province. Religious discrimination exists in some form in eight provinces, but Ontario alone has formally increased its discriminatory funding of Catholic schools (by extending through legislation, approved by all three political parties, the full funding of Catholic schools to the end of high school from the previous level of grade ten), while at the same time refusing to provide any funding whatsoever to religious schools serving less-advantaged minorities. (Imagine the international uproar if Northern Ireland were to fund Protestant schools and give no support for Roman Catholic ones, justifying the action on the grounds of political conditions in 1867.) At the same time, Christian education has been totally removed from the public (non-Catholic) sector, in a province where the majority claim Christian affiliation and a significant minority regularly participate in Christian worship. Ontario has the largest Jewish population in Canada, which supports independent Jewish schools totally ineligible for public funding. It also has Moslem schools.

As for effort, the attempts at reform made to date by the most recent Liberal, NDP, and Conservative governments have been inept at best and wrong-headed at worst. No attempt has been made to encourage the development of academically intensive elementary schools, or to give parents a choice other than Progressive education. The ministry itself is still seen, rightly or wrongly, as supporting Progressive ideas, if only by default. Premier David Peterson's Liberal government initiated the ill-fated project to destream grade nine. To be fair, its intention was not to undermine academics by introducing Progressive methodologies into the high school, but rather to provide a thorough education for all fourteen-year-olds, as recommended in a report from the prominent Liberal journalist George Radwanski. To work, the project required that the middle schools provide rigorous teaching according to clear standards, so that students would enter grade nine with at least minimal academic accomplishments. No effort was made to bring about this massive reform, and responsibility for its implementation was inherited by the succeeding NDP government.

The NDP objective was to make the high school more Egalitarian, with more equal outcomes among the social classes and particularly between blacks and whites. It is unlikely that the Rae government intended to introduce Progressive ideas (subject integration and collaborative learning) into grade nine any more than did its Liberal predecessor. It is well established (if not generally known in Canadian educational circles) that Progressive instruction increases the differences among individuals, the antithesis of both Radwanski's and Marxist intent. (Common sense suggests that if the teacher's impact is reduced, then children will learn more in proportion to their parents' direction.) Nevertheless, it is unsurprising that, once implementation was left to academics and administrative members of the establishment, the result should be an attack on direct instruction in grade nine and a lessening of emphasis on academic achievement. The actual results, in terms of either achievement or inter-racial and inter-class success, are unknown because that information would require extensive achievement testing and the collection of data by race and social class, both – ludicrously in the context – politically incorrect. Absurdly, inappropriate policies are promulgated to address informally observed and imperfectly defined problems, with outcomes that can never be known.

Policy announcements by the current Progressive Conservative government show an inadequate understanding of the educational problem. At various times it has promised a computer on every desk, as if a machine could replace a teacher of the basic skills; compulsory cooperative education for every high school student, to allow every-one to play at work without actually getting involved in either a genuine skill or a school-to-work program; and vague evaluation plans that will cost far more than the available national tests, without necessarily meeting the basic criteria of effective and useful testing.

Ontario has numerous reform groups, some of whose members remember education in the province before that system was disman-tled, some who have experienced schools in other provinces or coun-tries, and a number who have managed a good education within the province despite the Progressive reforms of the last thirty years. Some reformers see faint signs of a break in the power of the estab-lishment, while others believe that it will wait for the current waves of opposition to pass, just as it did in the mid-1970s.

Of the three provinces in the lowest tier, Newfoundland has been dealt the most cruel hand by nature, but the most recent reform has not been well targeted. Nova Scotia and Ontario have managed to ignore their potential and create educational systems considerably worse than their people deserve. I had difficulty placing Newfound-land and Ontario in the same tier. Newfoundland could arguably be ranked in the second group, on the basis of its achievement in com-parison with its social background. On the same basis, Ontario could be placed alone in a fourth tier.

THE SLOW PACE OF EDUCATIONAL REFORM

If Ontario's record is as bad as I make it out to be, the reader will undoubtedly ask: Why has the public not resisted en masse, and why have successive governments of varied ideological stripe not done something about it? That is an important question not only for Ontario but, in varying degrees, for the other provinces too. The answer illustrates just how great are the obstacles to the improve-ment of an educational system.

It should be remembered that parents have a much greater effect on their children than schools do; this is particularly so when one narrows one's view to the relative differences in achievement among children. Those who do best usually owe more to their parents than to the teachers or schools they attend (after all, other children also attend those same schools with different results). Parents differ more than schools do, particularly in Canada, where there are few excel-lent and few disgraceful schools. Even Ontario's level of schooling is mediocre rather than disastrous. One of Canada's educational strengths is the relatively small – in international terms – gap between its best and its worst schools.

Parents ensure that their children learn some basic things. Generally speaking, those who help their children to the greatest extent have the most successful children; academic success is a relative matter. So the knowledgeable ones most capable of effective opposition to the establishment have the least direct stake in opposing it. The more successful that energetic, educated, middle-class parents are in improving the public system, the more that disadvantaged bright children, the ones who suffer most in mediocre schools, will benefit. The number of parents involved in reform movements is a small proportion of the dissatisfied. Even among persistent reformers, who are rebuffed by teachers, principals, administrators, and trustees, few continue their efforts after their children leave school.

Thousands of parents have tried to do something about the inadequacy of their children's schools, but they have met solid resistance and defensiveness at all levels of the system. I have been asked hundreds of times by parents what can be done to change their child's classroom, the school, or the system. My advice has evolved over the years. For some time now, I have, with regret, said that the most practical thing I can suggest is that parents concentrate on saving their own child and forget about the system, even the classroom, which certainly will not be changed in time for their child. Thousands of parents have reached that common-sense conclusion before and without me. Increasing numbers of them teach their children after school, hire tutors, or enrol their children in Kumon, Oxford, Sylvan, and other private after-schools. That decision sounds callous, even cynical. The reality is that general efforts to reform education have had little success and that it is neither cynical nor callous to help one's own child; rather, it is a parental duty.

Some parents are, of course, satisfied with things as they are. For example, many parents of young children are delighted to see how happy their children are and to be told how well they are doing, not having evidence to the contrary. Some share the school's philosophy that freedom and high self-concept are the most significant values. Even in the secondary schools, when the problems are more likely to be visible, parents may be content to look the other way while their adolescent coasts through school without doing very much to receive a meaningless graduation certificate; they realize that any attempt to make their son or daughter actually do something would likely lead to outright confrontation and rebellion. This quiet and unexpressed decision parallels that of teachers in the classroom who tacitly accept that peaceful indolence is preferable to angry confrontation. But corruption is not an isolated infection at home or at school; it metastasizes.

There are parents too who feel genuinely and reasonably that they have got what they wanted from the system. One morning I was talking about educational reform to a group of young journalists at the offices of the *Globe and Mail*. Towards the end of the meeting a senior editor came in. He knew a little about my ideas, enough to believe that they were wrong. Almost immediately, he interrupted me to say that he was delighted with the education of his daughter in the city of Toronto system. She had had the benefit of French immersion, and she had gone to one of the elite secondary schools (my term; he described it as the neighbourhood school, but he lived in an elite neighbourhood. It is not generally known that Toronto has two unofficial levels of secondary school, but there is strong competition, among principals, teachers, and students, to get into the upper tier.) This man's successful and well-educated daughter was going to Queen's University, Canada's leading university for the academic elite, in the fall.

I am strongly critical of the Progressive idea, but it does work, as will any idea, however mad, for many children and their parents. University is a zero-sum system: the same number of students are admitted, irrespective of variations in quality; there is no standard in Ontario, merely a fluctuating school mark dividing successful and unsuccessful contestants. Even in provinces with exams, little attempt is made to determine a standard for admission to a particular program based on carefully articulated prerequisites. Universities want a certain number of students, in rich and lean years. Queen's, by setting high cut-off points for admission, guarantees itself good students with minimal effort.

In any school system, there are administrators and teachers who work effectively irrespective of fashion. There was a story, apocryphal perhaps, when David Peterson was premier of Ontario, that his children's public school, close to Upper Canada College, was the only one in the Toronto system where teachers used direct instruction. Some parents know how to get what they want, others are just lucky, and a few are sufficiently influential to affect their school. Parents make the best choices they can for their children, and to a significant extent middle- and upper-class children come out of the Ontario system, as they do from any system, good or bad, socialist or capitalist, more successful in academic terms than do less-advantaged children.

At the other end of the social scale, many parents are unable to make the most of the school system. The reasons are obvious. They themselves are less educated and do not know how the system works. For many there is simply not an opportunity to visit the school and talk to teachers and principals, because of shift work or the lack of someone at home to care for the children when they might go. For others there is a fear, sometimes legitimate, that they and their opinions will not be taken seriously.

The reality is that most members of parent reform groups are middle class. Those children most poorly served by the system come from socially, educationally, and economically disadvantaged homes. In my experience, the active reformers have usually experienced directly an educational problem (most often a son who has failed to learn the basic skills adequately), or are particularly well informed and interested in the education system in general, often from a knowledge of what goes on in other provinces or countries. Understandably, their reformist zeal fades once they have saved their own child, perhaps by home or private schooling.

As for politicians, many sincerely want to improve the system. There are politicians in all the major parties who recognize at least some of the problems laid out in this book, and who would like to address them. In Ontario specifically, such ministers as Sean Conway (as well as Premier David Peterson), David Cooke (encouraged by Premier Bob Rae), and John Snobelen (supported by Premier Mike Harris) have all spoken sympathetically of some of the reforms necessary to address the province's educational problems. Similar statements can be made about other provinces. None of those politicians has cynically sacrificed schools to achieve some other nefarious goal. As long as we assume that educational problems stem principally from ignoble motives and bad people, there is little chance of improvement. I am critical of teachers' unions, but their leaders are for the most part convinced that they are acting in the best interests of education.

Some understanding of why previous reform efforts have failed is required if readers are to understand why only radical reform will prove successful. I have already stressed the ability of members of the educational establishment (faculties of education, administrators, department officials, and teachers' unions) to block proposed reforms that undercut their power and privilege, which they believe they use wisely. But there is one general proposition that requires emphasis. Most educational reforms proposed for the system require careful implementation; every school is supposed to be changed in time. But who is going to implement the reforms? The only possible answer is members of the educational establishment. This fact, more than anything else, explains why the best-laid plans of politicians go awry.

At the beginning of Margaret Thatcher's third term as Britain's prime minister, I met a member of her policy advisory unit who was involved in educational reform. He himself was, I was not surprised to hear, an economist, not a pedagogue. He told me that the biggest problem the English reformers experienced was being unable to find people to implement their programs, to develop their national curricula and their new tests. Nearly everyone technically qualified was philosophically opposed, this despite the strong public and media support for the reforms. The Labour government under Prime Minister Tony Blair supports most of the key Thatcher reforms in education, but they are still strongly resisted in the schools and faculties of education.

Canadian reformers want to have clear curricula consisting of sequential objectives. Quebec has such programs, but the numerous versions of Ontario's common curricula, right up to the 1997 version, influenced by educational reformer and economist Bill Robson, were a travesty of sequential curricula, the language program reading like a satire of a common-sense program. The sincerity of those involved is not in doubt; they did not set out to construct programs that would be impractical and unhelpful. But the question remains, "How high should objectives be set?" The answer of those in the system is, "At the level currently being attained." That is reasonable enough if one believes that the present system is performing well – and they do – but not if a vital reason for reform is that standards are set too low. What form should objectives take? The establishment's reply is, "One that will ensure that teachers teach the right (i.e. child-centred) way." Most reformers want straightforward evaluation of every student in the basic skills. Establishment-made tests are usually expensive and may have limited, ambiguous, self-serving results.

In the end, effective educational reform means change in the classroom; that is where learning, as a part of formal education, for the most part takes place. (I am not forgetting the important role of homework, whereby young people can reinforce what they have learned, apply it in different ways and settings, and, if they are fortunate, discuss it with interested parents.) But ironically, the last thing that educational reform should attempt is direct intervention in the classroom. The practical and ethical problems are too great in a pluralist society. What reform has to do is to set conditions where parents can choose the kind of education they want and make it difficult for those supplying the service to resist. And this transformation must somehow be accomplished without much dependence on the educational experts for support. Conditions in the classroom will change when teachers have a strong incentive to concentrate on their central purpose, the attainment of meaningful educational objectives in a moral, productive, supportive, and pleasant ethos. At first sight, failure to address teaching in the classroom directly looks like a recipe for paralysis. Change must take place in the classroom, but governments cannot and should not direct teachers' pedagogy and the school climate. That paradox explains much of the failure of past efforts, but it is not irresolvable.

To bring about reform, we have to change our basic assumptions. It is simply not sensible in a pluralist democracy at the end of the twentieth century to imagine that all schools can be altered according to a single new and improved model, whether Technocratically computerized or Progressively humanized. We simply do not agree on what is better. Previous reform efforts have tried to follow a single approach, and they have not worked. Meanwhile, more and more parents are choosing alternative schools, either inside or outside the public system, with which they are more satisfied. The question implicitly addressed by the bureaucracy is not, "How can we best give parents what they want?" (a seditious question from the point of view of the establishment), but "How can we prevent parents from leaving the system?"

One size does not fit all. There is no single ideal school for every parent in a pluralist democracy, Technocrat and Progressive, Individualist and Traditionalist, Culturalist and Egalitarian. Continuously changing the whole system to the flavour of the year is impossible even if it were desirable. The so-called pendulum in education, which I think has wobbled near the Progressive end – I hope it is the end – of its arc for a long time, is mocked by teachers with the mantra "This too shall pass." We need schools reflecting the abiding wishes of parents and the public will, schools that change with changing knowledge, appreciation, and understanding, but not with fads promoted by the experts.

In sum, the obstacles to genuine educational reform are daunting. They include the following:

1 The children most seriously harmed by ineffective schooling usually come from disadvantaged families that are the least able to influence the system.
2 The majority of middle-class children do relatively well and have good access to places in colleges and universities based on that relative standing.
3 There is solid resistance to change from an entrenched educational establishment that is committed to the very things that reformers most want to change.
4 The public system is a powerful quasi-monopoly, and so there is little internal or external incentive for fundamental reform. Teachers

who see, and talk in private about, the poor practice in their own or their children's schools are muffled; it is "unprofessional" for them to become whistle-blowers, according to their union's code of "ethics." Reform groups of teachers have to tread very carefully.

5 Those most aware of the inadequacies of their children's schools compensate for them by means of after- or private schooling.

6 Even the best-intentioned politicians have to act through layers of bureaucracy within a four-year term; they wrongly assume that their policies will have some of the impact intended without negative side effects.

7 The provinces with the least-effective schools also have the least-effective systems of student evaluation, and so the scale and the individual nature of the problem are hidden from the public and parents respectively. Ineffective provinces choose expensive, but uninformative provincial tests over available and more economical national ones.

8 Differences among home backgrounds and in parental support, a major effect on student performance, obscure both the cause and the outcome of ineffective schooling.

9 There is fundamental disagreement at all levels of society about what schools ought to be doing.

WHAT NOT TO DO

In the following pages I outline prescriptions that are sometimes advocated for the reform of elementary and secondary schools. The ideas are not all equally misguided; they have thoughtful supporters with a carefully developed rationale. Giving any of them a high priority, however, at best diverts educators and the public from the reforms that Canada really needs; at worst it points them in the wrong direction.

Social Engineering

Schools should not be used in an attempt to make people fundamentally different from what parents, as good citizens, and society as a whole want them to be. All schools should reflect the basic ideals of the pluralist democracy; anything more specific should be consistent with parents' personal ideals. Most ideas for social engineering come from the neo-Marxist left; these concepts have a surprising continuing influence in the media given such a discredited and unpopular ideology. Schools are told that they should produce equal outcomes among certain selected (but not all) social groups. It is a belief that has taken strong hold among our media and with liberal politicians; even conservative politicians seem afraid to confront it directly.

The idea is a bad one because it would, if implemented, destroy the family. The influence of the family on children's lives is erased or marginalized when parents cannot raise their offspring with some responsibility for the results. Not everyone agrees with that assertion, but note that advocates of equal outcomes among groups never publicly admit that their success requires the destruction of family influence. Opponents of their ideas are instead characterized as conservative, bigoted, and prejudiced. The equal-outcomes idea cannot work in a genuinely free society because the more that schools are made the same, the more that differences in school success are automatically attributable to variations among individuals and their backgrounds. When attempts are made to slow down the more competent children, to hold them back, their parents intervene to help them privately or put them in schools where they will not be kept at some mediocre level. Those who reject Egalitarian schools for their own children include leading Egalitarian politicians and academics. Left-wing politicians have long made educational choices that they deride as elitist when others make them. Strongly left-wing Stephen Lewis and Michele Landsberg famously sent their son to Upper Canada College. More recently, British prime minister Tony Blair, following a long tradition of prominent Labour politicians, has rejected local comprehensives in favour of a grant-maintained (i.e. opted-out) school for his son. Moe Sihota, a minister of education in British Columbia's NDP government well known for his rhetorical defence of public schools, at the same time, in 1996, sent his daughter to an independent school, as did a prominent minister in Rae's NDP government in Ontario.

There are sound reasons for these politicians' choices. Parents should not be faulted for making legitimate and legal decisions in the best interests of their children. The problem arises when Egalitarian education for ordinary people is legislated, from which the rich, including prominent leaders, are exempt, in the same way that Egalitarian health care exempts the rich, including the prominent politicians who defend their policies. Egalitarianism is increasingly recognized, outside academia and the media, as a bad dream, particularly since the skeletons of corruption and nepotism have been discovered behind the Iron Curtain. If prominent Egalitarians refuse to sacrifice their children on the altar of their ideology, why should the mass of parents who do not even believe in it? Those on the left are not alone, of course, in their wish to mould society to their model.

Anyone with a clear set of educational beliefs to be applied universally to everybody else's children is equally guilty of intended social engineering.

The alternative is not inequity and unfairness. Equality of opportunity (as distinct from equality of outcomes) is an important criterion for evaluating a school system. One way to promote it is indeed to send all children to the same common school with the same curriculum. (Obviously, there will always be a few very exceptional children who cannot benefit from the common curriculum, but some countries hold these to a small fraction of the whole.) In a homogeneous society with strongly consensual goals, that is a defensible policy; but Canada is not such a society. An alternative is open access for all young people, not just the rich and influential, to a wide variety of educational options.

Obviously, I do not categorize my own Traditional, Cultural, and Technocratic philosophy as a bad dream. But there are two important differences, one a matter of judgment, the other a matter of fact. First, Egalitarianism is not of equivalent quality and worth to the Western Judaeo-Christian tradition, as most Canadians agree. A broader statement of the principle is that all value preferences are not of equal worth, but rather a matter of personal choice. This is not the place to argue that fundamental philosophical point; sufficient to state here that most Canadians agree with it. Second, I am not advocating that all schools be made over in the Traditional, Cultural, and Technocratic manner which I personally consider desirable. Such schools should be available to those who want them, just as those who differ should have access to their own preferences. The area public school should be based on the ideas of the majority or plurality in the larger society, neither on my personal preferences in education nor on those of any expert elite. There can be no objection to Egalitarians choosing schools run on their principles, but that concession is of no interest to the Egalitarian minority, for the good reason that their authoritarian ideology demands that all schools be run on Egalitarian principles. How can all be equal if some are allowed to choose not to be so? In that sense, the Egalitarian choice is different from the others. Therefore any concession to true Egalitarianism implies a further step towards the one-size-fits-all model. In contrast, it is perfectly reasonable to request or accept a computer-based school of choice without prescribing Technocratic common schools for everyone.

An important theme of this book is that Canadian elementary schools are dominated by a single philosophy, not at all the Egalitarian viewpoint (to which there is much empty lip-service) but rather the Progressive. The latter philosophy is far from being a consensual choice of the Canadian public, and even if it were, its imposition on a pluralist society would be wrong. Where Progressivism assumes cult status, it becomes a form of social engineering, based on therapeutics (educators are not instructors but therapists able to care for children harmed by parents and the environment). More succinctly, teachers, and their expert advisors, know best what every child "needs," a favourite Progressive word indicating the final authority of their belief system. Parents are told not to put their own "wants" before the child's "needs," which only the experts understand. In the classroom, the greatest danger of social engineering comes from the Progressive idea. In terms of legislation, influenced so heavily by ideologues in academia and the media, the greatest danger comes from Egalitarianism.

It is simply not sensible to assume that groups of young people should all end up the same, in terms of jobs, interests, income, values, politics, or schooling. People make some decisions independently – we all waver between choices, sometimes making the actual choice almost by chance. Most decisions are also heavily influenced, directly and indirectly, by family, friends, background, sex, teachers, books, chance encounters, or, above all, personal values. The idea that schools should somehow overcome all those influences and encourage all groups to think and act alike is destructively naive. What the state can do is to provide parents and young people themselves with informed choice in schooling.

Mechanization of Schooling

Mechanization is only helpful to the extent that it assists schools to achieve their educational goals and objectives. Yet for years efforts have been made to introduce computers into schools as though something magical would happen if children could use them or, better still, had a computer on their desks or, more recently and best of all, have access to the Internet.

For some children, particularly boys, computers do have an instant appeal and provide an intrinsic incentive to learn. But there is no evidence that the availability of computers is itself a great boon. They can help with drill, but they require close supervision. Computers can assist learners to gain access to databases, but at best that function is similar to using an encyclopedia and usually not comparable with reading several different expert sources. There are some valid teaching programs, but one rarely hears of computers being used to achieve important educational objectives; rather, computers and databases take on a life and a justification of their own. Books are subject to editorial and public, critical review. Entries in databases may be mistaken or deliberately false. It is to be hoped that the predicted replacement of books by massive computer databases in school libraries never comes to pass.

Central authorities should not decide how children learn; they should be concerned with developing clear objectives and checking their achievement. It is just as big a mistake to believe that purchasing computers will of itself advance educational achievement as to think that setting up child-centred classrooms is a a substitute for discovering what children have actually learned. They are both examples of unsupported faith in ideological propositions. They are both based on undeclared world-views not shared by millions of Canadians.

Certainly, every young person should learn to use a computer correctly and should leave school computer-literate. Even those limited objectives have not been universally achieved after more than a decade of intensive implementation of computers, and still there is talk of computerization being the educational answer. The explanation is obvious: computers tend to be used for the things that they can do most easily and that give the student the most freedom. The results are uneven; a few students do become extremely skilful, some from using computers at home, others from access at school. Many learn almost nothing.

Simply put, most young people require a teacher to see that they learn, to inspire them, and to provide the assurance and discipline to keep the learning process on track and evaluate what they have learned. It is not reasonable to expect all children and adolescents to learn independently. Most parents cannot even be sure their children are completing their homework adequately. The ready availability and attraction of computer games, not to mention unimpeded access to pornography and sadism on the Internet, are, at the least, distractions from educational learning.

A few secondary schools have become mechanized, in the sense that learning depends significantly on computerized resources. Such individualized programs should be an alternative available to students, but there is no evidence that such approaches will appeal to or work for the majority. They also represent the ultimate demise of the school as community.

There is clear evidence that mechanization is the preferred route to reform in parts of the United States. Todd Oppenheimer describes the cutting back of other school subjects to make room for computers as educational malpractice ("The Computer Delusion," *Atlantic Monthly,* September 1997). He gives examples, such as New Jersey reducing school grants while allocating $10 million to computers, a single school district in California spending $27 million on them, and schools replacing art and music by computers. In Canada it is diffi-cult to identify such movements within our large, secretive school districts, but there is no doubt that library, music, and art programs, among others, are in decline, while computers proliferate. The fact that young people should be taught to keyboard (at, say, the age of twelve) and should know how to use a computer when they gradu-ate, is no reason for the unfocused, unevaluated spread of computers throughout the grades.

This is an area where teachers in particular and educators in general are least to blame. For every district administrator who wants to boast about having more modern computers than any other district, there are ten teachers with considerable scepticism about their educational value. Unfortunately, parents are probably more likely than teachers to demand more mechanization; after all, does not everyone know that computers are the future? This is another reason why every school should be publicly accountable for its results; evaluation cannot prevent mistakes being made, but it is an invaluable antidote.

Organizational Reform

The most popular reforms are organizational. Almost every province and a great many school systems have undergone major structural reorganizations. For the most part, these neither save the expected amounts of money nor improve education. Combining school dis-tricts has helped to remove the remaining vestiges of community in the more densely populated areas where most Canadians live. School districts are increasingly redundant, except for the provision of technical support services (and increasingly for most of those too); they have lost their core reason for existence, that is, their sensitivity to local parents.

Reorganization usually does not have any direct harmful impact, except where surviving local communities are affected (by the loss of a small school board or, more seriously, by the loss of a school), but there are negative indirect effects. Reorganization is often expen-sive, sometimes it becomes an excuse for adding personnel, and it always diverts attention from more important reforms and often gives authorities an illusion of educational progress.

A well-educated school board member assured me that his enor-mous suburban board was reorganizing to decentralize authority.

For many years, decentralization and school-based management have been fashionable talking points in Canadian school systems. I was surprised at the trustee's assertion because I knew the system well as a tightly regulated, hierarchical bureaucracy. He told me triumphantly that they were moving to a system of area superintendents reporting to the director of education. What he imagined to be decentralization was actually the addition of another hierarchical layer, the definition of bureaucratization. Principals, teachers, and parents were being removed even further from the point of authority, not given more control.

This is not to suggest that any existing organizational structure should be considered sacrosanct. Over time, it is possible that other provinces should follow New Brunswick's lead in getting rid of school boards altogether. In the current context, however, Ontario's plan to greatly reduce the number of school boards makes little sense. It is not that the existing organization is particularly efficient or supportive of community; on the contrary, it is inefficient and excessively bureaucratic. Rather, the belief that simply moving to larger boards will save money distracts attention from the need to shed many bureaucratic layers and services. It would have been easier, and more politically palatable, to have followed the Quebec route of setting the budget for administrative positions. Simplest of all would have been to limit funding to school boards and allow schools to receive direct funding if they chose, bypassing the school board altogether.

A good principle is that organization and administration should react to conditions. They are means, not ends. If parents find a small local school ineffective because there are too many grades for the few teachers to teach effectively, then closure is an obvious solution. Shutting the school by central decision because it is "too small" or "too expensive" usually indicates an overly rigid and centralized system of operation.

Centralization or Decentralization?

This book may appear to be advocating decentralization, with more authority for the school. If readers have reached that conclusion, they have misinterpreted the text. Centralization is a current and generally unhelpful trend in all provinces, but decentralization is not necessarily the answer. Too many educational policy questions are posed as a choice between two alternatives. Suppose that a province were to reduce the size of its educational department and eliminate school boards, giving crucial authority to the local public school.

This move would be just as harmful in the long term as a totally centralized system such as Japan's (a system that suits that country but would not be appropriate in pluralist Canada). Local monopolies are no more intrinsically desirable than central monopolies. Parents are more open to tyranny from a local majority or special-interest group lacking the restraint of regulation than from a more disinterested and distant central bureaucracy.

Simple decentralization of the current system from the province to the school would not be a step forward. If the teachers' unions retained their power, they would in many cases come to run the schools more directly; if they did not, there would be the danger of inappropriate hiring and firing of teachers and principals (on the basis of personality conflict and contest for power). We should remember three things from the New Zealand experience of decentralization, with which I nevertheless have much sympathy. First, that country is much more socially homogeneous than most of Canada, so the danger from special-interest groups is less. Secondly, New Zealand's reforms include parental choice of school as well as powerful parent committees. The third observation is that running schools by parent committees is, even when it works well, no panacea.

The alternative of centralization is no more attractive. A weakness of the New Brunswick reforms, with their superficial appearance of decentralization, may prove to be that the three layers of parent committees will become ineffectual pawns of a hierarchical bureaucracy, parental powers simply being advisory. Even if they do not, it is unlikely that the different layers will be in agreement. New Brunswick's system already suffers from hardening of the arteries, and the reform, instead of opening the schools to local change and competition, may increase the cholesterol level in the system. Individual parents are still without authority or choice and have lost the right to vote with regard to education.

Most Canadian teachers are professionals and expect to have control over their working lives. Excessive centralization and excessive decentralization (to parent committees) both threaten that professionalism. Equally important, they both endanger the legitimate interests of parents. There should be a balance of administrative authority over the schools, between society, on the one hand, and parents collectively, on the other. Within the school there should be equilibrium between parents and staff. In the classroom the teacher should have major authority over the organization of instruction and day-to-day management.

Such balances, inevitably precarious, are most unlikely in a pluralist society, unless there is room for competing interests at the school level. That is what pluralism means; there are different values within a single society, locally as well as at a more remote centre. If a society is essentially homogeneous, such as those in Denmark, Germany, South Korea, and Japan, then a balance may be achieved at the centre between society and parents collectively because there is little difference between the two: parents are society. In Canada the Amish, Seventh-Day Adventists, Orthodox Jews, Jamaican immigrants, Roman Catholics, and, yes, even the so-called chattering classes are not society. These and other groups represent only parts of the mosaic, and the common factors binding them together are relatively few, but vitally important. The same is generally true of the other English-speaking developed democracies.

Although both extreme centralization and extreme decentralization of the system within a pluralist democracy are unhelpful, both centralized and decentralized components of authority are necessary. Education is an extremely important and sensitive endeavour with many competing interests; checks and balances are needed. The reforms recommended here will see both a tightening of control at the centre to ensure that schools do not offend what makes us a free, democratic, pluralist society and also increased authority for parents, as individuals and groups, manifested in greater educational choices. In short, we should have centralization in education to maintain the fundamentals of society and protect our values from extreme individualism, and decentralization to ensure that parents have primary authority over the education of their children within society's reasonable limits.

The reader may wonder how the balance between centralization and decentralization proposed here differs from the status quo. The current balance, founded in the nineteenth century, is between society's interests, represented by the provincial department, and local community interests, represented by school districts. But the school districts are no longer based on community, and the power of large bureaucracies and teachers' unions are products of the twentieth century. The balance of power has tilted away from parents. It is that balance – between parents and the centre – that requires restoration, while the power of special-interest groups, whose claim to represent the interests of all students is illegitimate, is reduced.

The issue of the centralization or decentralization of authority is a key one for reformers to consider. The lopsided nature of authority in education is a major cause of our problems. Most provinces wrongly see the issue as too much decentralization and the answer as more centralization: the greater regulation of schools by government. That would be a tragic mistake.

RECOMMENDATIONS FOR REFORM

Learning from Other Countries

This book has dwelt heavily on the Canadian situation, with only occasional references to conditions elsewhere. But our educational problems are similar to those faced by other countries, particularly the English-speaking, pluralist democracies. Nonetheless, Canada, like all countries, is unique, and it would be unwise to imagine that we could import a school system in the belief that it would work for us as it does in its native land. Defenders of the status quo jump from that reasonable statement to the conclusion that we can learn nothing from anyone else. They do not exactly say so, but the standard riposte to any comment on a favourable feature in some other country is a sneer about a real or imagined aspect of that country's school system.

Mention England, and the response is likely to be, "But we don't want a class-based system here." That country's system is, even today, more class-based than ours, but we should recognize the mote in our own eye, the increasing social divide in urban and suburban Canada as reflected in the public schools. We can can learn something from England's reform experience without aping its system of "public" (i.e. private boarding) schools, a relatively insignificant element in Canada.

Cite Japan, and one will be told about that country's terrible suicide rate as a result of examination pressures. In fact, its suicide rate is falling while ours is rising, and the rate among young males is lower than ours. Mention the United States, and one will be reminded of ghetto schools for blacks. Yet there is more vibrant reform in that country than in any other, much of it addressed to the needs of the disadvantaged.

From the Pacific Rim, particularly Taiwan, Singapore, and Japan, we can learn something about the effective elementary classroom and the sequentially developed program. North American observers of these classrooms are impressed by the emphasis on learning, by the high level of student interest and attention, and by the happiness and satisfaction evident in young people as they learn. These characteristics are particularly important when one recalls that the Canadian problem of achievement develops at the beginning of school. Defenders of the child-centred classroom assert that Asian parents give their children much more support at home. That is true; one of the reasons is that they know what their children are supposed to be learning and that they are expected to help them. Few Canadian parents understand what their children should learn because there are no clear, stated objectives. They are also often given the impression that they should stop pressuring their children and leave education to the experts. But Canadian parents are becoming more like Asian ones, assuming more responsibility for their children's learning; they should be encouraged to do so.

From the Netherlands, we can learn that permitting religion in the schools is not socially divisive. Whenever the subject of religious schools arises, the standard argument of the educational and intellectual elites (which are, not coincidentally, highly secularized) is that, even if some choice is desirable, it should not be based on religion because religion is socially divisive (consider Northern Ireland, India, Bosnia, or Sri Lanka). On that basis one could argue that the public school is a disaster by pointing to the old Soviet Union or today's American big-city schools, in Chicago or Detroit, for example. The idea that religion in education could be divisive in Canada is farcical. Religion is so marginalized in this country that it is the one distinguishing characteristic that can be scorned with the approval of the politically correct police in our media and universities. But the argument, however fallacious, must be addressed because it is so often raised.

The Netherlands has a history of antagonism between Protestants and Catholics that is considerably older and stronger than Canada's. Today, as in this country, religious commitment has waned, and ideology is more important in Dutch political life than religion. For over seventy years, the Netherlands has funded both secular public and religious schools on the same basis. Parents choose the best school using religion as one of several criteria. In some places, for example, the public school is the most liberal and child-centred; in others it is not. Where are the terrible consequences? If the secular elite in Canada were really concerned about religion in education being divisive (as distinct from opposing religion on philosophical grounds), then surely they would be particularly upset about the growing divide based on language, with francophone schools becoming much more entrenched in Canada outside Quebec and with the phenomenal growth of French immersion, which is socially divisive on class lines, within the anglophone population. Generally, the secularists who oppose religious education support both francophone schools and French immersion. The proposition that Canada is threatened by religious, rather than linguistic, division is so ridiculous that it is difficult to believe that it is so widely supported (or at least proclaimed) in the media. Surely no one thinks that it is Quebec's dying Catholicity which separates it from the rest of Canada.

Australia is a pluralist democracy with British traditions similar to Canada's (but without our francophone element). Its states in their powers resemble Canadian provinces, but they have gone further than any province in providing genuine choice. Roman Catholic schools in Australia have the same status as schools of other religious orientation, as is the case in British Columbia and Manitoba. More than one-third of Australian students are enrolled in partially government-funded independent schools. Traditionally, the country has had a sharper division than Canada between its working and middle classes. In recent years, as the proportion of students enrolled in independent schools has grown, that divide seems, if anything, to have weakened. I am not implying cause and effect; both changes are likely attributable to the Americanization of Australia and the weakening of the unions as trade becomes global. One could even argue that the influence of Australia's elite private schools has declined as the number of students enrolled in independent schools has increased. (The exceptional problem of England's caste-like upper class is precisely its small size and its impermeability.) While there is no evidence of increasing religious division in Australia, there is confirmation that the growing numbers of independent schools draw upon a predominantly and burgeoning middle- and upper-class clientele. The same trend can be seen in American and Canadian public school systems, with sharper divides between middle- and working-class schools. This pattern is very obvious in the city centres (Toronto, Winnipeg, Saint John, Montreal) and in the suburbs (North York, Brampton, Mississauga, River Oaks, Outremont, Dorval, Baie d'Urfé). One advantage of religious schools is that they tend to be less class-based than neighbourhood and academic ones. Practising Roman Catholics and Protestants are spread across class lines. Some Protestant denominations and sects are identified by social class, but community often provides an alternative base of security (e.g. the Salvation Army, Jehovah's Witnesses, or Seventh-Day Adventists).

The replacement of religious by class division is the result of a culture built on materialism: religious identification is weakening, while economic differentiation is increasing. Workers know the make (and status) of the car driven by their colleagues, but less often their religious affiliation, unless they dress distinctively or take unusual holidays. Some Canadians will be horrified at the idea that a third or more of students could be enrolled in independent schools, forgetting that over 40 per cent of Ontario students already attend schools other than regular public ones.

New Zealand is a more homogeneous country than Canada, with just one substantial ethnic minority, the population of Maori and Pacific island descent. It has demonstrated that the educational roof does not collapse if one has no bureaucracy at all between the centre and the school. I am not recommending that radical change in Canada, but the New Zealand experience of strong parental control illustrates that giving real authority to parent committees does not pave the way to chaos. (My own preference would be to allow parents to delegate authority if they wished.)

England demonstrates the many different ways in which school choice can be promoted with some imagination. It has traditionally funded Roman Catholic, as well as the established Church of England, schools. The country now has a few secondary technical colleges that operate outside the state school system. A key reform has been the right of parents in state schools to vote to become grant-maintained institutions, receiving funds directly from the central government. (I shall refer to these as direct-grant schools; "direct grant" has a different meaning in England.) Although grant-maintained schools are not numerous, the right to leave the system has had a healthy effect on educational bureaucracies, which have to serve their schools if they are to survive. If English bureaucracies concentrate on serving themselves instead of the schools, they can expect them to leave. England also provides a good example of comprehensive evaluation systems that collectively make schools highly accountable to the public. Like Canada, it has an intensely Progressive educational establishment, and its experience in introducing reform illustrates how quickly an establishment can move to block or impede genuine change. Reliance on a single set of reforms (such as changing the curricula and introducing tests) would be foolhardy. Telling parents that their school is ineffective is not much help if there is nothing they can do to escape it. One of Tony Blair's first acts as prime minister was to preside over the closure of a school on the grounds of academic incompetence.

While there is not a great deal we can learn from our American neighbour, its wide range of efforts at experimental reform does add to our knowledge. The Chicago experience, in what has been called the worst school system in the United States, shows us that simply delegating authority to local schools will not of itself lead to general improvement. The unsuccessful efforts in other parts of the United States to promote the common school by forcibly busing students between suburbs and urban centres show that parents will not accept the sacrifice of their children to the alleged interests of others. (If

minority students come to dominate the school, then white, middle-
class parents flee, either to private schools or by changing their place
of residence.) Generally, the once-popular assumption that black and
Hispanic minorities can best be helped by enforced integration with
whites is under serious question; even the National Association for
the Advancement of Colored People is split on its long-held commitment to school integration as the answer to blacks' educational problems. There is some evidence that black and Hispanic communities
may be better off with their own schools. On the other hand, the
Milwaukee experience shows that *permitting* minority students to
choose to attend predominantly white suburban schools and independent schools can also be helpful.

Most of all, we can learn from the American experience with student evaluation. The introduction of high-stakes tests as requirements for high school graduation has a powerful effect on what goes
on in schools, but one with both positive and negative aspects. It
seems better to allow students to qualify for the various graduation
standards at points along the way rather than only at the end, unless
there are clear markers all the way through high school. In Canada,
Quebec successfully applies markers, with clear grade-by-grade
objectives, continuously from the seventh to the eleventh grade, with
key exams in the final two years. New Jersey's High School Proficiency Test may be passed (and is by a high proportion of students)
in grade nine. Simply applying a universal test out of the blue in
grade twelve makes the stakes too high at that point and distorts the
instructional program during that year. California has no tests, but
demands that core objectives be integrated into the school curricula
and be assessed locally. The problem in that state is inadequate
implementation.

One cannot take any foreign blueprint and simply impose it on a
Canadian province. At the same time, to ignore the helpful and
unhelpful experience of others is foolish.

Choice

Of all the desirable reforms, genuine choice is the key. My book on
educational choice (1992) provides a more comprehensive discussion
of its meaning and definition in a pluralist democracy than I can
provide here. If there is one central theme to this book on reform, it
is that in Canada today choice is the most indispensable element. A
greater degree of choice is currently available in the provinces that
come out best from interprovincial comparisons – Alberta, British
Columbia, and Quebec – than in the ones that place worst. Yet the

proportion of students in regular, secular public schools in British Columbia (over 85 per cent) actually exceeds that in Ontario (not much over 60 per cent). The key is not the numbers in different schools, but the range of genuine choices.

Critics are quick to attack the emphasis on choice and to defend the public school against a conspiracy to privatize it and incorporate it into the business sector. Vouchers, they say, would lead to a sharp differentiation of schools on the basis of ability to pay, with the middle classes paying additional fees to purchase something better than the increasingly inferior school available for the voucher. Privatization and the voucher system have never been implemented anywhere in the world, and they are not proposed here. Canada has public, as well as both funded and unfunded independent, schools; they should continue. It is irrelevant to argue that one particular form of choice will be harmful. This book contends that no kind of monopoly can, by definition, meet the varying legitimate desires of a pluralist society.

Neighbourhood public schools should remain free of commercial interests, just as they should continue to be (or become) free from other sources of special interest – from groups of enthusiasts advocating environmentalism, gay rights, sexual freedom, religion, unions, laissez-faire capitalism, or the right to life. At the secondary level, the open discussion of important public issues is legitimate, but it should not be appropriated by a special interest, even if it is one that is widely held by enthusiasts on a school's teaching staff, such as a strong belief in environmentalism. Schools are threatened today by a host of special interests from inside and outside. The issue of choice based on deliberated, publicly announced principles is independent of vouchers and privatization; the Netherlands, as one example, makes major choices available, all within a public program.

Choice is vital for several reasons. As long as the idea that one size fits, or should fit, all is perpetuated, the principle that parents should have a major influence on their children's education is necessarily violated, unless they are able to reach a consensus about what they want. Once they disagree, which they usually do, authority is left, deliberately or by default, with those who provide the service. The only fundamental, substantive argument against choice is that society has or should have a strong consensual determination to develop a common and essentially homogeneous culture. There are unquestionably large numbers of Canadians who do hold that belief, but those who do, and who probably form a majority in some provinces, cannot agree even among themselves on what that culture should be.

There is a close analogy to the common school ideal; many Canadians like the idea of such a school in their neighbourhood, but there is no agreement on the basis for that school. To be cynical, one could say that they want a school based on their educational world-view which serves their local community. The implication of blind selfishness is unfair; a few decades ago, very likely when parents themselves went to school, that was not an unreasonable wish. But Canadians should be careful not to adopt the American heritage for their own. The common school has never been an important part of the Canadian tradition, and Canadians who glorify their own local public "common" school of the past in one breath are likely to mention the rival Catholic school in the next.

Choice is not a radical idea that Canadian reformers are trying to force on a system which is grounded on the principle of the common school. Eight provinces, unlike all the American states, have never had a common school, and the two exceptions are in the forefront of partially funding independent schools. Only a few extremists on the left seriously advocate the creation of a system of monolithic comprehensive schools. The idea that Canada would abolish funded and unfunded independent, Roman Catholic, and French-immersion schools and combine francophone and anglophone schools as bilingual institutions is unthinkable.

This book has illustrated a patchwork quilt of choices and policies, depending on the province. There is no agreed line between the public (meaning publicly funded) and independent school. The Maritime provinces come closest to the common-school ideal, but even they have traditionally operated de facto Catholic schools and in recent years have moved to increase choice by strengthening the unilingual francophone sector and initiating French-immersion programs in the elementary schools. The practical policy question facing Canadian provinces is not, "Should we allow choice?" In every province there are choices, although they may be limited by one's religion, wealth, language, or place of residence. The policy questions are, "Which choices should be permitted, and under what conditions?" Choice, balanced by the interests of society as a whole, is right (as distinct from a right) in a pluralist society. It is wrong for the state to determine, deliberately or not, that young children should be raised, for example, on the basis of high self-concept and the pursuit of personal self-fulfilment in a morally and socially permissive – the reader may substitute "tolerant" – climate, unless there is clear consensual support for those values. It is also wrong for the state to rule that certain Christian denominations should have state-supported schools while other Christian denominations and Jews and Moslems do not.

A second argument for choice infuriates the defenders of the status quo. A major theme of this book has been that the strong monopolistic or quasi-monopolistic control of publicly funded schools by a largely unelected, unofficial educational establishment is the major barrier to reform. Why is compulsory union membership legislated for virtually all teachers? Why are teachers paid on the basis of (often irrelevant) qualifications and experience without regard for competence, grade level, or specialization? Why do only a handful of school systems offer academically intensive alternative elementary schools, despite the fact that the schools which do exist are immensely popular? Why is there an enormous gap between strong public opinion during the past twenty years that there should be regular, external, standardized testing of all students in the basic skills and the reality of little or no valid and informative testing in so many schools? Why are provincial goals for education and program objectives often written in vacuous gobbledygook and interpreted by experts to mean what they say they mean, depending on the occasion and the audience? Why is it that Canada, one of the highest spenders on education, one of the most schooled countries, and with one of the most envied social systems in the world, can overall produce only mediocre academic outcomes, with large numbers of students either illiterate or severely handicapped in terms of mathematics and language? Why is it that programs of student evaluation developed in response to public discontent, such as recent testing programs in Ontario, the Council of Ministers of Education national program, and Nova Scotia's secondary school tests, frequently fail to meet basic criteria of utility and have very low stakes? Why is it that nationally the prevailing method of teaching skills in the primary grades is based on child-centred methods when there is compelling evidence that direct instruction is the single best approach? Why is it that few teachers graduating from teacher-education programs have been taught how to use direct instruction or how to evaluate students in an accountable manner?

The answer to these questions is essentially the same. The decisions are made, directly or indirectly, by representatives of the educational establishment: teachers' unions, departmental officials, members of university faculties of education, school district members, and educational administrators. Changing fundamental policies and practices would be offensive to one or more members of the establishment. None of the policies can clearly be shown to be in the best interests of students and their parents, but they are in the interests of some of those who are supposed to be serving the students.

Defenders of the establishment will respond hotly that many of the decisions in the list outlined above are made by politicians and elected members of school boards; that is so. The effects of the establishment's influence are so pervasive, controlling school boards' educational programs, for example, that it is vain to imagine that attempts simply to change the monopolistic system by regulation, legislation, or exhortation will have any effect. In Ontario a group of reform trustees actually gets together to resist the influence of the majority, which is dominated by the ideas of the educational establishment, represented most forcefully by the administrators who are supposedly paid to carry out the policies of the school board. The interests of different members of the establishment do not always coincide precisely. But there is tacit agreement to accommodate one another, particularly when it comes to preventing parents from gaining authority. Among prominent academics, teachers' unions, and organizations representing school board members and educational administrators, none has advocated any authority for parent committees.

The only hope for genuine educational reform lies in choice, through which parents would be provided with real opportunities to choose the kind of schooling they wanted. Put very simply, one cannot expect the educational establishment to dismember its own creation, of which it is genuinely proud. The establishment is not composed of bad people who need replacing: they believe in what they are doing, and they believe that the establishment knows best. Short conversations with educators about reform and reformers soon elicit examples of parents making bad choices (in their eyes), just as conversations with reformers produce stories about authoritarian behaviour on the part of the establishment.

I am told that I imagine conspiracies where there are none; that I conjure up the existence of an establishment. I have not spoken and written about conspiracies, in which I do not believe. A powerful establishment has no need to conspire; its members for the most part either think alike on the major issues or reach a consensus for the sake of peace with other members. By an establishment, I do not mean a secret society whose representatives meet behind closed doors to make educational decisions. I simply mean that the powerful groups in Canadian education have reached a political accommodation that is satisfactory to themselves.

It is possible that Canada is particularly prone to establishment control. One thinks, for example, of the lack of public debate among the political parties on such vital policies as bilingualism, equalization formulas, multiculturalism, and the Charter of Rights and Freedoms, about which there has been consensus among the various elites. The strongest evidence of an elitist establishment in Canada lies in the history of the Charlottetown constitutional accord. It was supported by all the major political parties of the time, by provincial governments, by the dominant media, and by leading academics, but it was resoundingly defeated by the people in a referendum.

Those still unconvinced of the existence of an establishment should ask themselves who benefits from failure to implement the reforms implicit in the list of policy questions above? Who is strongly opposed to real reform? Union officials and senior administrators receive the highest salaries in elementary and secondary education. In Ontario even the pensions of these highly paid people are exempt from the $60 000 maximum affecting ordinary Canadians. It is not the public or parents who will suffer from reform. On some policy issues, the establishment does get strong support from allies outside education (e.g. national unions and the "chattering classes") but not from the public. Members of the establishment are ordinary, decent human beings who make judgments within their context just as others would. They do not decide that their security is more important than the interests of parents and students; they truly believe in the value of the system. But which of us works actively to lower the value of our own responsibilities, or our pensions? The problem is that the system lacks checks and balances, and power tends to corrupt.

There are many other reasons for reform that supplement the two central ones: the ethical reason that parents should be able to influence their children's education and the practical one that an unbridled educational establishment acts (inevitably) in its own and its members' interests, including the propagation of its own educational world-views, rather than in the best interests and world-views of parents and their children. An additional factor is the decreasing confidence of teachers in the system, as illustrated by low morale and the rush to take early retirement when it is offered. I hear many anecdotes about teacher dissatisfaction. While writing this chapter, I heard from a teacher who is dismayed by the behaviour of newly appointed principals, who, she believes, are actively encouraged to manipulate (in her words, "lie to") teachers as they manage change – change that is unrelated to the students they are supposed to be serving, but which instead reflects current fads. There is some evidence for this charge of situational ethics in three recent doctoral studies of principals carried out by students at OISE: Elizabeth Campbell in 1992, Jonathan Black-Branch in 1993, and Lillian Hrabchak in

1995. Each examined different aspects of schools – Campbell the ethical base of administrative behaviour, Black-Branch the effect of the Charter on schools, and Hrabchak managerial bias in teacher-principal relations – but all came across unprofessional behaviour in principals that resulted as much from following fashionable practices and policies as from inevitable human failure.

The unions assert that the main reason why teachers are upset is the financial crunch, combined with the threat of change. That is part of the truth, but the reality remains that the system no longer holds the confidence of either parents outside or teachers within, some-times for similar reasons and sometimes for conflicting ones. Gov-ernments may take a cleaver to the educational system because, in the face of a powerful establishment, it seems the only way to make the desired financial cuts. The result is angry teachers and students who suffer from often ill-advised choices. Obviously, the radical reforms that I suggest will also cause upheaval and distress, but when teachers and parents are more able to choose their own stable and orderly school environments, both will be more satisfied. More-over, the reforms I recommend, even if implemented together, would take time to have any effect.

In the end, however, the centrality of choice comes down to two things: choice is common sense and is right in a pluralist democracy where there are important and legitimate differences of belief about the best education for young people, and practically and politically, it makes sense because it will increase the numbers of parents and teachers who will be happy with the environment in which the chil-dren of the former work and the latter teach. As a result, schools will be able to develop a stronger sense of direction, low-quality schools will not survive, and education will gradually improve in the broad sense of the word.

Limits on Choice

There are fundamental values underlying the democratic state that no publicly funded school should be permitted to oppose or subvert. It should be possible to reach a strong consensus on them. I believe that they would be something like the following:

1 consideration for others; a peaceful means for resolving disagree-ments; acceptance of those holding world-views different from one's own
2 belief in the fundamental equality of human beings irrespective of race, ethnicity, and religion; no restriction of access to a school on the basis of those characteristics

3 the unacceptability of teaching the superiority of or hatred for any group or individual on the basis of race, ethnicity, sex, or religion
4 access to various forms of knowledge and truth, including an accessible and well-stocked library and resource centre
5 support for democratic government and rejection of violent means to influence or overthrow it
6 the teaching of basic skills for literacy and numeracy, together with the general knowledge, habits, and attitudes required for good citizenship
7 use of an official language as the main vehicle for teaching and provision for instruction in the other official language
8 evaluation by the province of the implementation, practice, and effectiveness of the application of these principles

It is important to note that the second principle does not in any way prevent the establishment of religious schools. They would not be able to use religious or denominational membership as a criterion for admission, but parents and students would have to express their willingness to accept the climate and culture of the school.

Those are the fundamental social values for education upon which almost everyone will agree. They do not represent the most deeply held values of most (or any) people. Readers should not expect to find their own educational values and goals represented, unless they are shared by almost every other Canadian. It may be argued that the list is too strong, or that it is too weak. That is a practical question to be addressed by extensive consultation. The aim of such consultation would not be to obtain agreement of what should and should not be in the list; that is impossible in a pluralist society. Rather, the purpose would be to put together as long a list as possible without significant minority opposition. My judgment is that a responsive, democratic government would not be able to go much further, and that it should not settle for much less.

Types of School in a System Based on Choice

There is no single model of choice that will by itself lead to adequate reform – neither partial funding for independent schools nor charter schools within the public school board. A range of models should be considered; large provinces should permit them all, smaller provinces a key selection to guarantee freedom of access and end unfair discrimination.

The area public school The traditional public school should be strengthened, not terminated. Every student should have the right of access to what I call an *area public school*. By that, I mean the normal public elementary, middle, or secondary school, to which students would be zoned. There would be a few exceptions to this general right of admission; students whose disability is so great that either they themselves cannot profit from the school or their presence interferes with the learning of others would not be admitted. The area public school should also have the right to suspend and expel students for cause. Necessarily, the average distance that students would have to travel to such schools would increase with the growth of other kinds of schools. That problem would be offset over time as the average size, particularly for high schools, decreased. There would also be schools within schools; so every school would not always have its own building. Transportation would be free to the zoned area public school. The additional cost of increasing the average distance to area schools would be offset by the reduced cost of students in schools of choice, where transportation would be paid for or partially supported by parents.

The goals and objectives of the area public school would be stronger and clearer than those of the typical public school today. The reason for that is simple. The average school today is usually reduced to low doctrine because of the lack of consensus about what it should do. Because a few parents may sue if strong disciplinary action is taken, all students suffer from a permissive atmosphere. Because some students have poor attendance and refuse to work, the general academic climate is affected. Laziness is infectious and can easily be caught by teachers. The area public school would reflect a set of consensual beliefs and objectives determined at the provincial level (not at the level of the school district or the zone served by the school). These would reflect a good majority of the population (in provinces such as Saskatchewan and Prince Edward Island) or a plurality (most likely in Ontario). The higher the doctrinal content, the greater the number of parents who would seek alternatives; the lower the doctrine, the lower the affiliation of any parents and the lower the standard of work.

What follows is an example of a set of goals that might evolve for a province's area public schools:

1 acquisition by all of the basic skills of reading, writing, and mathematics
2 a high level of academic achievement in the sciences, geography, history, mathematics, literature, and a second language and the use (in reading and writing) of the English (or French) language
3 development of physical fitness, an understanding of healthy living, and psychomotor skills and interests in healthy leisure activities

4 development of healthy aesthetic expression, appreciation, and understanding in literature and the arts
5 development of the social skills of cooperation, leadership, and positive interaction with others
6 development of sensitivity to and knowledge of one's own and others' religious, moral, and cultural values
7 inculcation and modelling of the virtues of truth, justice, courage, consideration for others, and humility, together with the values and habits of personal responsibility, industriousness, friendship, courtesy, humility, self-respect, and an openness to life
8 preparation for work or for postsecondary education, in learning, skills, and work habits, including the use of the computer
9 a high level of discipline, work habits, courtesy, and cleanliness and dress appropriate for work at school

The more that one adds to those goals, the more parents and students one excludes. The more one subtracts, the lower the school's doctrine and the lower the level of commitment. Some readers may think that the set of goals I have suggested represents the status quo. They should examine more carefully what actually happens in the average local school.

Area schools would have a parent committee (sometimes known as a school council) composed of a parent majority elected by parents in a secret ballot (not at a meeting), a teacher minority elected by teachers in the school by secret ballot, the principal, and, in secondary schools, a student nominated by the student council, who would not be involved in personnel matters. The parent committee would have the responsibility of developing school policy and overseeing its implementation within the limits of provincial and district policies, together with the authority to prepare the school budget and select the teaching staff and principal. Over time, as trust grew, one would anticipate a high level of delegation to the principal and staff in many schools. A strong area public school, based on the public will rather than the establishment's interests, might well gain much stronger support than the current local school. It will only do so, however, if there is sufficient competition to force the school to change in order to meet the public will, or face rapid erosion of its enrolment and therefore of its teaching staff.

Provincial open enrolment In addition to the area public school, parents should be allowed to choose any fully funded public school within the province. In practice, the choice would be limited by geography and available transportation, but the principle is important. For example, some students might live with friends or relatives during the week in order to have access to the kind of education that they and their parents wanted. The choice of any school (other than the zoned area public school) should not entail the right of free transportation, except where it is constitutionally necessary (as is the case for some pre-existing schools for religious minorities, e.g. Roman Catholics in Alberta). Provincial regulation should limit abuse of the right to choice. For example, regulation should limit transfers without the two principals' agreement to one per student per school year.

Alternative schools (or programs)   Alternative schools or distinct programs within area public schools would be those supported by the school district for some special emphasis; they would not be area public schools, and no students would be zoned to them. Most likely, the initial options would predominantly fall into the following categories: existing French-immersion schools and programs; existing schools of the arts and vocational schools; new and existing academically intensive schools; and schools with a religious orientation. They would come about either by the district recognizing the demand for an alternative and investigating its viability or by the lobbying of parents. The authority and responsibility for the schools' administration would lie with the district. Transportation policy for schools would be developed (and implemented) at the provincial level. In principle, it would be subsidized or "user pay" with a special dispensation for parents unable to pay the fee.

Alternative schools would follow provincial and district regulations for area public schools, except for the special dispensation based on their difference. They would essentially follow the goals and objectives for the area public schools, with time allowed for the special focus. Their parent committees would be permitted to develop specific policies (in the area of discipline and dress, for example) to emphasize their unique qualities. It is unlikely that the Supreme Court would disallow alternative religious schools that were clearly distinguishable from area public schools and had open access, given the Edmonton precedent. There have been less-developed precedents in Ontario, near Fort Frances and near St Catharines.

Charter schools   These schools would be more independent of the district than the alternative schools. The charter would be a legal agreement whereby the parent committee would take over the running of the school from the school district for almost all day-to-day purposes. A majority of parents in an existing school could vote, or a group of parents large enough to make a school viable could petition the local district, for a school based on specified pedagogical principles. The rationale would typically be similar to that for an alternative school, but the parents would be seeking greater independence and more direct authority. If the local district rejected the demand, they would have the right to petition the provincial department directly for funding. The department could not unreasonably reject a petition, but it might require a connection with another school district if the home district refused to cooperate.

The school program would be based on that of the area public school with any deviations listed in the charter. The motives for charter schools might include greater autonomy from the local bureaucracy, greater financial flexibility, greater program variation than the district would accommodate in an alternative school, or experimental research. The levels of administrative, program, and financial independence would be also specified in the charter.

A group of charter schools, not necessarily in the same district, might over time come together in an affiliation or even form their own school board, comparable to existing Roman Catholic separate and minority-language boards, but without additional funding.

Existing religious and official-language schools   Existing francophone and Roman Catholic school districts would remain unchanged, except that their schools would have the same rights as public schools to request alternative or charter status. For example, some Roman Catholic schools might request charter status on the grounds that the district policies were insufficiently "Roman Catholic," there being a concern among some Catholics that their schools are being secularized. Denominational and second-official-language school districts would retain their constitutional authority.

Provincially supported independent schools   All provinces should adopt the policy of partially funding independent schools. Such schools provide the strongest guarantee to the average parent of genuine choice, free from the control of the educational establishment, at limited cost. If alternative and charter schools are to become effective choices, school districts and provincial departments must face the reality that they will lose many students (and their financial support) altogether if they do not cooperate. Already, many school districts deliberately block alternative schools for reasons of practice and principle. Those who believe that school officials have no imagination are confounded by the array of bureaucratic difficulties when they bring forward a proposal for an alternative or charter school based on greater academic demands and direct instruction.

As a basis for the partially funded independent school, the best model is British Columbia's, with varying degrees of financial support determined by the application of reasonable criteria. The formula for support of independent schools should have three components: the school's wealth, as reflected in its fees and budget; the program offered (e.g. elementary, secondary, or vocational); and the closeness of the school's program to the provincial curriculum. Students might potentially bring to the school a total grant up to 80 per cent of the average public school grant for the same program. (Ten per cent might go for administrative, inspection, and evaluation services, and there would remain a minimum gap of 10 per cent so that independent schools would always be less well supported by the public than public ones.) That maximum would be reduced if the parent body was unusually affluent, or if the school program departed substantially from the official provincial curriculum.

One criterion that could usefully be applied to ensure greater equality of educational opportunity is a stipulation that, in order to qualify for a provincial grant over, say, three thousand dollars per student, bursaries would have to be available for those unable to afford the fees. Funding for independent schools is usually phased in over time; as enrolment increases, the savings to the province offset the cost of the grants. In Ontario, for example, a beginning might be to allow residential property taxes for education to be directed to a pool of approved independent schools, with the pool to be applied on the same pro rata basis as the provincial formulas for public schools. Visible support by choice, applying a principle long used for Catholic schools, would probably be the most politically acceptable.

Students in an independent school for severely handicapped children would receive a grant well above the regular program grant, as would students who required special attention because they had been expelled from other schools and could not be accepted by area or alternative schools. The per-pupil grant would parallel that for similar students in public schools.

In substantive terms, this is the single most important reform. Independent schools are difficult for the establishment to control. On the other hand, there is evidence that public funding reduces the level of commitment (or community) of parents. The conditions for increased grants are also seductive.

Direct-grant schools The greatest drawback to alternative and charter schools is that they can be and are blocked by bureaucratic means. To operate, they require the goodwill of administrators and school board members, who tend to have an interest in their not operating, and who see their own empire and authority being reduced. The request for alternative status is seen as a statement of rejection. Partial funding of independent schools usually begins at a low level (because funding is initially a new cost). In time, it is the best guarantor of freedom for parents, but it takes time to have an effect. If the proposed school is very different from the area public school, it may be rejected on the grounds of unorthodoxy; if its purposes are similar, it may be rejected on the grounds of redundancy.

The direct-grant school would be a public school whose parents have voted simply to receive funding directly from the provincial government instead of through the local school board. There is no model of this kind in Canada. It should be a choice of last resort and be introduced two or three years after the other options. Public notice, however, should be given of its future introduction. If the other choices are offered sincerely, and if the area public schools really match the public will, there should be very few schools choosing direct-grant status. That status would require that the school become responsible for all aspects of its operation (although there is nothing to prevent it negotiating areas of support with the school district for an agreed cost). If the school choosing direct-grant status has been designated as an area public school (there should be a limit to the proportion of such designations within a school district), it would have to either remain an area public school, following the appropriate policies, or demonstrate to the department of education that no great disadvantage would be created for parents who wanted access to an area public school. Funding for the direct-grant school would be the amount spent per pupil for the equivalent public school, less the cost of inspection and provincial evaluation of students.

This reform may appear confusingly redundant, but it is necessary if the other choices are to be offered in good faith and if school boards are to be forced to divest themselves of their large bureaucracies. Once schools have the option to purchase services for themselves, school boards will discover the virtue of efficiency. Direct-grant status is in effect a trump card held by parents to influence authoritarian school boards. In terms of giving area public schools an incentive to improve, this reform is probably the single most important.

Objections to Choice

There are five major objections to choice. Social division is often referred to as balkanization by left-wing educators. That is an ironic term if one recalls that Yugoslavia's common school under authoritarian

Communism accomplished nothing to allay ethnic hatred and violence in Croatia, Serbia, and Bosnia. Despite its enforced common schools, the country is now divided on ethnic lines. Communist authoritarianism has not suppressed ethnicity anywhere else, either in the Balkans or in the old Soviet Union.

Canadian schools are already divided on the same lines as society generally – language, geography, and social class. If there remains any religious division in Canada today, it is between Roman Catholics, the largest religious group in the country and the only one with national political clout, and others. Catholics are, for obvious political and historical reasons, already well looked after educationally in the parts of Canada where they were originally most numerous. Overall, religion today is an insignificant line of division, even between Orange Protestantism and Catholicism, in a country where language, ethnicity, province of residence, social class, race, and political ideology are far more important causes.

The second objection is one of cost. It is argued in some provinces that two systems (Roman Catholic and public) are expensive enough without adding others. We are in fact in the process of adding a third in most of Canada outside Quebec, a francophone system, under heavy pressure from our activist courts. The error in this objection is a simple failure of imagination. The assumption is that the state should be funding school systems, when it makes far more sense for both economic and educational reasons for it to stop funding systems and to move gradually to funding schools chosen by parents for their children. The state would then determine the appropriate student grant for various programs and provide funding on that basis, either through a school system or directly to the school. In this way, provinces would have total control of costs. Unfortunately, imagination with regard to education has not been Canada's strong suit.

The third objection is that choice makes the system too complicated in terms of administration and of parental decision making. Alberta already has most of these choices, and England has more than those suggested here. Both jurisdictions spend less on schools than does Ontario with fewer choices. As more authority and responsibility are delegated to the school, there is less, not more, required of bureaucracies outside it. As for decision making, most parents, at least in the short term, would continue to choose the area public school or the closest Catholic school (where one is available) as at present, particularly if there was a hope it would move closer to the collective public will as a result of direction and competition.

In time, school districts should follow the excellent example of North York in Metropolitan Toronto and provide detailed information about every school. In densely populated regions, there would indeed be many choices, but it is condescending to tell parents that they will be confused if the state allows them too many choices for their children. It is worse than condescension, it is breathtaking arrogance, to tell Jewish and Moslem parents that support for their own schools would make things too confusing for them.

The fourth objection is the doomsday scenario that choice will lead to the death of the area public school. It is odd that those who defend the virtues of the *status quo* at the same time claim that extension of choice will lead to a mass exodus from neighbourhood schools. No one can forecast accurately what will happen, with or without fundamental reform, over ten or twenty years. My guess is that the area public school will be strong in most of Canada, once it is reformed to reflect the public will, with between 30 and 50 per cent of the population preferring a secular education. If my conjecture is wrong and the area public school gradually loses public support, either because it fails to reform or because parents prefer a school to which they can give strong commitment, it will have died for good reason: because hardly anybody wants it. While most alternative schools would be stronger communities than the area public schools, the more Technocratic (mechanized) alternative and charter schools would not be community-based. Further, the continuing decline of community, not only in schools but also in public life, suggests that many parents, particularly the mobile and cosmopolitan middle class, do not regret its loss. I have argued that community should not be dismembered by the state, not that all parents should be compelled to choose a school based on community.

The fifth objection is that choice exaggerates the differences between groups of parents; so the educated middle class will make good choices, and uneducated, working-class minorities will make bad ones. A variation of this argument is that choices will not be available for disadvantaged groups. There is more than an air of nanny-state-knows-best condescension in this contention. The evidence is rather that if choices are structured intelligently, people in all parts of society will try to gain advantage for their children. For example, magnet schools in St Louis have attracted blacks rather than whites, presumably because the former are more dissatisfied with their local schools than are suburban whites with theirs. A careful study has been made of the choices available in Milwaukee, one paying tuition to private schools for minority students and the other allowing them to attend public suburban schools (John F. Witte and Christopher A. Thorn, *American Journal of Education* 104 [1996]). Both programs are flourishing, the first oversubscribed; both involve mainly black and Hispanic minorities. There is indeed evidence that it is the more-concerned parents who make the choices, but the fact that the establishment objects to minority parents having the same kinds of choices now made, even in Ontario, by the more affluent is revealing. These two popular and successful programs were opposed vigorously but unsuccessfully in the courts by the State Department of Public Instruction and the state teachers' union.

So once again we return to the argument that all parents should be reduced to some low common factor, an idea that is exploded by experience, which shows that even the most eloquent Egalitarian advocates are likely to choose special help for their own children. Few Canadians believe that parents should be prohibited from helping their offspring. The disadvantaged poor are probably just as anxious as the more affluent to choose a good option for their children's education, if one becomes available. Parents living in North Vancouver and Toronto's Rosedale will be less anxious to move their children from the local area public school than will those in downtown Vancouver or Parkdale.

The Egalitarian argument, put forward by privileged, often self-appointed representatives of the disadvantaged, is contradictory and doomed to failure. First they argue that choice is simply wrong and unfair. When it is pointed out that the rich, including rich Egalitarians, and privileged others (e.g. Catholics in some provinces) make choices for their children anyway, they reply that it should not be made easy for anyone else because the disadvantaged are unable to make good choices. When they are reminded that the disadvantaged eagerly make sound choices when these are available, they object that some do not. What leading Egalitarians really want is for everyone to have the schooling that they themselves prescribe (while they see nothing wrong in their exercising a private choice for their own children). The idea that people genuinely may want different things either escapes these individuals or is rejected because they do not not approve of the other things that people often want: in particular, religion, whose influence on education the media elites particularly detest.

There is an important philosophical difference between those who favour choice and those who prefer a public monopoly with a few choices approved by the establishment. On the one hand is the belief that parents should have the authority to influence their children's schooling, and with that authority a sense of personal responsibility; on the other hand, the belief that parents should not be allowed to make their own choices because some of them will make "bad" ones (notably religious choices, which should be disallowed). Therefore, the state should make available only "suitable" options on the basis of expert interpretation of children's "needs."

Both sides should agree that genuinely bad and mediocre options, unwanted by any reasonable parent, should not continue, whether these are schools of choice or neighbourhood schools. The educational establishment has a record of readily accepting mediocrity and turning a blind eye to incompetence. Its attitude to parents has been one of benign paternalism to the compliant and hostile authority in the face of truculent independence.

Authority of the Provincial Department of Education

Under the reform plan proposed here, the de facto authority of the provincial department would increase in most provinces. In some of them, the central goals, objectives, programs of student evaluation, and inspection systems are so vague and weak that authority is in practice delegated to the school district, hence the excessive growth of school district bureaucracies. These policies would be firmly placed in the hands of the central authority, as they are in most other countries. Even in the United States, where the state has traditionally been weaker in the field of education than the Canadian province, many states are now taking charge of these central policies. The provinces would also assume fundamental responsibility for the terms of employment of teachers (collective agreements), for the funding of various kinds of schools, and for ensuring the collection of the data necessary to provide meaningful information to school administrators, teachers, parent committees, and parents. The increase in authority requires little, if any, increase in the number of employees. Some provincial activities are unnecessary (such as the production of instructional programs, as distinct from program objectives), some are duplicated, and others should be delegated to private institutions (e.g. production of standardized tests of achievement).

The changes required here would be radical for some provinces, but less so for others, such as Alberta, British Columbia, and Quebec. In time, the inspection of schools would become a provincial, rather than a district, responsibility. There would be some loss of work in the departments of education because responsibility would increasingly be delegated to schools and because large numbers of regulations (of approved texts, for example) would simply disappear.

Authority of the School District

The school district would typically lose authority to the province. At the same time, decentralization of authority to the school would come mainly from the school district, rather than from the province. Thus the authority of the district over time would be greatly reduced, with little power over major policy issues, which are rightly provincial (or even national) in nature, or over the distinct character and day-to-day running of the schools, which would be the responsibility of the parent committees and the principals.

The ultimate survival of the school district is already in question, as the New Brunswick reforms illustrate. Its role, if it survives, should be one of support for, rather than direction of, the schools. In the short term, it would look after the hiring and dismissal of personnel (but not the selection of teachers and principals), the administration of collective agreements, the supervision of different schools of choice both in anticipation of and in response to parental wishes, the distribution of students and programs among schools in accordance with provincial policies on choice, the construction of new schools, the sale of school buildings, the closing of unsatisfactory institutions (which might reopen as schools with different direction), the expulsion and transfer of students, and the in-service professional program for teachers. In time, as schools took over more responsibility, the remaining authority could well become managerial in nature and not require an elected school board at all, but simply a regional administrative office. This change would make the school district less discriminatory in its hiring practices. There would be no need for the director of education (school superintendent) to determine the educational world-view of the schools (typically Progressivism); so it would be possible for Orthodox Jews, Muslims, and Baptists to take the position, without worrying that their own children did not attend area public schools, which in many places would enrol a minority of students.

Transportation should be integrated for all schools and, in many cases, with municipal and private bus services as well. A regional transportation agency (as in Britain) could handle the integration far more efficiently than school districts. Where possible, school buses should be organized on a grid system (more like that of a municipal bus service), so that students would take the most convenient route to whichever school they attended. Bermuda's integrated municipal and school bus service is a model on a small scale for such an arrangement.

My guess is that school districts would survive for the foreseeable future, at least in dense urban and suburban regions, where the choices of school and demands for buildings are likely to be most complex and competitive. In rural areas, where the effective choices other than the area public school would be few, the parent committee might effectively replace the school board, particularly if the board was large and distant, as it increasingly is. If, however, the only remaining substantive responsibility of the school board was the administration of choice and the distribution and construction of schools, it might be better handled by a government agency that would be able to overview all publicly funded schools, irrespective of their category. School boards inevitably have their preferences and biases and at best represent the majority of voters, whereas choice is intended to provide support for legitimate minorities.

Program

While program is centrally important in education, it becomes a less crucial reform issue once there is a free choice of school. Institutions whose programs are badly delivered will simply lose students. The school which thinks that it is a great idea to split all the grades or to combine grades five and eight will simply change course, unless the idea is vastly more popular than it is with the parents who talk to me. More generally, schools with innovations that work and improve achievement will flourish; those that are mediocre or worse will lose their students. A good teacher transforms a poor program; a bad one subverts a good program.

Provinces should follow the Quebec model of program development. Sequential sets of objectives by grade should be published for each subject. The standards must be both demanding and achievable by the majority of students. They should not be set according to current levels of achievement. Rather, they should be based on the best national and international practice, for example, on those of Alberta, Quebec, Singapore, or Switzerland. In the senior grades, three standards should be set in academic subjects: for students seriously considering entering university, for those continuing to college, and for those aiming to graduate from high school and move directly to work. The provinces might also develop sets of lesson plans to teach the objectives (as Quebec does). The lesson plans should be available as optional aids, the objectives as policy. Schools should be left to determine the organization of the program, such as subject or grade promotion; combined college or university preparatory classes, with two distinct programs in small schools; and subject separation or integration. Teachers should allowed to determine the teaching methods best suited to the objectives and their students.

The controversial program areas of family-life education, sex education, and literature should be a matter of careful consultation with parents and special approval by the parent committee before they are implemented. Individual parents should be given the right to withdraw their children from courses in these areas and have them follow alternative programs. At the secondary level, if required, there should be alternative literature courses in area public schools. For example, one might have a traditional, academic emphasis (including Shakespeare, Austen, Dickens, Conrad, and Steinbeck) and another with a more contemporary emphasis. The right to withdraw should remain, and students should be able to take individual programs independently in accordance with the reasonable wishes of their parents.

Student Evaluation

The province should set minimum standards for external student evaluation. External standardized tests of the basic skills should be administered to every student at least three times in grades one to eight and once in grades nine to twelve. Only severely disabled students and those who have almost no knowledge of the official language should be excused. Individual results should be reported in writing to parents. The outcomes of schools, grouped with those of similar schools, should be made public. In general, the idea of using independently developed tests (such as the Canadian Achievement Tests and the Canadian Tests of Basic Skills) is a good one, because it avoids reducing tests to the actual levels of achievement in the weaker provinces.

Schools should be encouraged to test regularly to assess progress in the sequential provincial curricula. Provinces should make available sample tests and examinations to give teachers, parents, and students an idea of provincial standards and expectations. Parent committees should determine how frequently examinations are written in middle and high schools. Minimum standards should be developed for high school graduation in core subjects, and the graduation certificate should be accompanied by a transcript showing levels of achievement, record of attendance, physical fitness, and a citizenship rating. High school competency tests should be used as a condition of graduation.

Provinces, individually or in partnerships, should set examinations and/or tests in subjects used for admission to university, with the results automatically made available to universities to which students apply. The students' performance on exams should be combined statistically with their performance in school (as is the case in Quebec), and that combined record should be used for the granting of scholarships and bursaries, both federally and provincially.

Academic and School-to-Work Programs in Secondary Schools

If the instructional problem is greatest in the primary grades, the issue of organizing the program is greatest in the secondary school. Perhaps the least-recognized implication of educational research is the failure of the comprehensive secondary school. It seemed common sense to most people (including me for many years) that the comprehensive school which offered a wide variety of course options would provide a more equal opportunity and allow more young people to graduate from high school with a variety of skills, while still possessing the competence essential for every citizen. It turns out that that expectation was false.

There are successful comprehensive schools, but they are usually either small and do not offer fully comprehensive programs, or they are predominantly middle class and therefore not really comprehensive in either clientele or program. For the most part, community schools that are functional (i.e. those serving a genuine community) or provide value (i.e. by self selection) and offer a simplified, coherent program are more successful academically than comprehensive schools, not only in terms of average achievement but also in terms of a smaller gap between higher and lower achievers. Types of such schools include small rural, religious, and independent. (I refer here to comparisons of students of similar social background.)

The problem seems to be that the cafeteria-style high school permits students to take the easy options, which is what many do. And so many students graduate without any worthwhile accomplishment, and often with poor attendance patterns and work habits as well. The non-university programs are "dumbed down," get a bad reputation, and are deserted by the more ambitious. As increasing proportions enrol in so-called academic programs, these too are reduced to a lower level so that most can "pass." Bad currency drives out good.

The solution is not to exclude large proportions of students from secondary school (as was the pattern in most countries, including Canada, until the 1950s), but to provide opportunities only for the successful achievement of standards, not for simply putting in time. Gradually, as enrolments drop and school buildings are replaced, small schools (with enrolments around 600 to 800 and no larger than 1000) should replace large ones in urban and suburban areas, but that reform is obviously long-term. What can be done immediately is to change the range of options in the secondary school. It is also possible to reduce the level of individualism by creating discrete schools or programs within schools (at the price of reducing the numbers of levels and subject options).

Beginning by grade ten, there should be a demanding university-entrance program with clear standards for admission and exit. The admission standards should immediately not be set high, but should be raised over time, with fair warning to the elementary schools. Students should have the right to fail, but no right to success. A program should be made available in high schools to prepare those who have not been prepared for a tough academic program by the elementary and middle schools. Initially, students may need two years in the preparatory program to make up for what they have not learned at the elementary level. Some will not have the interest, the ability, or the commitment. The exit standards should consist of clear program objectives evaluated in part by provincial tests and examinations. Colleges and universities should be provided with both school and examination marks, preferably combined.

One easily administered organizational pattern would be to make the grade nine academic program open to all who choose it, as it typically is now. Admission to high school would be available to all students who completed grade eight satisfactorily, but movement to the academic program in grade ten would depend on meeting publicly recognized standards. Those who did not want to enter the academic program would be able to choose between a bridging program, to get them ready for grade nine academic, or programs leading to college or high school graduation with a particular skill or work experience.

Currently, a large number of non-university-bound students are enrolled, in the final grades of high school, in so-called academic courses that are diluted sufficiently to allow them to scrape through, or in non-university-oriented programs often called general or basic courses. Those two options (of sitting through academic programs dumbed down for the purpose and taking imitation academic courses without required standards) should be eliminated because of their essential fraudulence. Instead, depending on the nature and size of the geographical community and its schools, an array of demanding options, should be made available. Some examples include a college-oriented (i.e. community college, non-university) program should be offered with clearly defined academic standards in the basic skills, developed in consultation with the colleges offering non-degree programs; vocational programs, where there is local demand for certain kinds of workers without highly sophisticated skills; and part-time work, part-time school programs where students would be employed at a basic wage in a job where there is the possibility of regular employment after graduation, while they simultaneously take the core courses required for high school graduation. Many students may choose the college program as a substitute for the current general academic courses, without necessarily expecting to enter college, but their success would at least be governed by clear exit standards in the form of examinations.

Those unable or unwilling to reach those standards would choose among a variety of practical programs leading immediately to work, but they too would have to meet basic standards for high school graduation. Other requirements should be developed in consultation with local employers. At the moment, few students choose vocational options, even when they are available, because the low demands of pseudo-academic programs and the nebulous dream of well-paid, white-collar employment are far more attractive than the discipline of welding or sheet-metal work. The level of academic work taken by students in vocational programs would vary with the student and the program.

In short, I see three graduation standards – university entry, college entry, and high school graduation – each with clearly written objectives appropriate to its standard. Area high schools (the common schools available to all students everywhere) would generally offer at least one program in all three categories, but schools of choice might offer just one or two. They might decide to separate the programs physically, but there would have to be clear, flexible routes for students to move between programs by meeting the necessary academic standards. Alternative, charter, and direct-grant secondary schools would not be permitted to restrict entry at grade nine on the basis of entrance tests, but like the area schools, they would be able to limit access to the university preparatory program beginning in grade ten to those with the prerequisite skills for success on the basis of reasonable public standards. They too would have requirements for admission and could accept eligible applicants from programs in other schools.

Enterprising school boards and provinces should experiment with vocational centres, as developed in a few places in the United States. These centres are operated more on the line of colleges but are for young people between fifteen and nineteen who have not graduated from high school. They would offer both intensive job-preparation programs and direct, structured preparation for high school graduation. They would be intended for those who had experienced difficulties with the secondary school regime and wanted to try something more like a private vocational program which combined practical outcomes with considerable independence. The centres would offer a second chance to such students. The emphasis would be very much on individual job-training and on meeting high school graduation standards, rather than on community and extra-curricular activities. This would be a highly Technocratic option.

This proposal is an elaboration of the Danish system. Some readers will object that it introduces streaming, even perhaps that it is like the old high school entry exams. It does imply separation (streaming) of students at age fifteen, but they are currently de facto separated before that age anyway (by the level of their courses and their level of achievement). The plan provides clear end points and open, flexible, structured means of reaching them. Students choose what they want to do, but are not allowed simply to continue in a program when they have failed to reach the requisite standards. They can keep on trying if they wish and can transfer into a high-level program by achieving the appropriate entry standards.

Reform of the elementary system (by letting parents choose schools that emphasize direct instruction and by having parent committees run area public schools) is designed to reduce the level of difference among students in the middle grades. Any observant teacher in grade seven or eight can name many students who have little chance of entering university because their reading and math skills are two or three years below grade level. The evidence is that many students will respond positively when faced with realistic standards; if nothing is expected, nothing is what they produce. Elementary schools will be encouraged to achieve published standards and secondary ones to monitor them. It would be misleading, however, to imply that such changed arrangements will greatly increase the numbers entering university or becoming professionals; there are limits to the availability of all forms of employment. What policy can provide is fairness, accessibility, clarity, openness, and clear public standards; currently, public high schools merely provide accessibility.

The pattern described above is based on a four-year high school, from grade nine to grade twelve, which would be my preference. The same principles can be adapted to different organizational patterns. Currently, Quebec is probably closest to the spirit of the recommendation, even though a typical *polyvalent* secondary school in that province serves grades seven to eleven.

Teachers and Their Unions

The legislation establishing mandatory union membership for all teaching positions should be repealed, and instead teachers should be given the right to join or not join a union. The immediate effect will be slight, because it is to be expected that most teachers will voluntarily join the union of which they are currently members, as was recently the case in British Columbia. Nevertheless, the change would make flexibility possible. For example, some charter and direct-grant schools may be staffed by imaginative teachers who would be willing to try different ways of organizing their salaries and promotions. Making union membership voluntary also restores a fundamental freedom that should be available to everyone, particularly to professionals.

I should like to see the right of teachers in public schools to strike replaced by other means of dispute settlement, notably final-offer selection, as discussed in chapter 3, but I recognize that the Supreme Court may legislate otherwise. As financing becomes centralized, it is likely that salary schedules will be influenced or determined at the provincial level, as they are now in some provinces. When that happens, the opportunity should be taken to permit the kind of salary arrangements discussed in chapter 3, based on differential staffing. As school districts become less powerful, or perhaps cease to exist altogether, it should be possible for more flexible agreements to be made at the level of the school. If and when provincial agreements replace district ones, care must be taken to build in provision for alternative arrangements. Ideally, the provincial agreement would consist of optional contractual arrangements for remuneration, with choice to be made at the school level.

Any progress in this area will be slow and tortuous, and fiercely opposed by the unions. Most teachers are used to their unions and understand that, whatever their faults, they have delivered good salaries and pensions. Legislative and contractual changes by themselves will have little direct effect, but they will gradually permit a change in atmosphere from an archaic, industrial one (modern industries, such as telecommunications, are not run in this way) to a more professional environment. They will make it easier for alternative and direct-grant schools to try different approaches.

Early Childhood Education

This book has focused on elementary and secondary education from age six to eighteen, and the program and organization of the preschool have not been discussed except in passing. The cost of preschool programs accounts for a significant proportion of the budget allocated to schooling, without making a major contribution to the ultimate educational standards achieved by young people. Organized on the assumption that mothers are at home to dispatch and receive their children at odd hours during the day, the current programs are as obsolete as they are expensive. They are staffed by fully qualified teachers, paid according to the same salary scales as teachers of high school history. Clearly, there would be room for significant cost savings if pre-school programs were turned into early education centres, operating from 8.00 a.m. to 6.00 p.m. on a cost-recovery basis. Special programs, integrated within the early education centres, should be provided at no charge for disadvantaged children, beginning at age four; programs should be designed to prepare them directly for academic work in first grade.

In the long run, provinces will have to come to terms with the complex issues of education for those under six. There is growing evidence that very young children can be influenced by structured intellectual development; presumably the ineffectiveness of pre-school programs results from their failure to stimulate intellectual curiosity. There is also evidence that having a mother at home is an important social advantage for a young child. Philosophically, some people favour making demands on children at an early age, while others prefer pre-school to be a time for imagination and unstructured play. Advantaged parents are increasingly providing their children formal instruction at home or in private schools. Any public program must make unpleasant and expensive choices. In the meantime, the current system could be made less costly and less ineffective.

Funding Education

Partial equalization of spending across provinces should be accomplished by a federal-provincial tax scheme, with distribution of revenue among provinces on the basis of the size of the age cohort, an approach discussed in more detail in chapter 1. Basic services should be covered by national taxes and provided in a single grant that would replace the current equalization payments and the Canada Health and Social Transfer. Deductions from education grants would be made on the basis of the true market value of residential and commercial property province by province. Educational property taxes should be assumed as equalized according to a three-year rolling average based on 80 per cent of the true market value. Commercial property taxes should be pooled provincially.

Funding should be allocated provincially on the basis of the numbers of students genuinely enrolled and the types of programs. Enrolments in special programs should be carefully monitored and capped if necessary. In Ontario an initial step in the partial funding of qualifying independent schools should be the setting up of a pool for independent schools based on residential taxpayers' requests to support independent (as distinct from public and Roman Catholic) schools.

The student, the school, and the family should be seen as the important units of analysis, not the district. Grants should be made by school rather than by district, even if they are provided through the district. Salaries of teachers and school-level administrators should be separate from the general school grant, because they are close to being fixed costs if the schools are unionized. Parent committees, with genuine authority over discretionary budgets, should be informed of how much the school and school district are allocated and where the money goes. All school-district expenditures should be open to public scrutiny.

The discrimination between richer and poorer districts found in Ontario should be reversed. There should be higher grants to schools with a large proportion of disadvantaged children, such as those coming from low-income families. Great care is needed in determining differential program grants. There is no self-evident reason why French-immersion programs or even English as a second language should be more expensive than regular ones. There is a tendency for programs that are highly funded to proliferate. Probably, the best plan would be to keep the formula very simple, providing more money for students: in grades nine and up, for students from families below the twentieth percentile in family income; in schools and programs both for the severely disabled and for those requiring focus and discipline; and for those in vocational programs. Parent committees should be encouraged to raise money for their schools locally in order to help create a communal bond and to pay for individual school priorities. School grants should be reduced by a percentage of the money raised by schools above a provincially determined ceiling.

The reform of teacher education could save a considerable sum if fees were raised and most students enrolled in part-time programs, combined with school internships. One year of full-time teacher education is quite sufficient for those who prefer that option.

Ontario and Quebec are probably the only provinces where significant financial savings can be made overall without harming the fabric of education. In some of the other provinces, there is room for the transfer of spending from lower-priority areas (district bureaucracies) to higher priorities (such as ending discrimination in school support and improving the supply of texts and library materials) and for better-targeted payments to teachers; but these changes would produce little or no net saving. In the Atlantic provinces, an increase in spending is more justifiable than a reduction, but that would require a change in federal-provincial arrangements.

APPLYING THE CRITERIA

Quality

Sceptical readers may agree with much of my analysis of the weaknesses of Canadian schools, but will still have doubts about the recommendations to reform them. It is always easier to agree about problems than about solutions. What guarantee, one may ask, is there that the radical changes suggested here will actually make things better?

Quality is the first criterion usually applied to the school system. Will the reforms really make our schools better? Obviously, the answer will vary depending on whom one talks to. Bear in mind that we do not all agree on what is "better." There are three important ways in which I believe the reforms will make schools better. First, the area public schools, attended by the largest number of students, should gradually improve in the sense that they will necessarily move closer to the public will or face the loss of their student body. Their goals and objectives will substantially reflect the Cultural and Technocratic world-views most widely held by members of the public. The currently dominant Progressive outlook will have a much lower presence. The transformation will be most marked in the primary grades because instructional methodologies will change, but the secondary grades will become more focused on substantive (rather than ephemeral) objectives; currently, only those going on to postsecondary institutions are given tangible academic objectives and clear incentives. An important aspect of quality is that the school should reflect the public will.

In second place, the increased and more-representative choices available will provide a higher proportion of parents with the kind of education that they want for their children; the prevailing attitude that there is something wrong with parents when they reject the experts' prescription will be weakened. Progressive parents need have no fear that their children will be compelled to attend increasingly Technocratic schools. There are plenty of teachers who would be delighted to teach in Progressive alternative, charter, or direct-grant schools.

The third way in which schools will improve is that extensive assessment of the changes that schools actually bring about in students will make accountability unavoidable. Above all, parents will be able to vote with their children's feet. Knowledge does not automatically bring about action and improvement, but accompanied by genuine choice, it will be a powerful incentive and catalyst. In the short term, public accountability is the most powerful inducement for improvement. In the long term, genuine choice and the greater accessibility of independent schools are likely to be more potent.

"That's all very well," the reader may respond, but what about objective quality? Will achievement improve nationally? Will discipline be stronger? Will young people be better prepared for their futures? Those are the hard questions. When the state tries to decide what people ought to want, it does not do a very good job in a pluralist society where wants are so varied. It usually ends up providing what the experts think students should have. That is how we got into our current mess. But if the public generally and parents as individuals have authority, how do we know that they will make more-effective choices, in terms of objective criteria?

The reality is that parents are, and will remain, the greatest educational influence in every sense on their children. No educational reforms will quickly change parents, but they will give them a greater sense of responsibility for their children's education. What the reforms will do is to permit them to bring about the changes that they want for their children more effectively. Those parents, rich or poor, who really desire a strong academic education for their children will find it easier to get. Some parents, for good reasons or bad, are not strongly committed to an academic education, and their children will be less affected by the academic reforms. As members of a pluralist democracy, Canadians, including the experts, should accept that there are – and rightly so – severe limits on how much the state can force parents to think like "everybody else." Miseducation can be substantially eliminated, and minimum standards imposed. But in the end, young people are limited, as well as enhanced, by their family life.

If I am asked how much test scores will improve within five years of the implementation of the reforms I recommend, I cannot give the definitive answer that those who generally agree with me would like to hear. The room for improvement in British Columbia, Alberta, and Quebec is less than that in Ontario and Nova Scotia. The impact of reform will probably also be less – they have less to change. Ontario, an affluent province performing well below capacity with a highly motivated population, has the greatest opportunity for improvement. The less-affluent provinces are limited by their poverty and by the attitudes and values that often accompany disadvantage.

Despite my natural caution, the record shows that on occasion quite rapid improvements can be made. In some American states, organizational reforms and tough demands have had remarkable results. It must be admitted, however, that it is much harder to improve educational outcomes than it is to let them decline. I have seen good schools, both public and independent, which were built up over many years, seriously deteriorate in less than a year. The greatest opportunity for improved effectiveness in schools lies in the increased opportunity over time to reconstruct genuine community, with teachers, parents, and the majority of students pulling in the same directions.

Overall in Canada there has been a fairly steady decline in standards during the last thirty years. There have been ups and downs, and the pattern is far from uniform across the country; but the generalization is valid. Although we do not have good data, the limited information that we do have and the observations of employers and secondary and postsecondary teachers tell the same story. It will take a long time to put things straight. Turning the tide will itself be an important accomplishment in backward Ontario, the largest province, which drags down the national statistics. The social context should not be forgotten. If school reform takes place in a context where the social milieu and family structure continue to decline, a decline characterized by high crime rates, high youth unemployment, increasing divorce rates, a greater proportion of babies born to unwed mothers, and increasing recourse by young people to passive, sexually provocative, and violent media, then the educational reform of their minds, as distinct from school structures, faces an uphill battle. If it is accompanied by a social reconstruction, then it becomes part of a broader evolution.

The educational achievement of countries reflects the nature of their society. Canada, with levels similar to those in England and the United States, deserves outcomes that reflect its superior social conditions and its higher level of school funding. The reforms recommended in this book are intended to bring our system closer to our people's interests, hopes, and ambitions. Ontario parents are no less interested in academic achievement than are Albertans. Religious minorities in Ontario are no more of a threat to society than those in British Columbia. Canadian parents are not less interested than Germans and the Swiss in having their children find jobs when they finish their schooling. Increased parental authority will, over time, improve schools in the way that parents want; they have a direct stake in the outcomes. Nevertheless, a pluralist society may expect pluralist educational outcomes. That said, the combination of clear, sequential objectives, regular evaluation of student performance, teachers' accountability for results, genuine choice of school, and more non-union schools should lead to an overall improvement in academic performance and discipline within five years of the implementation of these reforms.

Efficiency

Canadian education is inefficient; we spend too much for too little. There are three major reasons for this outcome. Many school districts have bloated bureaucracies; teachers, on union terms, are paid salaries close to those of professions such as engineering and the law; and class size is determined by union agreements, rather than by assessments of effective teaching. The first problem should be the easiest to address, but administrators and school boards instinctively cut what is easiest to cut (e.g. instructional supplies and textbooks) or, if the easy cuts are insufficient, what will cause greatest public uproar and hence fuel a demand for more money.

The recommended reforms could be implemented over five years together with a reduction in spending in constant dollars in Ontario and Quebec. Unfortunately, it is simpler to cut costs directly across the board than to attempt to improve overall efficiency and effectiveness. For example, reducing grants to school systems is likely to have little impact on the problem areas of spending, which are safeguarded by union contracts or bureaucratic empires. There may be across-the-board cuts to teachers' salaries, making teaching a less attractive profession for the excellent people who are most needed. If there are teacher lay-offs, they are likely to be based on the last-in/first-out principle, which makes sense in a widget factory but not in an educational system.

The proposed reforms would make improved efficiency unavoidable. Those in the financial area would help to control spending. Povinces would determine the per-pupil grant in accord with the program, and adjustments, up or down, could be made annually. Districts would simply be unable to spend more money than they had. (If they did, they would be taken over by a provincial trustee. This problem has been faced in British Columbia.) School busing would be made more rational. The disparities among school districts in Ontario would be reversed, with more money going to the schools with the least-affluent, instead of the most-affluent, students, irrespective of whether they live in urban or rural areas. The disparities between provinces would also be slightly reduced.

There would be no automatic change to the terms of teachers' employment, but the way would be open for more imaginative and more efficient methods of employing, paying, promoting, and deploying teachers and teacher aides. Increasingly, they would teach in the kinds of schools where they actually want to teach, be these Cultural, Progressive, Technocratic, or Traditional, or some agreed compromise. The cost to government of teacher education would be reduced, as increasing proportions of would-be teachers enrolled in part-time programs as interns, paying for much of their training themselves and demanding value for money.

Whereas rapid improvement in quality is very difficult to guarantee, partly because people's notions of quality differ and partly because the conditions affecting it are so numerous and complex, improved efficiency is simply a matter of political will. That does not make it any more likely to come about; those with direct interest in inefficiency are well entrenched, a fact that allows extreme inefficiency in the public educational sector to continue to thrive.

Equality of Educational Opportunity

This complex idea was earlier defined as having two components: young people have a chance to move through the educational system to any level on the basis of ability and perseverance and without financial or other discrimination on the part of the educational system; and parents are able to determine the kind of education they want for their children, within the limits of the principles underlying a democratic, pluralist society. The proposed reforms are calculated to meet those two criteria. Critics will object more to my definition than to the obvious match between the two criteria and the recommended reforms. Their objections are likely to focus on two aspects.

First, they will argue that opportunity is meaningless if young people from some groups do not actually take advantage of it as much as those from other groups. The difference is one of fundamental values and cannot be resolved by argument. However, I am certain that the public does not support any attempt to determine equal outcomes among selected groups; the only open and effective way to do so is by means of quotas. Even the strongest proponents of quotas refuse to use that term because they know that the concept is strongly opposed by the public; they therefore use words such as "goals" and "targets." The reality is that various groups, like individuals, do have and always will have different values, beliefs, attitudes, and behaviours, which are translated into varying performance in school. For the most part, the differences have little to do with alleged, but unproven prejudice on the part of teachers, and far more to do with the different behaviour, preferences, values, choices, and prejudices of parents.

The area public school is designed to give the same opportunity to all, regardless of group membership (by race, ethnicity, religion, or social class). Those who believe that a carefully arbitrated set of values for the area public school agreeable to a majority or plurality is not for them may choose an alternative, whether it is a school developed for West Indian immigrants or one for Seventh-Day Adventists (neither of which may restrict admission by race or religion).

Some will object that the partial funding of independent schools is a subsidy to the rich; the reality is different. At the moment, access to independent schools in most provinces is restricted to those with a lot of money or an intense commitment to a cause (usually their children's religious upbringing). For example, most Canadian parents have to pay fees in excess of $6000 a year in order to obtain an academically intensive program for their ten-year-old child. This situation is highly unfair. Under the reforms, that choice would become free in an area public school, an alternative, charter, or a direct-grant school or be available at limited cost in a partially funded one. If the latter are compelled to provide bursaries to those unable to pay fees, then almost perfectly equal opportunity would be provided – more so than in any province today, even in Manitoba or British Columbia. The partially funded independent school will flourish only to the extent that schools in the public sector fail to reform. Canadians retain a historical commitment to the local school; their children are for the area public school to lose. If it does not improve, then it will surely and deservedly decline. Will the establishment publicly demand compulsory registration in schools that wilfully refuse to improve in accord with the public will? There has been little opposition from any quarter to the closing of obviously ineffective schools in England.

Secondly, Egalitarians will object that the more choices that proliferate, the greater the educational differences that young people will experience. There is much truth to that statement, although one should bear in mind the enormous differences that exist today between public schools in rich and poor neighbourhoods, quite apart from the varying experiences of children in the same classroom. Those who doubt this observation should look at the differences in average achievement levels, often exceeding two grade levels. (In other words, if your child in grade six attends a school with very low achievement levels, the average level of work in the class will be below grade five. If the child attends a high-achieving school, the average level will be above grade seven.) More to the point, most of the emerging differences will result from parents' deliberate expression of distinct values. A generally increased focus on achievement and evaluation, favoured by most parents, will gradually narrow differences in achievement as the best instructional practices are sought. My sense is that area public schools, overseen by parent committees, will themselves develop stronger common values than they currently have, for the simple reason that most parents want a stronger doctrine, rather than a weaker one. I believe that the schools which are most permissive, with fewest shared values, will have very small enrolments.

My experience in talking to educational reformers suggests that the greatest objection to the recognition of parental choice will be in the area of religious options. Editorial writers and columnists in Canadian newspapers sometimes endorse secular choice in education, but they usually draw the line at religious schools. Neo-conservativism (reflected by Technocracy and Individualism in education) and liberalism (reflected by Progressivism, the Cultural ideal, and Egalitarianism) are given voice in the Toronto-based media, but the social conservative (Traditionalist) viewpoint is unrepresented. There was no opposition from the media to the use of a plebiscite (with a narrow margin and poor turnout) to dilute religious rights in Newfoundland. But it is intellectually dishonest to support parental choice and exclude the one minority choice that parents are most likely to make. Most Roman Catholics, Jews, and members of the evangelical Protestant churches, constituting over 30 per cent of the population, prefer a religious school. It is part of the British and Canadian tradition. The main reason for its rejection is secular prejudice, which is found in the liberal wings of the mainstream Protestant churches as much as in the secular elites. Educational reform that deprives parents of what is most strongly desired by a large minority becomes an empty charade, as some American states, such as Massachusetts, have discovered.

One of the strongest reasons why parental choice makes for more effective schools is that the schools so formed become communities. Those based on experts' passing fads are unlikely ever to be effective or form genuine communities. Educational policies over the last few decades have, deliberately or incidentally, destroyed community. It cannot be rebuilt if its foundation is denied. The enemies of religion are often also enemies of community. Strong believers in secular ideologies (the state on the left and the free market on the right), they are suspicious of any viewpoints that do not fit their secularist mindset. In a pluralist democracy, minority beliefs that are not shared by the majority should be permitted, provided that they do not transgress the fundamental principles of the larger society.

CONCLUSION

Many titles have been suggested and considered for this book. The word "reformation" was chosen because it most precisely describes what is being advocated. Taken literally, reformation implies a putting together again, a new founding; that is what this book is about. Arguments about philosophical directions and methodologies are educationally important in a pluralist society, but practically and politically they are much less so. To pretend that such a large undertaking as schooling can and should change different direction every year or so is a failure of imagination. It is a double failure: a failure to understand how impossible massive reform of the classroom is and a failure to imagine the obvious alternative, that there does not need to be a standard classroom for everyone.

Reformation can also be interpreted as a synonym, perhaps a stronger version, of reform. Certainly, the book is concerned with reform. But everyone wants reform; there is simply no agreement about the best direction to choose. Today we live in a time when the old traditions have lost their universality. The Western democracies struggle to cope with rapid change, the maintenance of traditional democracy, the decline of religion, and the rise of pluralism. There are ongoing debates between individualism and community, between capitalism and some form of managed capitalism, between patriotism and globalism, between growth and the environment, between competing and sharing. The argument underlying this book does not necessarily reflect all those tensions, but it must be considered in that context. The larger Canadian society may have to confront a reformation, most obviously if Quebec decides to leave Confederation.

The proposed reformation of Canada's schools will strike many readers as too radical, too strong, and not appropriate for a country where accommodation and incrementalism are more common. Yet in some ways, this book is the least radical of any recent prescription. All universal cures demand that everyone take the same medicine. The reformation proposed in this book, like the Protestant reformation of the sixteenth century, leaves the established institution, the public school, relatively unscathed and eventually perhaps stronger and more competitive.

As befits a late-twentieth-century reformation, it is not a case of winner takes all. It will not destroy the local school, if that is what most parents prefer. Indeed, it will save the small community school threatened and invaded by the centralizers and the technocrats. The reformation allows those who do not want to change not to do so and those who see utopia in the full-colour computer connected to the Internet to follow that path.

It was not really radical, five hundred years ago, to suggest that Christians should find their own way to God, for that was precisely what Jesus had advised. Today it is not really radical to suggest that parents should have a major say in the education of their children, because they have traditionally been the children's principal educators. What would be radical would be to remove children even further from their parents by allowing the state and its experts to gain more control over what schools can and cannot do, leaving parents to stand on the sidelines as their children are made over in the name of an ever-changing secular god, whether it be self, money, or fulfilment.

I am not suggesting that the proposed reforms constitute a complete and precise whole from which any departure would be fatal. At the same time, the gradual implementation of small parts of the program over many years is doomed to failure. The early reforms would then be moderated, diluted, and subverted by the power groups. Those adversely affected would get together to resist later reforms, and the zeal to change would soon dissipate as problems and obstacles inevitably mounted and those in charge were replaced. Even the massive reforms in England, now nearly ten years old, are only slowly seeping through the system, and they continue to meet successful resistance from educators, despite their evident popular support.

The time when the state should determine all aspects of the schooling of every child has long since passed. Our educational systems are still buried in the late nineteenth century, when school districts acted as buffers between the provincial department of education and the community served by the school. There was or appeared to be consensus about what should happen in schools. They were either Catholic or Protestant, in fact if not in name. In the late twentieth century, there are more than two world-views, and the geographical community (in terms of educational or personal values) is obsolete, replaced either by individualism or by community based on common interests and beliefs unreflected in geography.

Today we need a new partnership between parent and state: not a fuzzy one where school officials bring parents on side by means of manipulative public relations, but one in which division of authority is carefully distributed and transparent. The state should collect taxes equitably and distribute funds to schools on the basis of fairness, effectiveness, and efficiency. It should establish the limits of freedom within the school in order to protect the fundamental values of a democratic and pluralist society. Equally important, politicians and officials should see themselves as agents of society, serving all its citizens, rather than as implementors of the latest manifesto.

The state should make available programs that provide a sound academic foundation and honestly prepare young people for work. It should ensure that a fair share of jobs is available to young adults by means of appropriate incentives. It should make available to every youngster a public school experience, free of the influence of any special-interest group and reflecting the public will of society and the interests of a majority or plurality of parents. Those who dissent from the neighbourhood public school, on the basis of legitimate educational preferences or world-view, should be able to obtain an education for their children in special schools in accordance with their own beliefs. All schools should be accountable for their activities and for their students' achievements, civic behaviour, and preparation for further education or work.

I am leary of the term "democratic" in an educational context because it is too often used to defend, by deceit, some narrow ideological interest. Would it not be truly democratic, however, if Canadian provinces were to lead the world in providing a system of publicly supported schools that genuinely addressed the varied interests and values of parents, at the same time as they met realistic aspirations of young people, all within the bounds of the core ideals of society?

APPENDIX

A List of Recommended
Educational Policies

Readers are invited to use the following lists to determine their own policy preferences, to judge where their province stands with respect to the major policy proposals, and to advocate change to local and provincial governments. An attempt is made to judge reasonable application of the policies in the various provinces (given in parentheses). Incomplete information or difficulty of generalization is indicated by a question mark.

Examples are for explanatory purposes only. The lists are intended to reflect in a summary way the policy implications of the reforms recommended in this book.

CHOICE OF SCHOOL

1   Parents are permitted to enrol their children in any fully funded provincial school, irrespective of religious or instructional orientation or school jurisdiction, without additional fees, provided that the children are qualified by age, possess any academic prerequisites, and are willing to abide by the rules and cultural expectations of the chosen school. (None)

2   Every student, with the exception of those duly expelled or suspended, has right of reasonable access, including transportation without charge, to a designated zoned area public school. (All)

3   There are alternative programs and schools, and charter schools where numbers warrant. (Alberta)

4   Designated area public schools may become alternative schools by agreement of a majority of parents and the school district. (Alberta)

5   Area public, charter, and alternative schools may become direct-grant schools (receiving their funding directly from the province) by a majority vote of parents. Direct-grant area public schools must adhere to the provincial and district regulations governing other area public schools unless

specific exception is granted by the province, in which case they cease to be area public schools. (None)

6   There is no discrimination in school funding on the basis of religion, denomination, or secularism, but all schools must adhere to a statement of fundamental principles appropriate to a pluralist democracy. (None; British Columbia and Manitoba do not discriminate between religions)

7   Independent schools receive partial funding provided that they meet reasonable requirements related to curriculum, per-student spending, student evaluation, and effective management. (British Columbia, Alberta, Manitoba, Quebec)

SCHOOL FUNDING

1   Area public and alternative schools are funded by the province on a per-pupil formula designed to meet the realistic requirements of different programs, with a basic per-pupil funding unit (bfu) based on a minimum average of 170 days of attendance. The bfu is augmented in the cases of students with extreme disabilities (e.g. bfu × 3); students placed in local behavioural programs or schools (e.g. bfu × 2); students in grades ten to twelve (e.g. bfu × 1.15); vocational students (e.g. bfu × 1.3); students living in census areas where family income is below the twentieth percentile (e.g. bfu × 1.15); it is reduced in the cases of students in part-time work, part-time school programs and other part-time students (e.g. bfu × 0.7 if the part-time school involvement is 60 per cent of full-time participation). Initially at least, funding for teachers' salaries and benefits is provided separately and adjustments made to the overall formula if the salaries are anomalous. Over time, the size of the acceptable anomaly is reduced. Funding for area public, alternative, and district-supported charter schools flows through the school district or provincial regional administrative unit. (British Columbia, Quebec)

2   Charter schools are funded by the provincial department or the school district based on the formula amount less an administrative overhead (the grant is divided between educational salaries and other expenses). (Alberta)

3   Direct-grant schools are funded directly by the provincial department by means of the formula less an administrative amount not greater than 10 per cent (excluding any costs for student evaluation). (None)

4   Partially funded independent schools are provided a per-pupil grant according to a formula reflecting parental ability to pay, program, and similarity of school program to provincial curricula. Normally, eligible schools (spending the same as or less than comparable fully funded schools) should receive between 50 and 80 per cent of the fully funded rate. (British Columbia, Alberta, Manitoba, Quebec)

5   Reasonable interprovincial parity of spending is ensured by federal-provincial agreements. A uniform national tax base covers a minimum of 80 per

cent of the national expenditure on elementary and secondary education, allocated to provinces on the basis of their share of the age six to eighteen cohort. A deduction is made from the provincial allocation to reflect the amount that would be raised by a three-year rolling property tax on residential and commercial property of 0.6 per cent of 85 per cent of true market value. (No)

6 No school district is permitted to spend more than 5 per cent above the relevant provincial funding formulas (except that initially an allowance is made for anomalous teachers' salaries). Additional funds raised by a school district (to a maximum of 5 per cent of budget) (1) are approved by a referendum of residents nominally or actually supporting the district board (e.g. public or Roman Catholic) and excluding residents supporting an independent school pool or a different district; (2) represent the same tax effort irrespective of the wealth of the district; that is, the percentage of additional residential property tax assessed to raise 5 per cent additional funding is uniform provincewide, with the province looking after the negative or positive balance in each case. (British Columbia, Quebec; some controls in most provinces)

SCHOOL PROGRAM

1 The provincial goals of education for area public schools are clear and straightforward. They represent a majority or a large plurality of parents and the public, and cover the academic, aesthetic, physical, social, moral, and school-to-work domains. (?)

2 The provincial objectives are listed by subject, with separate listings for different programs from grades ten to twelve. Objectives are clear, concise, and sequential. (?)

3 Area public secondary schools (or separate vocational centres) have school-to-work programs as an important focus. Part-time (paid) work, part-time school programs are available to all students. Vocational programs are available according to demand and local employment conditions. They include traditional trades, office work, hospitality, food services, agriculture, and horticulture. (Quebec)

4 Regional vocational centres are operated independently by the province, by community colleges, by school districts, or cooperatively. They provide direct job training and preparation for high school graduation for young people aged fifteen to nineteen. (None)

5 Cooperative programs designed to give young people an experience of the workplace are clearly distinguished from school-to-work programs. (British Columbia)

6 All area public schools offer challenging three-year university-entry and college-entry programs. (In small schools, two or more programs may be provided within split classes.) (?)

7 To graduate from secondary school, students must have passed, during the previous three years, strictly implemented minimum levels of academic achievement in language, writing, reading, mathematics, and general knowledge and meet a minimum standard of physical fitness. They must also meet provincial and school performance standards in selected subjects. (Students with a physical disability, permanent or temporary, may graduate, provided that there is a written stipulation of the standard(s) excused and the reasons for the exception on the transcript.) (None; Quebec comes closest)

EVALUATION

1 All students (with the exception of those with a severe disability or lack of knowledge of an official language) are tested by means of national standardized tests in the basic skills at least three times between grades one and nine, the first time of testing being no later than grade two. Districts or schools may be permitted to choose their tests, but provinces maintain records of equivalence among available tests for the information of parents and the public. (Quebec)

2 Canadian students wishing to enter university or college provide the relevant institutions with results of provincial, national, or international (e.g. International Baccalaureat) tests and/or examinations, either in the form of combined school and examination marks or with separate marks for each. (Alberta, British Columbia, Quebec)

3 Federal and provincial scholarships, bursaries, and grants (direct or by means of program subsidy) take into account performance on provincial or national tests and examinations. (?)

4 All test and examination results are available to the public by school. When published, the schools' results are grouped according to their demographic characteristics. (None; Alberta, British Columbia, Ontario, Quebec are moving in this direction)

5 Provinces require that all graduates reach the provincial standards. They may use provincial tests and examinations, they may make parallel sets of tests available for use by schools under assured conditions, or they may use inspection and spot tests to ensure quality control. (Quebec)

6 Tests or examinations are taken by all students, without exemption, at the end of every year or semester in academic subjects, beginning, at the latest, in grade nine. (None? Quebec comes closest)

TEACHERS

1 Differentiated staffing, with teachers classed as interns, teachers, and senior teachers, is permissible. (None)

2   Provinces develop, in consultation with teachers and parent committees and in negotiation with teachers' unions, a provincial framework for
teachers' salaries, with alternative salary grids based on some combination
of level (e.g. intern), experience, relevant qualifications (e.g. honours degree
in the senior subject taught), subject and grade level taught, and competence
(determined by the principal with the advice of a committee delegated by
the parent committee). There may be a main framework with other alternatives outside it or, if they are negotiated, several plans within the main
framework providing for local choice. Salaries are applied locally by the
parent committee in consultation with the principal. The basic framework,
with maximum and minimum salaries by level, minimum and maximum
days of work, and minimum and maximum instructional hours, is mandatory in all public schools (area, alternative, charter, and direct-grant). Teachers of demanding academic subjects and of grades seven to twelve are paid
more than general teachers in the primary and junior elementary grades.
(None)

3   Teachers have a right to join or not join a union of their choice. Schools,
not districts, are the basis for unionization. School staffs have the right to
veto any deviation from the main provincial salary framework, which is
negotiated provincewide. There is no deviation from the basic framework
without provincial and union approval. (None)

4   Provincial collective bargaining is resolved by final-offer selection,
based on provincially legislated criteria. (None)

5   Teachers, as professionals, choose their (ethical) methods of instruction, depending on the subject, the class, and their own preference. They are
accountable for the results of their teaching, in the context of their students'
previous levels of achievement and other contextual factors. (?)

TEACHER TRAINING

1   Teachers may take their education and training courses on a part-time
basis during a period of (paid) internship in a school, under the supervision
(mainly indirect) of a (paid) senior teacher. (None)

2   Interning teachers-in-training pay a minimum of 40 per cent of the
actual cost of their programs in teacher education. One-year full-time programs are also available. (None)

3   Faculties of education provide training, education, research and practice in a wide range of instructional methodologies, and knowledge and
skills in the area of student evaluation. (?)

4   Unfunded and partially funded independent schools may develop
their own requirements for teacher certification in their schools, in consultation with the department of education. (?)

DISCIPLINE

1   All schools, including area public schools, have the right to expel students for consistent unwillingness to complete reasonable assignments; repeated disobedience; violence or possession of violent weapons; the repeated use of or dealing in prohibited substances; major infractions (e.g. arson) of the school discipline code; or repeated infractions after reasonable warnings (e.g. consistent failure to attend class). (?)

2   Local schools or programs provide a strictly controlled environment for students who have been repeatedly warned, suspended, or expelled for reasons other than extreme or criminal acts. (None)

3   Special provincial boarding schools provide a highly controlled environment for students with serious behavioural problems which the home is unable or unwilling to address effectively. (?)

4   All funded schools expect and require regular daily attendance at all classes; acceptable work habits; courteous behaviour to all adults and fellow students; respect for property; and dress in accordance with the school code. (?)

5   Principals are in charge of discipline and order in the school, and may suspend or expel students in accordance with the school's due procedures irrespective of the students' status in the courts. (?)

PARENT COMMITTEES

1   Parent committees have a majority membership of parents, elected by parents of students enrolled at the school, and include teachers in the school, elected by fellow teachers, and the principal (voting *ex officio*). A student elected by the student council serves as a voting member for schools that include grade eleven or twelve, but he or she may not participate in or be informed about decisions relating to personnel. (Ontario, Quebec, New Brunswick)

2   The school's parent committee has primary authority over the policies of the school, within a framework of provincial policies and regulations; the areas include the selection of teachers and the principal; recommendations for the dismissal of teachers or the principal; development of the school atmosphere; dress and discipline codes; program organization; appeals from teachers, other employees, and students; and budget. (None)

3   The principal has authority and responsibility for the implementation of provincial and parent-committee policies; the evaluation and management of teachers; the coordination of classes and subjects; the scheduling of students, teachers, and facilities; the administration of texts, materials, library acquisitions, tests, and examinations; the discipline and attendance of students; and the day-to-day administration and management of the

school and its facilities. The school committee may delegate additional responsibility to the principal provided that there is regular reporting of activity to the committee. The principal may delegate and share authority, but not responsibility. (None)

4   Area public and alternative schools have parent committees according to the provincial regulations. Direct-grant and charter schools may negotiate their own policies and practices with the school district or province.

SCHOOL DISTRICTS
(OR PROVINCIAL REGIONAL OFFICES)

The school district has the following responsibilities:

1   to support parent committees in the development and implementation of policy;

2   to ensure that schools follow provincial policies and regulations;

3   to provide direct services to schools as appropriate and required, e.g. custodial and cleaning services, building maintenance, payroll services, finding qualified candidates for selection by schools, hiring of principal and teachers on the request of the parent committee, in-service training for teachers, food service, liaison with social and other local and provincial agencies, school supplies, dismissal of teachers and principal for cause (normally on the advice of parent committees), and liaison with the appropriate transport agency for the busing of students according to provincial policy;

4   to ensure school and/or program availability in accordance with parents' legitimate wishes where numbers warrant;

5   to allocate buildings fairly among area public, alternative, charter, and direct-grant schools;

6   to plan construction of new buildings and other facilities in accordance with provincial policy and direction where so delegated;

7   to assist in the development and allocation of a variety of school-to-work programs, including senior vocational programs, and to develop vocational centres in cooperation with community colleges, where numbers warrant. (None)

PROVINCIAL DEPARTMENTS (MINISTRIES)
OF EDUCATION

The provincial department of education has the following responsibilities:

1   to develop and publish provincial goals and objectives of education for direct application in area public schools and for the guidance of all provincial public schools;

2   to develop and implement policy with respect to a mandatory program of student evaluation (with possible additional voluntary components,
such as the annual testing of students in the basic skills); to coordinate and
implement interprovincial and international testing programs of samples of
students;

3   to develop and implement general policies and regulations for public
schools and the removal of unnecessary rules and regulations that interfere
with the reasonable autonomy of school committees and professional
teachers;

4   to ensure the provision of genuine choice of school where feasibile and
where demand exists;

5   to assume the responsibility of school districts where there are no such
districts and in the case of grant-maintained and provincial charter schools;

6   to assist in the development of a variety of school-to-work programs
(e.g. by negotiating the cooperation of employers in the part-time employment of students; by lobbying provincial and federal departments to develop
policies that will increase employment opportunities for youth and reduce
incentives to those over age sixty to remain at work);

7   to develop, implement, and monitor program funding formulas for
application to public and partially funded independent schools; to administer
arrangements for additional local funding at the request of school districts;

8   to certify teachers on the basis of their having satisfactorily completed
internships and a teacher-education program, including the compulsory
components of instruction and student evaluation; to cooperate with the
certification of teachers' unions according to labour law without the legislation of a closed shop or Rand formula;

9   to develop criteria for the development of provincial agreements with
teachers and a negotiated framework for application locally;

10   to develop teaching units in the curricula for optional use by teachers;

11   to develop in-service training programs for use by teachers on a mandatory (in the case of substantively changed curricula) or optional (e.g. alternative teaching strategies) basis;

12   to provide and allocate funds for new school buildings and to direct
the use and allocation of existing buildings where necessary (e.g. among area
public, Roman Catholic, francophone, and direct-grant schools);

13   to cooperate with the department of transport in the development of
a coordinated, efficient program of school busing, based on free (for area
public schools and constitutionally necessary choices), partially supported,
and full user-pay principles;

14   to collate and publish information, including student achievement by
school, subject and skill; subject, and program enrolment by type of school;
employment and salaries of all school personnel according to uniform categories, with those employed entirely in a school (i.e. by a parent committee)

distinguished from those working mainly outside the school (e.g. consultants); educational spending by uniform categories; student enrolment and attendance by school; teachers by qualifications, salary, and school; membership of parent committees; teachers' attendance by school, average absence, and reason for absence by day of week; categorized school budgets by school, enrolment, and type of school; incidence of suspension and expulsion (with reasons) by school; record of criminal charges (by offence) for offences committed on school property by category of person charged (e.g. student);

15   to provide an auditing and inspection service of all funded and partially funded schools, which may be delegated to school districts in part (a regular inspection schedule is not implied: random and selective systems should be used);

16   to place and operate school districts under trusteeship if they fail to maintain appropriate standards of education, fiscal probity, good management, and sensitivity to parental wishes. (None)

References and
Further Reading

Note: Abbreviated references to magazine and journal articles and most reports are included in the text. The books and reports listed here are generally available in major educational libraries and from the publishers. Entries with asterisks are not mentioned in the text, but are useful references for the reader who would like to pursue some of the ideas further.

Adams, Marilyn Jager 1991 *Beginning to Read.* MIT Press, Cambridge MA. A recent and balanced overview of the research on beginning reading.

Barlow, Maude, and Robertson, Heather-jane 1994 *Class Warfare.* Key Porter, Toronto. A lively defence of the establishment in education, with reformers categorized as part of the evil capitalist empire.

Bibby, Reginald W., and Posterski, Donald C. 1992 *Teen Trends.* Stoddart, Toronto. A unique look at the world of the Canadian adolescent, based on a national questionnaire.

*Bloom, Allan 1987 *The Closing of the American Mind.* Simon and Schuster, New York. A searing defence of the Cultural world-view in education; nineteenth-century liberalism.

Bronfenbrenner, Urie 1970 *Two Worlds of Childhood: U.S. and U.S.S.R.* Russell Sage, New York. A prescient recognition of the problems created for child upbringing when individualism replaces community.

Chall, Jeanne 1983 *Learning to Read: The Great Debate.* McGraw- Hill, New York. The second edition of a classic that records the research on phonics and other approaches to reading.

Coleman, James S., and Hoffer, Thomas R. 1987 *Public and Private High Schools: The Impact of Communities.* Basic Books, New York. The most important research for educational policy in over twenty years, with devastating implications for the large comprehensive high school that has become the Canadian ideal, despite its conspicuous problems.

*Crittenden, Brian 1988 *Parents, the State and the Right to Educate.* Melbourne University Press, Melbourne. A fine study of the relationship between parent and state in education.

Economic Council of Canada 1992 *A Lot to Learn.* Ministry of Supply and Services, Ottawa. This report and a companion volume listed under Newton et al. provide rare basic information about Canadian schools.

*Emberley, Peter C., and Newell, Waller R. 1994 *Bankrupt Education: The Decline of Liberal Education in Canada.* University of Toronto Press, Toronto. A strong defence of liberal – Cultural, in my usage – education, without addressing such practical problems as minorities and public and parental opinion.

Gairdner, William 1992 *The War against the Family.* Stoddart, Toronto. A rare and unrespectable (in Canada) argument against the anti-family movement of the last twenty or so years; liberal and left-wing critics joined forces to condemn it by means of personal attack, and a prominent Vancouver bookseller refused to stock it.

Herrnstein, Richard J., and Murray, Charles 1994 *The Bell Curve: Intelligence and Class Structure in American Life.* The Free Press, New York. Condemned by the leftist and liberal coalition, with the customary personal attacks; a short, but notorious section on race is less important than the hard-headed analysis of factors influencing problems of the underclass.

*Holmes, Mark 1988 "The fortress monastery: The future of the common core." In the *NSSE Yearbook*, part II, *Cultural Literacy and the Idea of General Education* (University of Chicago Press, Chicago). An argument that the Western, Judaeo-Christian educational tradition can only be saved outside a low-doctrine common school.

– 1991 "The values and beliefs of Ontario's chief education officers" and "A delicate balance: Leadership or stewardship". In *Understanding School System Administration,* edited by Kenneth A. Leithwood and Donald Musella (Falmer Press, London). A description of the first phase of research into different views on education of educated Ontario citizens, with emphasis on directors of education.

– 1992 *Educational Policy for the Pluralist Democracy: The Common School, Choice and Diversity.* Falmer Press, London. The case for choice of school within a Western pluralist democracy, with a detailed discussion of the problems of religion, ethnicity, race, and social class.

– 1993 *The Educator's Guide to Student Evaluation.* OISE Press, Toronto. A practical guide to assessment in the school, with an explanation of the uses of test and other results.

– 1995 "Educated dissent: Implications of policy disagreement for educational leadership." In *Effective School District Leadership,* edited by Kenneth Leithwood (State University of New York Press, Albany NY). The second phase of surveys – of educators, engineers, and nurses – with respect to educational policy).

– 1998 "A conservative education." In *After Liberalism* (Stoddart, Toronto).

– and Wynne, Edward A. 1989 *Making the School an Effective Community: Belief, Practice and Theory in Educational Administration.* Falmer, London. A practical guide to running a school on Traditional-Cultural lines, with a particularly relevant chapter by Wynne on the practical implications of community.

King, Alan 1989 *Canada, Youth and AIDS Study.* Department of Health and Welfare, Ottawa. Interesting data and establishment interpretation, with unintended insight into how schools become part of the social and family problem.

King, Alan J.C., and Peart, M.J. 1992 *Teachers in Canada: Their Work and Quality of Life.* Canadian Teachers' Federation, Ottawa. Interesting, rare data with establishment interpretation.

Lapointe, Archie F., Nancy A. Mead, and Janice M. Askew 1992 *Learning Mathematics* and *Learning Science.* Educational Testing Service, Princeton NJ. Clear, accessible data with remarkably little attempt to explain away the findings; authors are at arm's length from the participating countries.

Livingstone, D.W., D. Hart, and L.E. Davie 1995 *Public Attitudes towards Education in Ontario 1994.* OISE, Toronto. Simply the best longitudinal data in Canada; occasional left-wing slant in the wording of questions and in interpretation more than offset by the value of the data.

– 1997 *Public Attitudes towards Education in Ontario 1996.* OISE/UT, University of Toronto Press. The most recent opinion survey in the series.

*MacIntyre, Alasdair 1981 *After Virtue.* University of Notre Dame Press, Notre Dame IN. Impressive combination of Aristotelian and Christian thought applied to contemporary problems; this philosophy underlies my own educational world-view.

Newton, Keith, et al. 1992 *Education and Training in Canada.* Ministry of Supply and Services, Ottawa. Valuable companion to *A Lot to Learn*, listed above under the Economic Council of Canada.

*Nikiforuk, Andrew 1993 *School's Out: The Catastrophe in Public Education and What We Can Do About It.* Macfarlane, Walter and Ross, Toronto. Strong attack on Progressivism by Canada's best-known educational journalist.

Robitaille, David, and Garden, Robert A. 1989 *The IEA Study of Mathematics II: Contexts and Outcomes of School Mathematics.* International Studies of Educational Achievement. Pergamon, London. Good data; tendency to favour North American, as compared with European, educational policy in data interpretation.

Rutter, Michael, et al. 1979 *Fifteen Thousand Hours: Secondary Schools and Their Effects on Children.* Open Books, London. Classic, unduly optimistic study of school effects; illustrates most clearly, but tends to understate, the effects of high-stakes student evaluation on achievement.

*Solway, David 1989 *Education Lost.* OISE Press, Toronto. A brilliant, bitingly humorous look at education in the classroom, showing vividly what excessive Technocracy and Progressivism are destroying.

Teddlie, Charles, and Sam Stringfield 1993 *Schools Make a Difference: Lessons Learned from a 10-Year Study of School Effects.* Teachers College Press, New York. Probably the most up-to-date statement of research findings from effective-schools studies.

*Thiessen, Elmer 1993 *Teaching for Commitment.* McGill-Queen's University Press, Montreal. A philosophical argument that indoctrination need be no more a part of religious education than of education in most other areas.

Index